Healing in the History
of Christianity

Healing in the History of Christianity

AMANDA PORTERFIELD

OXFORD
UNIVERSITY PRESS

2005

OXFORD
UNIVERSITY PRESS

Oxford University Press, Inc., publishes works that further
Oxford University's objective of excellence
in research, scholarship, and education.

Oxford   New York
Auckland   Cape Town   Dar es Salaam   Hong Kong   Karachi
Kuala Lumpur   Madrid   Melbourne   Mexico City   Nairobi
New Delhi   Shanghai   Taipei   Toronto

With offices in
Argentina   Austria   Brazil   Chile   Czech Republic   France   Greece
Guatemala   Hungary   Italy   Japan   Poland   Portugal   Singapore
South Korea   Switzerland   Thailand   Turkey   Ukraine   Vietnam

Published by Oxford University Press, Inc.
198 Madison Avenue, New York, New York 10016

www.oup.com

Oxford is a registered trademark of Oxford University Press

Library of Congress Cataloging-in-Publication Data
Porterfield, Amanda, 1947–
Healing in the history of Christianity / Amanda Porterfield.
  p. cm.
Includes bibliographical references and index.
ISBN-13 978-0-19-515718-5
ISBN 0-19-515718-4
1. Spiritual healing.   2. Healing—Religious aspects—Christianity.
3. Miracles.   4. Healing in the Bible.   I. Title.
BT732.5.P67 2005
234'.131—dc22   2004029864

9 8 7 6 5 4 3 2 1

Printed in the United States of America
on acid-free paper

To Keith

Acknowledgments

Many people contributed to this book, both directly and indirectly. Martin Marty, Brooks Holifield, Grant Wacker, Randall Balmer, Susan Graham, and other colleagues in the American Society of Church History encouraged the project as I first began to develop it. Ron Numbers also supported the project from the beginning and sent me articles I needed to read. Denis Janz, Richard Horsley, Virginia Burrus, Derek Krueger, Daniel Bornstein, Peter Matheson, and Mary Bednarowski helped me think about healing in the context of the history of Christian practice. Cynthia Read at Oxford University Press gave the manuscript a detailed reading that improved it enormously. Her knowledge of the history of Christian thought is as impressive as her insight into what makes a good book.

Paul Flesher, Carolyn Anderson, Susan Frye, Bob Torry, and other colleagues at the University of Wyoming attended to early drafts of chapters, and my colleagues at Florida State University were equally generous with their time and help. I am especially grateful to David Levenson for opening his library to me and for helping me find my way amid the voluminous scholarship concerned with Jesus and the early history of Christianity. John Kelsay gave me considerable help in strengthening the chapter on early modern Christianity. John Corrigan, Brian Cuevas, Matt Day, Kathleen Erndl, Aline Kalbian, David Kangas, Martin Kavka, Nicole Kelly, John Kelsay, Amy Koehlinger, David Levenson, and Barney Twiss all helped me think about the placebo effect and the relationship between Christian healing and modern science.

Several graduate students made significant contributions to this book. At the University of Wyoming, Mary Dolan's belief in the importance of the book sped me on my way. At Florida State, Laura Brock tracked down articles I needed for the chapter on medical missions. Gene Mills responded helpfully to my request of an analysis of the manuscript with respect to Pentecostal thought. Kelly Baker, Jeff Danese, Michael Gueno, Warren Hope, Dave Isaacs, Marianne Lipsius, Michael Pasquier, and Howell Williams all helped me improve the manuscript. Joseph Williams wrote a seminar paper on charismatic healing that I drew from in writing the last chapter. I also drew from Thomas Lloyd's undergraduate paper on Internet prayer. Thanks to Michael Gueno for his work on the index.

Last but not least, thanks to Keith Hull for enabling me to express my thoughts more clearly and for many other things as well.

Contents

Healing in the History of Christianity

Introduction

Healing is a persistent theme in the history of Christianity, thread-
ing its way over time through ritual practice and theological belief,
and across space through the sprawling, heterogeneous terrains of
Christian community life and missionary activity. To focus on healing in the history of Christianity, as this book does, is to attend to
important elements of continuity amid the jumble of competing
doctrines, innumerable churches, disparate behaviors, and historical
developments.

When I embarked on this book, I did not anticipate the extent
to which I would come to see Christianity as a religion of healing.
My initial goal was to explore the history of Christianity without getting lost in the process. I chose healing as an organizing focus because of current interest in the topic, which I hoped would make my
study interesting to others, and because new ways of thinking about
religious practice and experience prompted me to take claims to religious healing more seriously than I had before.[1]

Although I was prepared to take the reality of Christian healing
seriously, I did not expect to find the history of Christianity so laden
with its signs. I thought I would find the emphasis on healing apparent in the ministry of Jesus marginalized in Christian history,
shouldered out by theologians and church authorities intent on
marching people toward salvation in heaven, but kept alive, on the
edges of ritual practice and belief, by common people desirous of
protection and escape from sickness, misfortune, and death. I also

presumed that the enormous variety of these popular manifestations of healing would overshadow any commonalities among them, and that relationships between these manifestations and official church teachings would be fairly tenuous. I assumed that my study would support the view held by a number of historians I admire that there are, in fact, many Christianities, and that reference to Christianity as a singular phenomenon is at best a convenience and at worst an aggressive, simplistic form of wishful thinking. I did not expect to find myself constructing the argument that attention to healing reveals remarkable similarities among different cultural expressions of Christianity and that healing has been a driving force in the construction of Christianity as an ongoing historical tradition.

This driving force is not easily conceptualized, however, because of its multilevel meanings and wide-ranging implications. At the most obvious level, Christian healing refers to cures accomplished in the name of Christ and through the agency of his Spirit and saints. Many Christians have testified to dramatic, miraculous cures, and missionaries and theologians have often pointed to them as evidence of the power of Christian faith and the truth of Christian doctrine. But dramatic cures represent only a fraction of what Christians have experienced and meant by healing. Much more commonly, Christian healing has involved relief of suffering and enhanced ability to cope with chronic ailments. Thus, medieval pilgrims often made repeat visits to healing shrines, apparently because such visits relieved suffering but did not produce a lasting cure.

Part of Christianity's appeal as a means of coping with suffering is the idea that suffering is not meaningless but part of a cosmic vision of redemption. Along with the actual healing that might be stimulated by faith in a higher power, this imputation of meaning to suffering has itself been a tonic. While the effectiveness of Christian practices as means to relief from suffering has contributed enormously to their popularity, the real genius of Christianity has been to embrace pain and disability and death and not to limit the meaning of health and healing to their expulsion. Thus, many Christians have accepted the onset or persistence of suffering as part of religious life, while also celebrating relief from suffering as a sign of the power and meaning of their faith. Beneath this apparent paradox, a fairly consistent tendency to experience suffering as a means of both self-understanding and communion with others has enabled many Christians to rest easier with pain and death, even as healing experiences have energized Christians, enabling some to defeat pain and death, at least temporarily.

Christians have often studied suffering, and sometimes even inflicted it on themselves, as an occasion for religious experience. In late antiquity, Christian holy men acquired sanctity through endurance of physical torture and transcendence of pain. In late medieval Europe, female mystics deprived their bodies of food to identify with the suffering humanity of Jesus. In twentieth-century Africa and the Americas, numerous theologians held up the sufferings of poor people as signs of the suffering Christ, arguing that attunement to these sufferings motivated people to confront social injustice and work toward creating a better world. Each of these interpretations of Christian suffering represents a different set of cultural concerns and historical developments; they also reflect the persistent Christian tendency to find religious meaning in suffering and to seek redemption on its terms.

In their attention to human suffering, many Christians have devoted themselves to caring for sick and dying people. Prompted by desire to emulate the compassion of Jesus and his healing ministry, Christians have launched countless agencies, institutions, and grassroots movements directed toward health care. In many of these efforts, Christianity and medicine have been deeply intertwined. Although sometimes competitive and even acrimonious, Christianity and medicine have often advanced together and depended on each other for support.

The implications of Christian healing extend in other directions as well. In its foundational meaning, Christian healing is about repentance and forgiveness of sin. Linkages between repentance and healing derive from Old Testament stories about the blessings of health, fertility, respect, and prosperity that accompanied God's forgiveness of Israel's sins after he called her to repent. God chastised Israel for her sins and turned her toward repentance with punishments of sickness, barrenness, disgrace, and misery. Thus, affirmation of a connection between sickness and sin lies at the root of Christian healing.

In some instances, Christians affirmed this connection by blaming people for being sick, as in the case of medieval Christians who regarded leprosy as a sign of sexual impurity. In other instances, however, Christians discerned surrounding forces of evil and sin as causal agents of disease and suffering. The gospel writers understood the healings performed by Jesus along these lines, describing them as acts that defeated evil spirits. Wherever Christians have laid blame, discernment of sin as the cause of suffering has contributed to visions of reality that place human beings and their sufferings at the center and that link relief of these sufferings to the purpose of creation.

Numerous versions of Jesus' call to personal repentance for sin developed over the centuries. Medieval Christians worked their way to forgiveness as one might follow a medical regimen conducive to health, undertaking acts of penance as remedies for particular sins. In the early modern period, Martin Luther's impatience with piecemeal penitence and attempts to bargain with God

led him to define grace as a completely unmerited healing act of divine forgiveness. In sixteenth-century Anglican churches, forgiveness of neighbors
was a requirement for admission to healing communion, and in the early
twentieth century, Episcopalians representing the Anglican tradition in the
United States incorporated psychotherapy as a means of developing forgiveness among communicants.[2]

As part of its impetus toward reconciliation, Christian healing has often
been associated with the construction and maintenance of social peace. At the
core of their social practice, Christians have built families out of strangers, and
the extraordinary success of Christianity as a world religion can be attributed,
in part, to this social feat. From the beginning, followers of Jesus understood
the formation of close communities as manifestations of Christ's healing
power. In addition to caring for the sick within communities and through
missionary outreach to others, Christians relieved isolation, expelled enmity,
and created familial love as expressions of the healing power of Christ.

While practices associated with religious healing created Christian persons
and communities, they also pitted persons and communities against hostile
forces. Beginning with Jesus, many have interpreted healing as a sign of the
coming Kingdom of God, and this interpretation in turn led many communities to separate themselves from the world. In several forms of Christianity
originating in the United States, for example, including Shakers, Latter-day
Saints, Seventh-day Adventists, and Pentecostals, believers conceptualized
their communal identity in opposition to the larger society and engaged in
healing practices that affirmed their communal solidarity, their moral purity
in anticipation of God's Kingdom, and their separation from the world.

Christians have compared the cohesive power of Christian community as
a kind of social peace akin to the organic harmony of a healthy body and even
used that comparison to justify the expulsion and punishment of outsiders.
For example, when the governor of the Massachusetts Bay Company, John
Winthrop, urged that the outspoken religious radical Anne Hutchinson be cast
out from the Puritan community in seventeenth-century Boston, he promoted
her eviction as a therapeutic measure to protect the social body and restore its
health. Winthrop envisioned his community in terms of mutual affection, lack
of dissimulation, and the willingness of each part of the body to serve the needs
of others. As "members of the same body," he wrote in 1629, "we must delight
in each other, make others' conditions our own, rejoice together, mourn together, labor and suffer together." Like many believers before and since, Winthrop understood harmony to be a defining element of Christian community
and he understood Christian community to be the living body of Christ. If "we

keep the unity of the spirit in the bond of peace," he promised, "the Lord will be our God and delight to dwell among us."[3]

Christians have invoked the transcendent authority of Christ as justification for conquering and even killing others, all the while believing in the compatibility between the healing power of Christ and his saints and their own efforts, as defenders of Christ and the saints, to eradicate evil. The judges of the Spanish Inquisition reasoned along these lines, as did religious partisans on both sides of the American Civil War. In 1862, Julia Ward Howe joined rousing anticipation of "the glory of the coming of Lord" and his "terrible swift sword" in her "Battle Hymn of the Republic," with an allusion to Christ's healing power: "With a glory in his bosom that transfigures you and me."

But violence is only one possible extension of the power manifest in religious practice and experience, only one way that individuals experience their group connection, and only one way that the social implications of religious experience get acted out. In numerous instances, the social mandates implicit in religious practice and experience have led Christians to challenge injustice and reform society. In numerous other instances, they have worked toward the conservation of social hierarchies and affirmations of existing social power. The healing power many Christians have experienced in the Eucharist has worked in many ways, sometimes enabling egalitarian friendships among people around the world, sometimes helping to maintain social worlds governed by ecclesiastical and political hierarchies.

The Resurrected Body

Images of the resurrected bodies of Christ and his saints have figured prominently in Christian healing throughout its history and can even be said to epitomize this healing tradition. In many depictions in art and literature, Christians have represented spiritual purification through images of bodily wholeness. Sensitivity to relationships between the body of Christ and the body of the Christian community, and between these and the bodies of individual believers, have played crucial roles in many different expressions of Christian healing.

Resurrection has not always meant denial of death or future exoneration and revenge, although these interpretations are plenteous enough. In innumerable ways and contexts, Christians have experienced eternal life as a vitalizing presence in this life, akin to the vitality of life itself—what the medieval theologian Hildegard of Bingen called "greenness" (viriditas). Christians in many different times and places have found eternal life to be a lived reality, something more than, or even different from, intellectual beliefs about the future or metaphysical beliefs about the triumph of spirit over flesh. Visions and visceral experiences of the living presence of the resurrected Christ have often stimulated feelings of vitality in believers, as well as hope of resurrection in the hereafter.

This is not to say that the full meaning of Christian resurrection, at any time in history, can be reduced to a celebration of bodily health. Probably the vast majority of Christians has understood bodily resurrection to mean life after death. But powerful images of bodily health reside within the concept of resurrection and in its depictions in Christian art and literature. In many healing practices undertaken by Christians, the images of physical health embedded in stories and pictures of resurrection have operated as invigorating signals for sick people and their caregivers.

Christian healing has revolved around signs of resurrection and eternal life, enabling people to feel rejuvenated, tranquil, and grateful to be part of a vision of reality that culminates in union with God. In many different times and places, Christians have found the healing signs of Christ in the midst of sickness and death and embraced human suffering as a site of transcendence where the signs of God's presence were likely to appear. Missionaries have paid special attention to sick and dying people, working to convey experiences of Christ's resurrection and eternal life to those perceived to be in dire need, but also to relive such vitalizing experiences for themselves through proximity to sick and dying people.

Religious Healing as Experience and Practice

Christianity is not the only religion in the world concerned with healing and its connotations. Far from it. Healing is part of many, if not all, religions and goes a long way in explaining why tendencies to be religious, and capacities for religious feeling and ideation, seem to have evolved as instinctive parts of human nature. But even in the context of long-standing, worldwide demands for religious healing, Christians have distinguished themselves. Often borrowing techniques and ideas from other religions and from numerous forms of medicine, Christians have time and again disseminated their religion as a means to healing and eternal good health. Christianity's success as a world religion has much to do with its attractiveness in this regard and with its effectiveness in promoting a whole range of salutary benefits and behaviors.

Religious experiences are always related to social life, at least indirectly.

The forcefulness and objectivity that Christians have associated with the authority of Christ derive not only from experiences of transcendence, but also from the social relationships that structure religious life and support those experiences of transcendence. Like other forms of religious experience, Christian healing situates people in community and establishes expectations and relationships. As religion scholar Catherine Bell argued, the social expectations and relationships involved in religious practice are not just means to an end, but often ends disguised as means.[4] For example, when a baby is baptized, people who attend the ceremony act as if their purpose in coming is to witness the sacrament of baptism, which involves sprinkling of water and utterance of sacred words over the baby. But at a less obvious yet no less important level, baptizing the baby is also a means to the end of gathering and maintaining the community.

As anthropological studies of non-Christian religions have shown, candidates for healing often become symbolic objects in a ritual process of communal integration and group solidarity. In some instances, this process can succeed whether or not the patient recovers. For example, in her study of religious healing rituals among the Kodi people of East Indonesia, the anthropologist Janet Hoskins discovered that the power of these rituals had more to do with the "moral unity" and "aesthetic impact" they generated in the people gathered to witness them than with any actual cure in the patient. Hoskins observed, "The group is recreated and reconstituted" during rituals of healing, "often over the body of the patient and often without much hope of alleviating his suffering."[5]

Similar phenomena can be found throughout the history of Christianity. Like other forms of religious healing, Christian healing stabilizes and consolidates communities through manifestations of transcendence that invigorate people. Dying people have often conveyed the healing power of Christ to others and become symbols around which communities have gathered.

Christian healing can be distinguished from other forms of religious healing in its appeal to Christ as the transcendent source of healing and prime symbol of personal and social integration. As a religious practice, Christian healing has involved many diverse actions, including prayer, pilgrimage, penance, laying on of hands, participating in sacraments, and venerating saints, relics, and icons. In the context of this diversity, the basic dynamic that begins to explain how Christianity has actually worked to make people feel stronger and find relief and comfort is the personal relationship that believers experience with Christ. As a person embedded in the memories, imaginations, and thinking habits of Christians, as well as more objectively described in scripture, community, liturgy, prayer, song, visual art, and the lives of saints, Christ has

motivated countless people to understand themselves in relation to his likeness. Much more than belief is at stake here. The experience or anticipation
of union with Christ is a religious practice and only partly a matter of belief.
Christian healing is more about a sense of relationship to a divine person than
about doctrine, although doctrine has been important in preserving and stimulating this sense of relationship and defining its boundaries. If many have
been healed because they believed, others believed because they had been
healed.

Scientific Approaches to Hope and Healing

As anthropologists and scholars of religion open up new ways of thinking about
healing in terms of religious experience and practice, new scientific interest in
healing as a biological process leads to better comprehension of how religious
experience and practice can stimulate bodily strength and vitality. Recent advances in brain science enable new understanding of the ways that relief from
stress can affect all of the systems and functions of the body, from heart rate,
blood pressure, digestion, and immunity to improvements in the exercise of
thought, speech, and memory. Increasingly specific, empirical knowledge
about the bodily effects of stress and relief enables appreciation of the role that
despair and hope play in sickness, healing, and health and the role that cognition plays in maintaining hope or inviting despair.

In the 1970s, the discovery of endorphins—natural morphine-like substances released by the brain that decrease pain—pointed to the existence of
chemical reactions within the brain that might be emotionally triggered. The
subsequent discovery of neurotransmitters—chemical message carriers
prompting nerve cells to respond to and regulate each other—advanced scientific understanding of the brain chemistry involved in the autonomic nervous system and its role in managing heart rate, blood pressure, stomach acid-
ity, intestinal churning, and other bodily functions. Fear can stimulate these
functions, which figure in anxiety, depression, and other mental states. Of
course, there is an enormous gap between experiencing these conditions and
analyzing their chemistry, or between interpreting their expression in particular forms of human culture and acknowledging their biological nature. Yet,
brain science offers new understanding about how fear, and the relief from
fear associated with religious hope, can affect the whole body through the
nervous system and body chemistry. This understanding is already altering the
way many people think about the advantages of religious belief and practice.

In one line of inquiry developed since the 1970s, based on the premise that human brain function is similar to that in other animals, researchers showed that rats could be conditioned to suppress their own immune system. Rats injected with an immune-suppressing saline solution learned to associate their immune dysfunction with drinking saccharine-sweetened water, which experimenters produced at the time of injection. After several rounds of this conditioning, experimenters offered sweetened water to the rats without injections. Remarkably, the rats died from immune dysfunction at the same high rate, apparently because their bodies learned to associate immune failure with drinking sweet water.[6] In subsequent experiments involving the positive effects of expectation, rats conditioned to associate a flashing green light with rescue from drowning in a bucket of water swam longer, and stayed alive longer, once the light flashed than rats not so conditioned. Researchers concluded that the conditioned rats perceived the green light as a signal of safety that enabled them to keep swimming and not succumb to helplessness.[7]

Discoveries like these have helped make obsolete the mind-body dualism that has so often shaped Western discussions of religion. A century ago, someone as respectful of both science and religion as William James could dismiss "medical materialism" as irrelevant when it came to religious experience. Impatient with the animus to religion he perceived among materialists eager to dismiss Paul's conversion on the road to Damascus as an epileptic event, or Saint Teresa's mysticism as hysteria, or George Fox's preoccupation with martyrdom as a symptom of chronic bowel complaint, James argued that materialist interpreters could say nothing at all about states of mind of which they approved and only caricatured those of which they disapproved. In "its attempt to discredit the states which it dislikes, by vaguely associating them with nerves and liver, and connecting them with names connoting bodily affliction," James complained, scientific materialism was "altogether illogical and inconsistent."[8]

Among medical researchers and psychologists a hundred years later, the situation has changed. Today, interest in the salutary effects of religious belief and practice far exceeds interest in its pathological aspects, and empirical studies demonstrating positive correlations between religious involvement and health are growing at a much faster rate than studies demonstrating negative correlations. Bolstered by advances in brain science and erosion of the Cartesian dichotomy between mind and body, a major shift in scientific and medical attitudes toward religion occurred in the last two decades of the twentieth century. This shift led to new empirical findings about the positive effects of religious practice on recovery and longevity.[9]

Overall, these recent studies do a better job of showing how well religion works as a contributor to the reduction of biological stress than they do of exploring the limitations of religion with regard to health (or anything else).

They also tend not to concern themselves with common factors underlying a range of human activities that might make religious involvement comparable to athletic involvement, say, or active engagement in music, or satisfying sex. Despite their incompleteness and partiality, however, these studies make it easier than ever before for a wide range of people, believers and nonbelievers alike, to consider and appreciate the salutary biological effects of Christianity. In other words, it is now possible, as never before, to take religious healing seriously as a real and important biological phenomenon. This is not to claim that biological discourse is able to comprehend the fluidity and multivalent character of religious experience, but simply to say that biological researchers have made religious healing more comprehensible.

Ancient Theories of Natural Healing

Although important breakthroughs in the biology of healing have occurred in recent decades, the notion of healing as a natural process goes back to ancient Greek medicine. Beginning in the sixth century BCE, and probably earlier, philosophers attempted to describe the natural world in rational and empirical terms. Expanding on the notion ascribed to Thales (640?–546 BCE) that water is the essential element of nature, Greek philosophers developed the theory that the human body, like the rest of nature, is composed of four elements: water, air, fire, and earth. These elements came to be associated with four humors whose moist, dry, hot, and cold qualities coexisted in the human body in a more or less balanced way. The school of medicine associated with the Greek philosopher Hippocrates (c. 460–c. 370 BCE) stressed the importance of observing patients for signs of humoral imbalance. The Hippocratic injunction to do no harm presumed nature to be essentially self-balancing and self-healing. In Hippocratic medicine, the physician's primary task was to stimulate and support the humoral balance involved in the natural process of healing.

The Greek physician Galen (c. 129–200 CE) supplemented the humoral theories of Hippocratic medicine with anatomical knowledge derived from dissection of animals and expertise as a surgeon for gladiators. Galen's anatomical theories lasted fifteen hundred years, until the Flemish surgeon Andreas Vesalius (1514–1564) used human autopsies to prove many of Galen's theories incorrect. As a philosopher, Galen argued that everything in nature, including every plant, animal, and organ in the human body, had a predetermined purpose. Galen's emphasis on nature's teleological design fit well with theological ideas about divine providence and contributed to the authority of Galenic medicine throughout the Middle Ages.[10]

Though essentially materialist, the empirical approaches to medicine derived from Greek medicine often coexisted and intermingled with religion. In ancient Greece, temples dedicated to the god Asclepius supported physicians as well as priests, who interpreted dreams and performed other rituals aimed at healing. In medieval Europe, medicine and religion often intertwined, although their relationship was sometimes rocky, mostly because of theologians bent on maintaining Christianity's claim to superiority over medicine. From the medical side, the therapeutic effects of religious belief and practice were often acknowledged, and even the most thoroughgoing empiricist might respect religion as a helpful assistant to nature that promoted expectations of recovery. In this regard, the pragmatic principle attributed to the tenth-century physician Isaac Judaeus justified the physician's endorsement of religious hope: "Always make the patient feel he will be cured even when you are not convinced of it, for it aids the healing effort of Nature."[11]

The Placebo Concept and Its Limitations

The placebo concept emerged in the context of just this attitude. "The placebo effect" refers to the power of suggestion and to the role that positive expectations and symbols of hope can play in stimulating relief from stress and natural processes of recovery. Researchers have sometimes invoked the placebo effect to describe the enhanced feelings of well-being associated with religious healing. However, the shortcomings of the concept have led scholars in several different fields to leave it behind in order to construct more adequate explanations of the agency involved in religious healing.

The term derives from *placere*, literally "to please," used in Catholic vespers for the dead. In medical practice, placebos were inert substances administered to placate patients, and for centuries they were widely used; ships' doctors, for example, kept supplies of talcum powder on hand, fully aware that the powder was an inactive substance, but also that its administration was often soothing. One historian even went so far as to claim that "the history of medical treatment until relatively recently is the history of the placebo effect."[12] Given the fairly rudimentary state of premodern medicine (limited anesthesia, inaccurate knowledge of human anatomy and infectious disease, and counterproductive treatments such as purgation, leeching, and blistering), the use of placebos was one of the physician's most effective treatments. Patients commonly attributed relief to them, and at least they did no harm.

More heroic forms of medicine were often disastrous. The case of George Washington's sore throat, probably exacerbated by pneumonia, exemplifies the dangers. As one writer described the treatment Washington received, "Because he could afford the best cure available, he was given a mixture of molasses, vinegar, and butter, and then made to vomit and have diarrhea. But he lapsed. In desperation, his physicians applied irritating poultices to blister his feet and his throat, while draining several pints of blood. Then he died."[13]

Beginning in the sixteenth and seventeenth centuries, new discoveries in anatomy contributed to dissatisfaction with the adequacy of humoral diagnosis and to a growing tendency to depersonalize the work of empirical observation. By the nineteenth century, corresponding shifts in medical focus occurred as physicians attended more to diseases and less to patients, and more to efficacy and less to placation. Even as partnerships between religion and medicine developed in modern hospitals staffed and supported by religious people, growing embarrassment among medical practitioners about appealing to religion (or any other form of placation that might seem like trickery) hampered acknowledgment of religion's contributions to healing. By the mid-twentieth century, this embarrassment led many medical practitioners to avoid administering placebos. Not denying the frequent relief associated with them, physicians came to regard the use of placebos as a form of deception and thus ethically dubious.[14] Placation slipped from being one of the principal goals of medical treatment to a marginal and suspect endeavor.

At the same time, a number of researchers were studying the role that suggestion played in a wide range of treatments and attempting to measure this "placebo effect." In the context of huge growth in the development of pharmaceutical agents in the mid- and late twentieth century, some researchers were simply interested in subtracting placebo response from a medicine's "true" efficacy. But others were interested in the placebo effect itself. Several studies showed that the strength of this effect correlated with the size of a pill and the severity of treatment, indicating that the degree of potency expected produced a corresponding degree of result. Thus, a placebo administered as if it were morphine reduced postoperative pain more effectively than a placebo administered as aspirin.[15]

Other studies pointed to the *performance* of treatment as the primary stimulus of the placebo effect. As several studies showed, patients who submitted to treatment often got better, even if the treatment was not medically justified. Two notorious studies performed in 1959 and 1960 tested the efficacy of a surgical procedure, then in vogue, that involved splicing the internal mammary artery to relieve angina. Patients in the control group underwent a sham operation for chest pain that involved incision under anesthesia but no arterial splice. A high percentage of patients receiving the sham operation reported relief from angina, as did a comparable number of patients who got the full treatment.[16]

In the 1960s and 1970s, the psychiatrist Jerome Frank played a leading role in conceptualizing the power of suggestion. In one set of experiments investigating the doctor's role in creating or enhancing a placebo effect, Frank discovered that the doctor's expectation of patient relief significantly heightened the placebo effect, whatever treatment was administered. Expanding on this discovery, he focused on the situations in which placebos were administered, showing that context was an even more significant factor in stimulating relief than the patient's own temperament or personality type. He summarized this aspect of his work in 1974: "The extent of response to a placebo depends primarily on the interaction of the patient's state at a particular time with certain properties of the situation."[17]

Frank's book, *Persuasion and Healing*, was the first to develop the long-standing religious implications of the word placebo into a full-fledged theory about the relationship between the placebo effect and religious healing. Viewing the placebo phenomenon as supporting and stimulating the natural process of self-healing, Frank called attention to the interdependence of psychological and other biological processes, and to religious healing as a model from which physicians should draw in developing their bedside manner. Noting that religious healers "minister to many more sufferers throughout the world than do physicians," Frank emphasized that religious healers see "illness as a disorder of the total person, involving not only his body but his image of himself and his relations to his group." In other words,

> instead of emphasizing conquest of the disease, they focus on stimulating or strengthening the patient's natural healing powers. They believe that this can be done by the ministrations of a healer who, whatever his methods, enters into an intense relationship with the patient. In contrast with scientific medicine which, while paying copious lip service to the doctor-patient relationship, in actuality largely ignores it, all nonmedical healing methods attach great importance to it. Those operating in a religious context, which includes all forms of healing in primitive societies and faith healing in industrial ones, also see themselves as bringing supernatural forces to bear on the patient, with the healer acting primarily as a conduit for them.[18]

Scholars of religion have picked up on this way of thinking about how religious healing works. Among historians of Christianity, Peter Brown wove findings associated with placebo research into his discussion of holy men in late antiquity. In his discussion of cures performed by these religious virtuosos, Brown called attention to "a process of 'focusing'" on symbolic objects that imparted "reality and efficacy to what were thought of as the inscrutable workings of providence." Many cures attributed to holy men, he observed, involved "the administration of an innocuous *placebo*," often just water, "that is charged with the blessing of the holy man." Brown also noted that holy men emerged as a distinct class in late antiquity, often as supporting agents of medical science. Just as patrons of civil service inserted themselves into certain situations "not to disrupt the law but to make it work," Brown argued, so "the blessing of the holy man did not suspend the normal workings of Byzantine science and [its] sophisticated methods of dealing with life in the world, but merely strengthened the processes of decision-making involved in the application of these skills."[19]

In his discussion of the cult of the saints, Brown investigated the "imaginative dialectic at work" in the healings that took place at shrines dedicated to saints and their relics. Drawing on accounts written by Gregory (539–594), the bishop of Tours in Merovingian Gaul, Brown observed a clear relationship between the healings Gregory reported in his own life and the sufferings of his patron saints. "The very intimacy of the emotional bond between the believer and his invisible companions," forged amid the breakdown of Roman society and the emergence of new modes of identity, established an emotional equation between the believer's sufferings and those of the saints. Thus, Gregory found relief from a terrible sunstroke headache by submerging his head in the spring where friends of the martyred St. Julian had washed the saint's head after decapitation. In a further development of the same logic of symbolic focus and religious suggestion, material objects representing the sufferings of the saints became vehicles for healing. Gregory found relief from a painful eye infection by applying drops of water taken from the sockets where persecutors of St. Benignus had set the martyr's feet in molten lead.[20]

In recent years, some researchers have questioned the validity of the placebo effect as an explanation for anything. Among these critics, defenders of mystical or supernatural power have viewed the concept as a threat to their belief, and not without reason. In one effort to defend and protect the mystical powers of Native American shamans from the profanation of secular analysis, religion scholar Lawrence Sullivan emphasized that Native religious healers "would be offended by the idea that their healing powers depended on the placebo effect." Perhaps with reference to other forms of pollution dumped on Indian reservations, Sullivan called the placebo effect "a toxic waste site."[21]

Scientific researchers also challenged the validity of the placebo effect, with some suggesting that it be completely discarded. Their challenges call attention to the difficulty, even impossibility, of separating the effect of any specific placebo from the effects of numerous factors, including the healing processes that would naturally occur anyway, with or without a placebo.[22] This criticism is especially useful now, when some religious believers are designing scientific experiments to demonstrate the existence of supernatural forces.[23]

Scientific challenges to the placebo effect are useful means of appreciating just how difficult it is to isolate the therapeutic effects of religion from other factors. As scholars of religion well know, religion involves cultural attitudes and behaviors that define a person's outlook and participation in the world. Given the presence of cultural markers and social mandates implicit in religious experience, it is hard to imagine how an experiment could be designed to separate religious healing from its social and cultural components, or to stabilize the fluidity, subtlety, and multilevel aspects of religion long enough to measure them in any meaningful way. How would any research design control for all the religious and cultural factors involved in the recovery of some people and the failure to recover in others? Or even begin to distinguish religious factors, such as belief in eternal life through Jesus, from the effects of other culturally inspired phenomena that might have therapeutic effects, such as belief in the dignity and importance of individual life, support from family and friends, job satisfaction, or artistic pleasure and accomplishment?

If attempting to isolate religion from culture is impossible, attempting to separate the biological effects of religious belief and practice from other biological factors may be equally so. Religion may work to strengthen the immune system in many individuals, but how could this ever be conclusively proved? How could any research design completely isolate the effects of religion on the immune system from the effects of exercise, diet, and DNA, or from a constitutional tendency to optimism and healthy-mindedness?

Of course, the confluence of biological, religious, and cultural factors could be viewed as an important discovery rather than an unsolvable problem. Viewed constructively, it could be taken as evidence of the inseparability of mind and body and of the biological rootedness of both religion and culture. To admit this rootedness hardly implies that religion is either trivial or simple. Biological approaches to religion are a long way from anything like an adequate understanding of religion's complexity, fluidity, or historical development.

In another important criticism of the placebo concept, cultural anthropologist Thomas Csordas raised the question of whether it really offered much by way of explaining how religious healing worked. Referring to the placebo effect as a kind of "black box psychic mechanism," Csordas argued that it was nothing more than a label for a poorly understood process of therapeutic efficacy, a rhetorical device that obscured the mysterious nature of religious healing by subsuming it under a name—as if naming it was an explanation. Leaving placebo terminology aside, Csordas defined religious healing as a restructuring of cognition and memory. He emphasized the role of religious performance as the means by which this restructuring was accomplished. Religious performances stimulated transformations of memory and cognition, he argued, that in turn could have real emotional and physical effects. In a case study, he looked at the practice among charismatic Catholics of falling backward in an ecstatic state into the arms of fellow worshippers, and at experiences of relief from suffering and disability associated with that practice. He concluded that the process of being bodily handled and cared for in this way was crucial to the experience of healing in that setting. In a ritual context full of symbols of Christian redemption, relief from suffering, and bodily wholeness, the visceral event of releasing one's body into the arms of members of a Christian community—symbolically, the body of Christ—triggered profound cognitive transformations that, in turn, produced both immediate feelings of enhanced well-being and improved long-term health.[24]

Pentecostal lore about being slain in the Spirit includes stories of people "falling out" and cracking their heads on the backs of wooden pews without ill effect. Some Pentecostals regard catching people when they fall as an innovation reluctantly introduced as a precaution against lawsuits. However the practice of falling out developed, the presence of an intimate and responsive community seems to be an essential ingredient.[25]

In his discussion of the efficacy of charismatic healing, Csordas argued that it involved "an existential immediacy that constitutes healing as real" as well as "a cultural legitimacy that says healing is possible." The existential immediacy derived from the embodied nature of the experiences and from their "kinesthetic flow," which enabled participants to feel the vitality and force of their healing experience. In these and other expressions of Christian healing, the therapeutic relationship was central. Symbolism alone did not produce healing.[26] As cultural anthropologist Charles Briggs argued, some sensory engagement in a relationship with a person or force that is simultaneously beyond and within the self must occur for the symbols to have the kind of impact, or make the kind of difference, that people associate with divine power.[27] This kind of engagement with God begins to describe the transforming agency that Christians have often associated with healing.

Healing in Relation to the Person of Christ

In the chapters ahead, I accept religious healing as a real biological phenomenon, although one prey to pious exaggeration. I acknowledge that many Christians have found strength and relief from suffering, fear, and anxiety through
encounters with Christ and his saints, and I strive to locate these encounters
in their cultural and historical contexts. At the same time, a good deal of continuity is revealed—much more, frankly, than I expected to find. I argue that
healing has persisted over time and across cultural spaces as a defining element
of Christianity and a major contributor to Christianity's endurance, expansion,
and success.

As an ultimate goal, I aim to show that religious experience and practice
are vital forces in human culture and history and that Christianity's popularity
over time and appeal across a variety of cultures have much to do with these
forces. Christian experience and practice are extraordinarily diverse and always
reflect particular historical and cultural situations, yet they also share a common focus on the person of Christ—or, if not always on Christ directly, then
on the saints who emulate and intercede with him and partake in his identity,
or the Holy Spirit that conveys his healing power. Depictions of Christ, his
saints, and his Spirit are diverse, but their status as persons, or as agencies of
persons, persists even as their more specific aspects vary.

A sense of relationship with Christ goes a long way in defining what people, over centuries and across geographic space, have meant when they have
claimed to be Christian. As any insider to Christianity knows, even the name
Jesus Christ carries emotional impact and has a remarkable tendency to elicit
confessional feeling and talk. He is the divine person felt by many to touch
and adumbrate their humanity.

I

Jesus: Exorcist and Healer

Among all the activities ascribed to Jesus in the New Testament gospels, exorcism and healing are among the most prominent. The Gospel of Mark, the earliest gospel, presents Jesus as a prophet known throughout Galilee for exorcism and healing, and Matthew and Luke build on this depiction. John does not refer directly to exorcisms performed by Jesus but does emphasize Jesus' role as healer. Taken together, there are seventy-two accounts of exorcisms and healings performed by Jesus in the four New Testament gospels, forty-one of which refer to distinct episodes. These forty-one episodes involve a variety of different literary forms, an indication of their independent origins. And ten of them refer to crowds of witnesses, an indication of the gospel writers' understanding that Jesus' ministry included highly visible, public acts of exorcism and healing.[1]

Beginning with Mark, the gospel writers portray Jesus as a charismatic healer. The touch of his hand (or hands) is extremely powerful; early on in Mark's gospel, Jesus' touch heals Peter's mother-in-law (Mark 1:31) and brings a girl back from death (5:41). At the same time, people want to touch Jesus; any contact with him is therapeutic. Sick people crowd around him, eager to touch him (3:10). Simply feeling "the fringe of his cloak" enabled a hemorrhaging woman to recover (6:56). Even more dramatically, Jesus confronts and expels demons and "unclean spirits" that possess people and drive them to distraction (1:24, 32, 34; 3:11; 5:2–10; 9:17–18, 20–22). In several cases, those demons testify to Jesus' power and authority over them. Moreover, Jesus commissions his disciples to exorcise and heal. Mark 6:7–13 reports that Jesus bestowed "authority over the unclean spirits" on twelve followers who proceeded to "cast out many demons, and anointed with oil many that were sick and healed them" (cf. Matthew 10:1; Luke 9:1).

The gospel writers distinguished exorcism from other forms of healing and recognized demonic possession as a form of affliction different from lameness, blindness, or leprosy. Thus, when Jesus left the synagogue, people "brought to him all who were sick *and* possessed with demons" (Mark 1:32). Despite this commonplace distinction between exorcism and physical healing, it would be a mistake to read into it a Cartesian dichotomy between mind and body or to suggest that the gospel writers viewed demonic possession as a spiritual problem wholly separate from the natural problems to which human beings were heir. From the gospel writers' perspective, sin lay at the root of sickness as the underlying cause of the malevolence to which all kinds of misfortune could be traced; so illness and disability clearly had spiritual implications, either as punishments from God or as manifestations of malevolent spiritual powers lurking about the cosmos.

The Problem of Miracles

From the beginning, people had difficulty believing in the exorcisms, healings, and other miraculous acts ascribed to Jesus, and even more difficulty understanding what these events meant. In the earliest accounts of Jesus, the problems involved in defining miracles and understanding what belief in them meant are not just mentioned in passing but essential to the construction of those accounts. The problem of miracles also runs through the history of Christian thought. This problem seems not to have prevented Christians from experiencing miracles. But it certainly has kept theologians busy and produced a fascinating history of scholarly debate.

In modern times, New Testament scholars often dealt with the difficulty of understanding miracles by stressing the greater importance of Jesus' teachings. Only recently have scholars found ways of understanding Jesus' exorcisms and healings that do justice to the gospel writers' insistence on their centrality without violating modern scientific understandings of material reality. To appreciate the significance of these new insights, it is helpful to see them in historical context, as part of an ongoing intellectual struggle in Western Christianity to develop a rational understanding of miracles.

For Augustine of Hippo (354–430), the North African bishop and theologian whose influence shaped a good deal of subsequent theology in the West, the foremost miracle of Christ was his "ascension into heaven in the flesh." The miracles Christ performed while on earth were evidence that he "was shown in outward appearance as a human being" but "in hidden reality he was God." After his ascension, "many miracles" followed "to testify to that one supreme miracle of salvation." And this supply of evidence for Christ's bodily ascension continued to flow: "Even now" Augustine wrote, "miracles are being performed in Christ's name either by his sacrament, or by the prayers or the memorials of his saints."[2]

While Augustine appealed to miracles as evidence for a rational argument about the transcendent reality of Christ and his presence in the sacraments and saints of the church, theologians in the East took a more mystical approach to the nature of Christ and a more experiential approach to miracles. For Basil of Caesarea (330–379), Gregory of Nazianus (329–389), Gregory of Nyssa (330–395), and other theologians around Constantinople who followed them, the Holy Trinity was not an ideal construct subject to rational understanding, as Augustine thought, but a community of divine persons whose reality could not be grasped rationally but only experienced through encounter and transformation. The community of divine persons venerated by Eastern Orthodox Christians included saints as well, and mystical encounters with their icons, often renowned for healing transformations. In the West, the healing powers of saints were also well known, and a great flowering of mystical expression developed in the late medieval period, partly as an alternative to the hyperrationalism of medieval scholastic theology. But the theologians in the West who followed in the path of Augustine did not embrace miraculous healing as a manifestation of mystical experience as straightforwardly as Eastern theologians did. In the West, miraculous healing was more often associated with manipulation of spiritual forces, and thus more vulnerable to condemnation as magic.[3]

For theologians in the Augustianian tradition, the rational approach to miracles as evidence for the divinity of Christ took an important turn with Martin Luther (1483–1546), John Calvin (1509–1564), and other reformers of the sixteenth century. Along with many Catholic reformers who criticized the Roman Church for exploiting people's belief in miracles, Luther and Calvin downplayed the significance of external signs of the spirit and argued that miracles had largely ceased at the close of the apostolic era.[4] Critical of what they perceived to be the magical elements of Roman ritual and their venal exploitation, Luther and Calvin acknowledged the healings performed by Jesus and his apostles as miraculous signs of divine authority, but wrote little about them.

Luther's voluminous commentaries on the Bible simply ignore the gospel passages that describe Jesus' activity as a healer. As far as ongoing miracles were concerned, Luther never doubted that God could and did perform them. But he completely rejected the idea that healing, or any other blessing from God, might be obtained by means of penance, prayers, saints, or any power inherent in the elements of the Eucharist. Rituals designed to inveigle Christ's favor, such as "pilgrimages, masses, invocation of saints, etc. would have found no place in the church," Luther declared, if people had not turned away from Christ as "mediator and high priest" and mistaken him for "a judge" whose opinion might be swayed by defensive argument or pleas for mercy. Faith involved submission to God, not manipulative efforts to change his will. "God works in us and we are passive," Luther declared, "like a potter, from the same material he can make a vessel either for honor or dishonor."[5] At the same time, Luther never denied humanity's need for healing or Christ's role in attending to that need. Human beings were sick, Luther believed, and no amount of effort on their part, or the part of their priests, could cure them. Only the perfect love of Christ, given freely by and through him, could save individuals from sin and make them well and whole.

Calvin, too, shifted attention away from the performance of miracles to God's underlying presence in all aspects of life, or, as he put it, "God's Preservation and Support of the World By His Power, and His Government in Every Part of it by His Providence." His famous work, *The Institutes of the Christian Religion*, only indirectly mentions the healing performances of Jesus, as in the reference to "miserable sinners, who sigh for the physician to heal the wounds of a guilty conscience." In his efforts to define the fundamental principles of the Christian religion and free it from what he perceived to be the corruptions of the Roman Church, Calvin followed Luther in rejecting the notion that Christians might rely on saints to intercede with God on their behalf. Like Luther, he argued that the sacraments "confer no advantage or profit without being received by faith." He also believed that God was parsimonious with miracles. With regard to Old Testament accounts of the sun stopping in response to Joshua's prayers and moving backward as an aid to Hezekiah, Calvin observed, "God has declared by these few miracles, that the daily rising and setting of the sun is not from blind instinct of nature, but that he himself governs his course, to renew the memory of his paternal favor to us."[6]

In denouncing what they perceived to be the magical rites and superstitions corrupting the Roman Church, Luther and Calvin criticized pilgrimages and other means of religious healing in which Christians had participated for centuries. If many believers persisted in practices that Luther and Calvin found objectionable, the reformers nevertheless succeeded in furthering a theological distinction between religion and magic that Christian apologists since the first century insisted on. But at the same time, the reformers' insistence on the necessity of faith pushed the meaning of Christian healing in a psychological direction. Although reformers condemned public performances of healing, they emphasized the importance of subjective feelings of suffering, repentance, and desire for relief and lavished more analytical attention on these interior events than ever before.

Protestant condemnations of magic and superstition contributed to new interest in the human side of religion and stimulated new affirmations about the need for Christ-like behavior in ordinary life. In the context of this early modern commitment to Christian life in the world, Jesus' own life acquired new importance as a model for human behavior. And by translating the Bible into common languages, encouraging Bible study among lay people, and placing Bible reading at the core of Christian worship, Protestant intellectuals in the seventeenth and eighteenth centuries opened the way for closer investigation of the earthly life of Jesus.

But this quest for the historical Jesus did not immediately lead to interest in his work as a healer. Early historical and literary studies of Jesus reflected the rationalist spirit of the Enlightenment as well as Protestant interest in the internal nature of faith. Well into the twentieth century, historical studies of Jesus only strengthened the development of earlier tendencies in Luther, Calvin, and other Protestant Reformers to downplay religious healing and marginalize miracles.

Beginning in the eighteenth century, German Protestants took the lead in the modernist quest for Jesus. In their effort to "demythologize" the New Testament, these Protestant scholars worked to separate the kernel of the Christian gospel from the husks of outmoded belief, with the goal of lifting up a Jesus whom modern men and women could embrace. Until the mid-twentieth century, when an infusion of Catholic scholars, Jewish historians, and students of comparative religions altered the terrain, historical studies of Jesus followed a path that corresponded to developments in Protestant theology that, if not original to Luther and Calvin, at least received emphatic expression in their writings. Working along that path, New Testament scholars minimized the place of exorcism and physical healing at the core of Jesus' ministry, explaining them, more or less simply, as evidence of his moral authority.

This line of thought came to fruition in the work of Albert Schweitzer (1875–1965), who argued that the forceful personality of Jesus commanded modern devotion, not "the thought-forms which were available to him" as a participant in an ancient culture. In *The Quest of the Historical Jesus*, published in German in 1906, Schweitzer urged his readers to overlook the magical beliefs characteristic of the culture in which Jesus lived. Instead, Schweitzer argued, Christians should celebrate Jesus for his full realization of "the moral will" inherent but latent in human beings everywhere. Because Jesus "grasped the entire truth and immediacy" of this moral will "and imbued it with his will and his great personality," Schweitzer believed, "he can help us to master it and to become moral forces for our own time."[7]

Schweitzer was acutely sensitive to human suffering; he believed compassion was a fundamental characteristic of Christian life and devoted much of his life to relieving suffering as a medical missionary in French Equatorial Africa. But he did not equate his medical work with the kind of religious healing that the gospel writers attributed to Jesus and his disciples. In fact, belief in that kind of healing was precisely what Schweitzer thought modern man needed to shun in order to realize the same moral will Jesus had embodied in his time. Thus, Schweitzer saw the core dynamic of Jesus' ministry as the expression of a remarkable personality: a man who acted powerfully for good in the world because his inner being was so morally pure and forceful. And he believed this interpretation of Jesus coincided with that of Paul. Schweitzer celebrated the "mystical fellowship with Christ" that he associated with the teachings of Paul and linked that fellowship to the internal ethical force Christians recognized in Jesus. In the fellowship of ethical personalities that joined Christians to Christ, Schweitzer explained, "everything metaphysical has an ethical significance." As Schweitzer hoped to do himself, Paul became one with his master, "demonstrat[ing] this ethical view of what it is to be a Christian by his complete dedication to service."[8]

Rudolph Bultmann (1884–1976), the most influential New Testament critic of the mid-twentieth century, carried Schweitzer's interest in the force of Jesus' personality further. Bultmann viewed the core of Christianity as an intensely personal, transformational encounter with God that could be distinguished from Hellenistic miracle cures, on the one hand, and from interpretations of Jesus as simply an ethical teacher, on the other. Bultmann acknowledged that accounts of Jesus' activity as an exorcist figured importantly in gospel depictions of his ministry, but he saw little relevance in that fact for Christians in his own day. Hoping to stimulate fresh experiences of God's ongoing activity, Bultmann followed Schweitzer in declaring that the quest for the historical Jesus should be abandoned as a theological enterprise. Rather than ensnaring modern Christian theology in disputes about what miracles Jesus might or might not have actually performed, Bultmann called for an existential understanding of the gospel message and symbolic interpretations of the healing activities and other miracles attributed to Jesus.

Drawing from the existential theology of the nineteenth-century Danish theologian Søren Kierkegaard (1813–1855), Bultmann saw God's relation to the world as a powerful, ongoing activity that required personal engagement. Following Luther's thought, Kierkegaard defined Christian life not as the performance of meritorious acts or assent to particular claims about the miracles of Jesus or the life to come, but as an internal response to the call of the Absolute amid a world of relative truths and meanings. For Kierkegaard, the only healing that really counted was that which responded to despair. Again following Luther, he defined despair as "a sickness in the spirit" caused by an unwilling "relation to the Power which constituted it." Only if one willingly accepted God as the power that grounded the self could one be healed of the despair that Kierkegaard called "the sickness unto death."[9]

Bultmann applied this Kierkegaardian understanding of man's relationship with God to his analysis of the New Testament. Rather than thinking of a miracle "as an event which happens on the level of secular [worldly] events," he argued that we should think of it "as happening within them." The healings attributed to Jesus in the New Testament might be taken as signals of this existential discovery, but Bultmann resisted literal interpretations of gospel miracles. He admitted that every act of demythologization involved an inevitable tendency toward remythologization. But as he explained in 1958, "Belief in the almighty God is genuine only when it actually takes place in my very existence." Indeed, Bultmann believed that "the question of God and the question of myself are identical."[10]

In reaction against this existential, theological interpretation of Jesus and his work as a healer, other scholars tried to put Jesus back in his own historical context by comparing his performances with those of other religious virtuosos in the ancient world. With the publication of Morton Smith's *Jesus the Magician* in 1978, this iconoclastic view of the historical Jesus became widely discussed. Wildly speculating that Jesus may have studied magical arts in Egypt, and that Luke's narrative of Jesus' early life was written partly to counter and suppress stories about such a sojourn, Smith described Jesus' initiation this way: after "undergoing a baptism believed to purge him of sin, Jesus experienced the descent of a spirit upon him—the experience that made a man a magician—and heard himself declared a god, as magicians claimed to be." Being driven by a spirit into the desert was "a common shamanic phenomenon," Smith argued, and part of the "picaresque existence" and "predictable life of a traveling magician and holy man" that, in Smith's view, Jesus fell into. Smith explained that Jesus' ability to control weaker minds resulted in psychological cures and other forms of showmanship that drew great crowds and made him seem godlike to his followers.[11]

Smith did not dispute the reality of these psychological cures, but he did not think very highly of them, either. Observing that medical scientists since the late nineteenth century had come to recognize the biological symptoms of mental illness and the positive benefits of hypnosis and psychoanalysis, he saw no need to follow the old rationalist approach of presuming "that miracles do not occur and that the gospel stories of Jesus' miracles were legendary outgrowths of the basic, historical material, to be pruned away by the critic in search of 'the historical Jesus.'" He acknowledged "that blindness, deafness, loss of speech, paralysis, and the like might occur as hysterical symptoms and be 'cured' instantaneously if the hysteria suddenly ceased." Just as "certain individuals were amazingly successful in quieting hysterical patients" in modern hospitals, so "Jesus' 'exorcisms' and 'cures' are now commonly thought to have resulted from the sudden cessation of hysterical symptoms and cognate psychological disorders."[12]

Written in 1978, before new appreciation of the Gospel of Mark as a literary achievement became prominent, before theoretical investigations of ritual in the study of religion had made much headway, and before brain biology and cognitive psychology made more fine-tuned understandings of anxiety, suggestibility, and somaticization readily available, Smith's references to hysteria sound quaint and anachronistic. In addition, his quotation marks around "exorcism" and "cure" seem patronizing, leaving the impression that disorders of mood or character, however intense, should not be taken too seriously. Nevertheless, Smith did acknowledge that ritual performance could have a powerful psychological effect. Noting that Jesus' cure of Peter's mother-in-law from fever is the first of the physical healings reported in Mark, he asserted that fever "often has psychological causes and responds readily to suggestion." He recognized, albeit in a patronizing way, that altered expectations can dramatically affect how a person feels. "The cure of Peter's mother-in-law is completely plausible," Smith admitted. "An old lady suddenly recovered from a fever when her son-in-law came back from synagogue bringing as a guest an attractive young holy man." Jesus "was doubtless accompanied by half a dozen of the congregation's most prominent members," Smith went on, "who would expect hospitality and see the condition of the house."[13]

Smith made an important contribution to the historical study of Jesus by drawing attention to Jesus' work as a charismatic performer. But his impatience with the theological influences shaping historical studies of Jesus resulted in a draconian agenda to debunk theological claims and cut Jesus down to size. In placing Jesus in the context of comparative religion and conceptualizing him as a shamanic figure, Smith advanced discussion about Jesus considerably. But his work also resulted in a major question, which he left unanswered: Why *did* Jesus stand out, at least among his followers and his enemies, from other wonder-workers of his day?

In a more recent popular study, Harold Remus took up the idea of Jesus as a shamanic healer and gave it a fresh psychological and pastoral interpretation. Citing medical and anthropological studies about the important role that expectation plays in health and illness, Remus presented Jesus as similar to many other healers, both in his day and in our own, whose personal authority and ability to empathize and communicate might stimulate recovery from illness. Remus compared Jesus to medical doctors who elicit trust in their patients and create hopeful expectations that help bring about recovery. Referring to Norman Cousins's popular work on the role that hope, purpose, and social support play in biological health, Remus claimed that Jesus' ability to heal was the result of the hope and purpose he instilled in his followers and of the sense of community he fostered. This claim has special implications for Christian ministers, Remus suggested, who carry on Jesus' healing work in their own work as pastoral counselors.[14]

According to Remus, Jesus was "a wounded healer" whose gift in healing others derived from his own experience of being wounded. Interpreting this concept in terms of Christian theology, Remus argued that the coincidence of healing power and powerlessness on the cross manifest in Jesus should be a model for all ministers of the gospel. Remus encouraged pastors to draw on their own experiences of grief and suffering and to use these experiences in their work as counselors who can help relieve psychological suffering in parishioners. Remus cited Henri Nouwen's 1972 book, *The Wounded Healer: Ministry in Contemporary Society*, and affirmed Nouwen's understanding of Jesus' life as a model for pastoral psychology.

The concept of "wounded healer" was not original to Nouwen, however, or peculiar to interpreters of Christianity. In fact, it developed first in the context of studies of shamanism in pre-Christian cultures. In a paper published in 1925 titled "Divine Election in Primitive Religion," Leo Sternberg called attention to experiences of dismemberment and sickness characteristic of shamanic initiation. And in an influential book on shamanism first published in 1951, Mircea Eliade cited Sternberg and devoted a whole chapter to "Initiatory Sicknesses and Dreams." C. G. Jung, in turn, cited Eliade's chapter on initiatory sickness in shamanism in his own discussion of "Transformation Symbolism in the Mass" in 1954. In Jung's interpretation, the Roman Catholic Eucharist carried vestiges of more primitive sacrificial rites performed by pagan priests as well as vestiges of initiation rites in which shamans assumed their powers in visions and dreams of dismemberment and self-sacrifice. All these religious rites, Jung argued, represented a process of psychological transformation that moved persons toward psychic wholeness and individuation. At the pivotal point of this process, the individual realized his potential to influence others by *"giving himself up."* In modern Western culture, according to Jung, the psychotherapist embodied this self-sacrificial process and carried forward the shaman's role as wounded healer. Remus took Jung's argument one step further: pastoral counseling was the Christian version of the psychotherapy of wounded healing.[15]

At the same time, Remus departed from Jung in making Jesus the most perfect exemplar of the self-sacrificing healer—not just one shaman among many. He turned to the gospels for evidence that, as the wounded healer par excellence, Jesus differed from other miracle workers of his day because of the humiliation he endured as part of his suffering. The problem of why Jesus suffered if he was the messiah was especially prominent in Mark, Remus noted, who could not explain why Jesus suffered so ignominiously, but simply repeated accounts of the secrecy and confusion surrounding Jesus' identity.

According to Remus, the later gospel writers attempted to resolve this problem, but their explanations only created new problems. Matthew explained the relationship between Jesus' power as a healer and his suffering on the cross by appeal to Jewish prophecies, especially those in Isaiah regarding God's chosen one, who "took our infirmities and bore our diseases" (Matthew 8:17; cf. Isaiah 53:4) and "will not wrangle or cry aloud, nor will anyone hear his voice in the streets" (Matthew 12:19; cf. Isaiah 42:2). For Matthew, Jesus' suffering and humiliation provided evidence of his role as God's chosen servant in fulfillment of Jewish prophecy, which also foretold the Jews' failure to recognize the Messiah in their midst. Luke, too, saw Jesus as the fulfillment of Jewish prophecies and emphasized Jewish rejection of him. Addressing Gentile readers, Luke explained Jewish rejection of Jesus as a necessary element in the unfolding of the gospel's larger destiny in the world. Thus, Luke laid the blame for Jesus' death on Jewish priests so completely that he made the Gentile Pilate say, "I find no crime in this man" (Luke 23:4), and then again, "I have found in him no crime deserving of death" (23:22).

Like the other gospel writers, Remus argued, John presented the healings performed by Jesus as evidence of his divine nature, authority, and power. But in John, more clearly than in the earlier gospels, these healings symbolize the eternal life Jesus represents and thus something far beyond temporary relief from sickness, blindness, paralysis, demon possession, or death. Thus, in John, the story of Jesus raising Lazarus from the dead (11:11–26) points to Jesus' own resurrection, to his ultimate power over death, and to the eternal life in which believers partake. In John, the suffering and humiliation that Jesus endures is part of a metaphysical process in which the Logos and Son of God take on human flesh and its vulnerabilities in order to redeem the world. In this context, the sicknesses and debilities that Jesus treated are symbols of mortality, and his miraculous healings are symbols of salvation from death.[16]

If John's symbolic interpretation of healing established the path that a good deal of subsequent theology would take, Remus called his readers back to prior accounts of Jesus' healings. In his effort to restore healing to its rightful place at the center of Jesus' historical ministry, Remus explained Jesus' ability to heal in modern, rational, scientifically acceptable terms and moved away from the supernatural explanations of religious healing that, to Remus, seemed to be an obstacle to modern understanding and practice.[17]

The Centrality of Miracles in Mark

While Remus found psychological meaning in gospel stories about Jesus as a healer that Christians today could use as a model for pastoral work, other New Testament scholars were employing new techniques of literary criticism to reconstruct the impact of Mark's gospel on early listeners and to emphasize the place of miracles in Mark's presentation of Jesus. For these scholars, confusion and controversy about the meaning of Jesus' miracles play a central role in Mark's depiction of the impact Jesus made on people and in Mark's strategy of drawing listeners and readers into active engagement with the presence of Jesus. In Mark's gospel, the healing acts of Jesus occur in the midst of confusion, not in spite of confusion, and prompt effort on the part of listeners and readers to wonder about them.

Most scholars now recognize Mark's stamp on the gospel tradition. But until fairly recently, his was the least familiar of the New Testament gospels and the least likely of those to be read in the context of worship. The relatively abrupt style, ironic thrust, and unflattering depictions of the disciples made it easy to pass over Mark in favor of more lyrical passages in the other gospels. The late nineteenth-century discovery that the authors of Matthew and Luke relied on Mark in writing their gospels laid the groundwork for renewed interest in Mark. In recent decades, New Testament scholars have employed contemporary forms of literary theory to understand Mark's gospel as a coherent and compelling narrative and to investigate its paradoxical approach to miracles. As a result of the rediscovery of its theological and narrative power, the Gospel of Mark has a hearing today that it has probably not enjoyed since the early centuries of Christianity.

Most scholars believe that the Gospel of Mark was written around the time of the Roman-Judaean war of 66–70. A rebellion against Roman occupation in Judaea brought on the war, which ended in Israel's devastating defeat and the destruction of Jerusalem and the Judaean temple. Mark reflects the apocalyptic ideas rampant in the midst of this catastrophic religious crisis and wartime situation. The gospel also reflects the confusion surrounding Jesus' identity among both Christian Jews and Gentiles drawn to Christian Judaism at a time when God seemed to have abandoned Israel, or punished her harshly for her sins. Scholars generally agree that Mark's gospel was written to help these people face misunderstanding and persecution and to give them "courage to live for the rule of God despite opposition and threat."[18]

New Testament scholars point to the coherence of Mark's narrative, its complicated design and deliberate gaps, which "create suspense, puzzlement, and the open ending."[19] Miracles play a major role in this design, and figure even more prominently in Mark than in the other New Testament gospels. Almost a third of Mark is devoted to accounts of miracles, including half of all verses in the opening ten chapters. In terms of "the sheer amount of space," Mark gives "proportionally more" to miracles "than any other early Christian document," according to New Testament scholar Christopher Marshall. In addition to their contribution to the suspense, puzzlement, and open ending of Mark, miracles symbolize recurrent themes and foreshadow later developments, especially Jesus' own resurrection. Restoration of health to individuals who are possessed by demons, sick, or incapacitated are the miracles Mark prized most, accounting for thirteen of eighteen miracles he describes.[20]

At the most obvious level, the miracles operate as a call to repentance and faith. At a deeper and equally important level, Marshall argued, they "convey a challenge to faith" that defies easy explanation and prompt the hearer or reader to greater "spiritual insight." Thus, the miracles in Mark are not straightforward testimonies either to the divinity of Jesus or to the disciples' faith. Several miracles provoke suspicion and animosity toward Jesus, not reverence (2:1–12; 3:1–6, 22–30; 6:1–6). Jesus warns people to keep silent about some miracles (1:44; 5:43; 7:36; 8:26), resists displaying them to show authority (8: 11–13; 15:29–32), and objects to credulous interpretations (13:21–22). Far from providing opportunity for the disciples to demonstrate their faith, Mark uses the miracles of Jesus to show that the disciples lack the insight into Jesus' actions that accords with authentic faith (4:35–41; 6:51–52; 8:14–21). In other words, the miracles performed by Jesus are puzzles that require a solution— and demand an effort of interpretation from listeners and readers.[21]

Clues to these puzzles in Mark's narrative all point to the coincidence between Jesus' identity as the Christ (literally, "the anointed one") and the appearance of God's Kingdom. As Marshall explained, the miracles are parables that reveal the eschaton (the end and fulfillment of time) in the person of

Jesus. They point to the person of Jesus and to the "salvation energy" he embodies and the healing power of this energy in all dimensions of human life: spiritual, physical, and social. As "dramatic parables which refer beyond themselves to the manifestation of God's kingly power in Jesus," the miracles in Mark, according to Marshall, "are only complete when those who witness them move beyond the external occurrence" of events and respond to them in kind, taking up in their own lives the reality of the in-breaking kingdom.[22] In other words, the problem of miracles, and the solution to puzzles presented by the parables, can be worked out only by stepping into the reality they suppose and by manifesting that reality in terms of one's own life.

The Jewish Background of Jesus' Healing

"In the world of Jesus," Geza Vermes wrote in *Jesus the Jew*, "the devil was believed to be at the basis of sickness as well as sin." This belief in the demonic origin of sickness reflected ideas about combat between good and evil, and about demons causing evil, that followers of Abraham's God picked up from Zoroastrian cosmology during the Persian rule over Palestine and Judaean settlements in the fifth and fourth centuries BCE. As these Persian ideas about evil developed among Israelites, the demand for exorcism and other forms of spiritual healing grew. Judaean communities at the time of Jesus attributed powers of exorcism and spiritual healing to biblical heroes of the past, including Noah, Abraham, Moses, and Solomon, and to the prophets Elijah and Elisha. They also attributed powers of exorcism and healing to charismatic holy men, like Jesus, who cast out demons and healed the sick under the oppression of Roman rule in their own day.[23]

In the communities where the gospels were written and first heard, belief in a cosmic battle between good and evil influenced understanding of the destruction of Jerusalem and of Jesus' work as exorcist and healer.[24] But first-century interpretations of both Jerusalem and Jesus also drew on an older theme in Hebrew scripture that interpreted disease and misfortune as God's punishments for sin and disobedience of his law, and health and prosperity as blessings from God in response to repentance from sin and recommitment to his law. In this traditional Judaean way of thinking, Israel enjoyed a special relationship with God. Israel personified the community of God's people, and legendary heroes in scripture represented this community and its personal relationship with God. In this way of thinking, healing meant restoration of social well-being for the people of God, as well as recovery of physical health for faithful individuals.

This linkage of sin with suffering so important for the history of Christianity derives from Judaean ideas, represented in Hebrew scripture, about how God communicates with Israel. The emphasis on forgiveness and insistence on repentance for sin that figure so prominently in the history of Christian healing also derive from Judaean stories about the relationship between God and Israel. Thus, Christian healing can be understood as an outgrowth of Judaean religion, grounded in scriptural traditions linking sin with suffering and healing with repentance and forgiveness.

Stories about the people of Israel made it clear that God would protect his people from disease and misfortune and reward them with health and prosperity as long as they adhered to their covenant with him. Moses explained in the Torah, "If you heed these ordinances," God "will love you, bless you, and multiply you" (Deuteronomy 7:12). Not only will you "be the most blessed of peoples, with neither sterility nor barrenness among you or your livestock," but "the Lord will turn away from you every illness; all the dread diseases of Egypt that you experienced, he will not inflict on you, but he will lay them on all who hate you" (7:13–15).

The prophets of ancient Israel expanded on what Moses said about the covenant requirement of righteous behavior and the consequences of adhering to or rejecting it. The prophet Isaiah addressed fellow Israelites on their day of fasting, crying out that it is wrong to observe religious fasts while you "oppress all your workers" (Isaiah 58:3). It violated God's law, Isaiah contended, not "to let the oppressed go free" and "not to share your bread with the hungry" (58:6–7). If you would only fulfill your agreement, Isaiah preached, "and bring the homeless poor into your house" (58:7), as righteousness demanded, God's blessings would rain down. "Then your light shall break forth like the dawn, and your healing shall spring up quickly; your vindicator shall go before you, the glory of the Lord shall be your rear guard" (58:8).

Historian Richard Horsley theorized that two different groups in first-century Judaism vied for ownership of this prophetic tradition. On one side, scribes, Pharisees, and priests affiliated with the temple in Jerusalem framed stories about the covenant with God, the Exodus from Egypt, and the exhortations of the prophets in terms of submission to ruling elites whose authority descended from David. In the past, Davidic rulers had even established grand tombs for the prophets in a gesture of unity that obscured the fact that a number of these prophets had been put to death for criticizing the behavior of Israel's rulers and challenging their authority. On the other side of the prophetic tradition in first-century Palestine, according to Horsley, the peasants of Galilee also claimed ownership of prophetic tradition and interpreted it differently. Galilean tribes had resisted Davidic rule and priestly interpretations of Mosaic Law at important moments in history, and some Galileans, perhaps including Jesus and his followers, equated the people of Israel with the people of Galilee, where the judges and prophets of old had lived.[25]

In Jesus' day, Horsley argued, even as they were beaten down by Roman soldiers and Jewish agents of Roman rule, Galileans could still remember their heritage as followers of Deborah and other heroic leaders who fought valiantly against the armies of Canaan. According to Horsley, this "little" tradition of popular religion revitalized by Jesus exalted the moral authority of the people who suffered oppression for the sake of their covenant with God. Like "little" traditions in other cultures, the Galilean interpretation of Israelite history was not a watered-down version of the "great" tradition of literate elites, but an alternative tradition that existed in tension with it. In the first century of the Common Era, this tension between Jerusalem and Galilee increased as the people of Galilee were forced by their own governors in Jerusalem to pay taxes and supply labor as tribute to Rome.

In the gospel accounts, Jesus and his followers engaged in performances of exorcism and healing that dramatized the restoration of healthy communal life and challenged scriptural interpretations advanced by priests, scribes, and Pharisees who defended Israel's ruling elite. In his exorcisms and healings, Jesus embodied the connections that earlier prophets had drawn between sin and suffering, forgiveness and healing, and righteousness and health. Thus, Jesus stood in the tradition of Jeremiah, who conveyed God's judgment on the people of Israel in the face of the growing power of the Babylonian Empire and the loss of political independence for Israel and Judah: "Your hurt is incurable, your wound is grievous. There is no one to uphold your cause, no medicine for your wound, no healing for you" (Jeremiah 30:12–13). But the potential to reverse this distress lay at hand. If Israel repented and returned to its covenant with God, suffering would disappear and good health—a metaphor for restoration of political power—would return: "I will restore health to you, and your wounds I will heal, says the Lord" (30:17).

Advancing a social justice interpretation similar to Horsley's, and also pursuing psychological interpretation of Jesus' work as a healer, the Catholic theologian and historian John Dominic Crossan argued that, for followers of Jesus, belief in a just God offered a way to overcome experiences of isolation, marginality, and dispensability provoked by the legion of Roman soldiers in Galilee and by the governors of Judaea, who exchanged the forced labor of Galilean peasants for the preservation of their own comfort, security, and status. With reference to recent studies of the positive effect that friendship, nursing, prayer, and trust in God can have in alleviating stress and bolstering health, Crossan argued that hospitable meals and other forms of companionship embodied the religious belief in social justice that Jesus and his followers made a transforming force in people's lives. Faith in a just God had political and even revolutionary effect, Crossan suggested, precisely because of its link to a larger, social context of meaning that affirmed God's presence in the world.[26]

Other scholars might not agree that Jesus was a political revolutionary, but most would endorse the emphasis Crossan and Horsley placed on the social context and social implications of physical healing, and most would agree that the restoration of community implicit in Jesus' acts of healing reflect his Judaean background. The image of the people of Israel as a corporate body—a person engaged in a relationship with God—is an important theme in Hebrew scripture, as are connections between sin and suffering and between forgiveness and healing. For the gospel writers and their war-torn communities, especially Mark, who emphasized the confusion surrounding Jesus' identity and the difficulty understanding what his spiritual power meant, Jesus embodied these themes in a poignant but ultimately encouraging way. As it did to the people of Israel in the Roman-Judaean war, suffering descended on Jesus despite—and because of—his special relationship with God. In the context of his Passion, and that of Israel, stories of his healing power, transforming love, and bodily resurrection gave courage to Jews who identified with him and to growing numbers of others as well.

Exorcism at the Core of Jesus' Healing Work

General agreement exists among scholars that the later gospels, Matthew, Luke, and John, were written at the end of first century, and that all four New Testament gospels reflect historical events surrounding the Roman-Judaean war and perceptions about Jesus more than a generation after his death. Nevertheless, many scholars continue to search for evidence within the gospels of the historical life of Jesus. In the "Jesus Seminar" convened by Robert Funk beginning in the 1970s, scholars assembled to vote on which gospel passages they considered to be historically authentic, and strong support emerged for understanding the historical Jesus as an apocalyptic preacher with a radical ethical message.[27] In the 1990s, a modification of this "talking head" version of Jesus developed among scholars interested in the historical Jesus as an actor who revealed God's Kingdom and its healing power by confronting and expelling demons. Thus, John Meier argued that Jesus combined exorcism with other activities in an odd way: "What made Jesus unusual, if not unique, was not simply his role as exorcist but rather his integration of the roles of exorcist, moral teacher, gatherer of disciples, and eschatological prophet all into one person."[28]

Other scholars argued that the gospel writers built ideas about Jesus' teaching on the foundation of earlier accounts of his practice as an exorcist and healer. For example, Edwin Broadhead argued that the exorcism stories are among the earliest and most authentic descriptions of Jesus' work that we have. His encounters with the demoniac in the synagogue, the epileptic boy, and the spirits who fled into a herd of pigs say much about the dramatic and troubled world in which Jesus lived and worked, according to Broadhead, as do the Beelzebub controversy and the temptation scene. The exorcism stories reflect a world full of menacing demons that not only caused full-blown possession, but also created an evil atmosphere that enabled sickness and disability to thrive. Stories about other wonderful feats performed by Jesus, as well as theological claims about his messiahship and about the meaning of discipleship, may be based on these more primary accounts of how he restored well-being to people by confronting and expelling the demons that invaded and inhabited the world of first-century Galilee.[29]

To elaborate on the primacy of exorcism in Mark, the encounter between Jesus and the possessed man in the synagogue (Mark 1:21–28) is the first event in Jesus' public life, and the one that sets the stage for the rest of his ministry. As Mark tells the story, Jesus began teaching in the synagogue as soon as he arrived in Capernaum. He spoke as an authoritative teacher and "astonished" people. While Jesus was holding forth in the synagogue, or perhaps on his way in or out, a man with an "unclean spirit" accosted him. The demon inside the man "cried out saying, 'What have we to do with you, Jesus of Nazareth? Have you come to destroy us?" The demon recognized Jesus, and what he stood for: "I know who you are, the Holy One of God.'" Jesus "rebuked" the demon, "saying, 'Be muzzled and come out of him.'" The demon obeyed, although not without making a scene: "The unclean spirit convulsed" the man, "and crying with a loud voice came out of him." The people of the synagogue were "amazed" at the way Jesus exercised command over this demon and spread the story of what had happened.

Mark's story about the Garesene demoniac (5:1–20) is even more violent, and Matthew and Luke tone it down in their retellings (Matthew 8:28–34; Luke 8:26–39). Confronting a possessed man wandering in a mountainous region of Galilee, unrestrained and "crying out and bruising himself with stones," Jesus demands, "Come out unclean spirit from the man!" The man kneels, "and crying out with a loud voice he said; 'What have I to do with you, Jesus Son of the Most High God? I adjure you by God, do not torment me.'" When Jesus demands a name from the demon, the reply comes back, "Legion is my name, because we are many." (In his analysis of the story, Meier argued that the bizarre account of Jesus sending the legion into pigs that run off a cliff and drown in the sea was added on later.)[30]

In both of these stories, Jesus and the demons challenge each other with names. Whether the demons are trying to defend themselves or the men possessed by demons are calling on Jesus for help, crying out the name of Jesus plays a central role in the story. The demons (or the men taken over by demons) name him Jesus of Nazareth and identify him further through his relationship to God: Holy One of God and Jesus Son of the Most High God. Jesus responds with overriding authority, commanding the unclean spirits to leave the men they possess, which they do suddenly and decisively.

In addition to depicting Jesus' work, the exorcism stories are bound up with questions and concerns about Jesus' identity. This issue of identity is of paramount concern for all the gospel writers and is complicated by theological claims and counterclaims. When Jesus heals a "blind and dumb" demoniac, the Pharisees (or, in Mark, the scribes) retort, "This man does not cast out the demons except by Beelzebub the prince of demons" (Matthew 12:24; cf. Matthew 9:34; Mark 3:22; Luke 11:15). Apparently because demons recognize Jesus, some people say that his power emanates from the dark side. Others say he is the apocalyptic Son of Man come to rule the earth.

References to the Son of Man in Daniel (7:13–14) frame all three accounts of Jesus healing a paralyzed man (Mark 2:8–12; Matthew 9:4–8; Luke 5:22–26). Adding to the confusion, in the story about crowds of people from several different regions coming to Jesus to be healed, Luke (6:17–19) follows Mark (12:15–21) in reporting that when demons expelled by Jesus identified him as the Son of God, Jesus commanded them to be silent. In his version of that story, Matthew (12:15–21) does not mention demons or anyone identifying Jesus as the Son of God, but reports instead that Jesus ordered the people he healed not to "make him known," in fulfillment of Isaiah's prophecy (42:2) about the servant of God who "will not shout or raise his voice, or make himself heard in the street." Similarly, Matthew (8:16–17) makes the story of Jesus casting out many demons after sunset into a fulfillment of another prophecy in Isaiah. Luke (4:40–41) follows Mark in making Jesus silence the demons who tried to identify him but goes further than Mark in making the demons say that Jesus is the Son of God and the Messiah, a term in Hebrew scripture meaning "anointed king" or "anointed high priest," a reference to official earthly leadership of the David monarchy. At the very least, the confusing titles and demands for silence suggest that the effort to classify Jesus was a matter of some importance, and some difficulty, both for his followers and his detractors.

Recognizing the significance of names, Broadhead pointed to the title

"Holy One of God" in some of the exorcism stories as a defining element of the earliest strata of gospel accounts. In Broadhead's view, the early forms of the exorcism stories come as close as anything to historical evidence about how Jesus acted. Broadhead argued further that important theological developments in the first century after Jesus' death can be discerned by tracing the editorial embellishment and revision of these stories.

Identifying four stages of interpretation, Broadhead classified straightforward accounts of Jesus expelling demons as stage 1. In these primary accounts, Jesus is called "Holy One of God," a name that epitomizes his authority as an exorcist. Examples include the stories of Jesus' encounter with the demoniac in the Capernaum synagogue and his encounter with the possessed Garasene, along with stories of other cures performed by Jesus that involve exclamatory phrases testifying to Jesus' command of spiritual powers.

Exclamatory phrases, especially the name "Holy One of God," serve as the platform for stage 2 stories, which link Jesus' work as an exorcist to his identity as Christ. In this second stage of interpretation, according to Broadhead, the exorcisms and other miracles performed by Jesus become evidence of the authority of his teaching about the Kingdom of God. For example, in Luke's (4: 41) account of Jesus expelling demons at sunset, the demons came out shouting at Jesus, " 'You are the Son of God.' But he rebuked them and forbade them to speak, because they knew he was the Messiah." Then, on the following day, he delivered teachings about the Kingdom of God.

In stage 3, subsequent interpreters built teachings about the nature of discipleship onto these earlier pronouncements about the Kingdom of God. In passages representing stage 3, explicit stories about exorcism do not appear, but earmarks of exorcism persist in Jesus' formulaic rebukes (Mark 8:34–9:1; Matthew 16:21–28; Luke 9:23–27). Thus, in Matthew 16:22–23, "Peter took hold of [Jesus] and began to rebuke him: 'Heaven forbid! he said. 'No Lord, this shall never happen to you.' Then Jesus turned and said to Peter, 'Out of my sight, Satan; you are a stumbling block to me.' "

In the fourth and final stage, the theme of discipleship becomes paramount, and demonic imagery is entirely reconceived. In Matthew 7:21–27, it is not enough to say, "Lord, Lord, did we not prophesy in your name, drive out demons in your name, and in your name perform many miracles?" Jesus explains, "Not everyone who says to me, 'Lord, Lord' will enter the kingdom of Heaven." In this story, incantations over demons are foolish and insufficient compared to true faith and discipleship, just as a house built on the sand of visible evidence is nothing compared to one built on the rock of faith. A similar development can be discerned in the fourth gospel, which contains no explicit reference to exorcism and in which language once associated with demons has lost its literal meaning and been reemployed to describe failed disciples and Jewish rejection of Jesus. Thus, traces of the exorcism story can be found in the story of failed discipleship (John 6:66–71), in which Peter calls Jesus by the ritual names used in exorcism, "Lord" and "Holy One of God," and in which Jesus uses the word "devil" as a veiled reference to Judas. In John's (8: 42) reinterpretation of the Beelzebub story (Matthew 9:32–32; Mark 3:22–27; Luke 11: 14–23), Jesus says to the Jews, "If God were your father, you would love me." "Your father is the devil," Jesus says, and you choose to carry out your father's wishes (John 8:44). " 'I am not possessed,' said Jesus; 'I am honoring my Father, but you dishonor me" (8:49).

Another specialist in gospel exorcism stories, Graham Twelftree, showed that, in addition to provoking fear and amazement through his exorcisms, Jesus showed a confident simplicity that made him a "very conspicuous" if not "innovative" figure. Although other Jews in first-century Galilee performed exorcisms, Jesus was unusual in exorcising by his own authority, or by authority of the spirit or finger of God. His dramatic representation of divine personhood was in no way ancillary to his teaching, according to Twelftree. Jesus' performance *was* his message: the exorcisms "do not illustrate, extend, or even confirm Jesus' preaching." They *"are the kingdom of God in operation."*[31]

This interpretation of the meaning of Jesus' exorcisms as real-time operations of the Kingdom of God resonates with arguments made by Christopher Marshall and other investigators of Mark who view the miracle stories in Mark as paradoxes that engage listeners in a process of spiritual discovery that culminates in the realization that Jesus embodies the Kingdom of God. And this line of interpretation is not confined to studies of Mark, as that gospel is not the only source of accounts about Jesus' work as an exorcist. The story of Jesus exorcising the mute (in Matthew, mute and blind) demoniac (Matthew 12:22–23; Luke 11:14), does not appear in Mark. Scholars believe that it derives from Q (*Quelle*), the "source" common to Matthew and Luke but unknown to Mark, which scholars reconstructed by comparing the three gospels. In addition to supplying a distinctive exorcism story of its own, Q knows about several of the same exorcisms Mark does (Luke 11:17–22), thus joining Mark in providing independent evidence of the importance of exorcism in the historical life of Jesus.[32]

Arguing that Jesus' reputation as a healer may have grown out of his work as an exorcist, Twelftree pointed to the central role that naming plays in the gospel accounts of Jesus' healings. Jesus' utterances as a more general sort of healer echo the name-calling that characterizes his interactions with demons. And the simplicity of the verbal formula, material aids, and ritual gestures involved in the healing stories resonate with the simplicity and confrontational style of his exorcisms.[33] Thus, the gospel writers show Jesus using some material aids, such as oil or water or his own spit, in his work as a healer, as well as simple, authoritative commands, such as "Son, your sins are forgiven" (Mark 2:5) and "Girl, get up!" (5:41). They also portray him touching people with simple authoritative gestures, such as stretching out his hand (1:41) or taking the girl by the hand (5:41). Twelftree classified these gestures as extensions of his command as an exorcist. The formula he uses in confronting demons is straightforward and relatively nonesoteric, such as "Be muzzled and come out of him" (1:25); "Come out unclean spirit from the man" (5:8); and "By the finger of God I cast out demons" (Luke 11:20). The demons respond in kind: "I know who you are, the Holy One of God" (Mark 1:24) and "I adjure you by God" (5:7).

Agreeing with Twelftree that Jesus conducted exorcisms that transformed people's lives and manifested God's power on earth, Christian Strecker cautioned against interpreting those dramas in terms of abnormal psychology. In Strecker's opinion, modern psychological notions such as projection, dissociation, and multiple personality disorder involve an egocentric model of personality that does not do justice to first-century perceptions about spirits "entering and indwelling or inhabiting" a person and simultaneously transforming the surrounding social environment. In Strecker's reading, Jesus acted like a demon, or a man possessed by one, as well as the antagonist of demons. If some thought he was possessed by Beelzebub (Mark 3:21–22), others wondered if he was possessed by John the Baptist, Elijah, or some other prophet (6:14–16; 8:27–28). As a man possessed—by the spirit of God, Mark believes— Jesus comes across as a man transformed by God who transformed the world and people around him. The boy with seizures becomes calm. The howling Garasene becomes a respectable man again. These reversals in behavior, Strecker argued, were social events. The reintegration of outcast people into society through exorcism signaled the restoration of God's covenant and the Kingdom of God.[34]

If exorcism, naming, and healing lie at the root of New Testament ideas about the meaning of discipleship and Jesus' messianic status, this root is obscured even in the gospels themselves, partly because of conflict and confusion over what Jesus stood for, and partly because of the inevitable reinterpretation of the past by each new generation and community. Still, foundational elements of exorcism, naming, and healing have persisted as defining elements of Christian authority. Appeals to the name and person of Jesus to cast out harmful forces have often produced healing, even as the historical and cultural contexts carrying his name and person have constantly changed.

2

Healing in Early Christianity

The religious movement originating with Jesus met with amazing success. Despite sporadic episodes of persecution, it gained thousands of adherents in the first three centuries after Jesus' death. By the end of the second century, small Christian communities had sprung up in most of the urban centers around the Mediterranean, as well as northwest and west into Germania, Gaul, and Spain, north and east through Syria into Mesopotamia, Bactria (now Afghanistan), and Persia, and further east to southern India. By 225, Persia had more than twenty bishops, and Christian communities appeared in Armenia and along the Euphrates, the Persian Gulf, and the Hindu Kush.[1]

In the sprawling, spreading Roman Empire, the pace of conversions grew after Constantine's vision of the sign of Christ leading him to victory over the city of Rome in 312. The emperor proclaimed religious toleration in 313, bringing the persecution of Christians to an end first in western, then in eastern parts of the Mediterranean world. The unification of the Empire in 324, the development of Constantinople as a center of Christian learning, and the establishment of Christianity as the official religion of the Empire by Theodosius I in 381 secured and extended the new religion's influence, which spread south into Ethiopia in the fourth century, across the Red Sea into Arabia, along the Silk Road into Syria and Persia, and further into Europe.[2]

The fourth century witnessed several important developments

related to the transformation of Christianity from being an offshoot of Judaism on the margins of the Roman Empire to its establishment as the official religion at the center of Mediterranean culture. Political endorsement brought an influx of new converts, along with wealth, influence, and support for new institutions and organizational structures. A demographic shift of poor people from villages to cities helped stimulate the systematic organization of Christian outreach to the poor and sick that had begun in the third century, and new orders of lay exorcists emerged to meet the demands of a growing population of seekers of healing. Political support for Christian institutions advanced the organization of Christian philanthropy and made possible the creation of hospitals.

The late nineteenth-century German scholar Adolph von Harnack was the first modern historian to recognize the importance of Christianity's reputation for healing to its early success. In recent decades, a number of historians built on Harnack's insight to argue that the new religion provided innovative forms of health care as well as rituals of spiritual healing that contributed to its attractiveness and figured importantly in its expansion.[3] Recent historians also pointed to the interest in medicine shown by early Christian writers and to the frequent use of medical metaphors in Christian discourse.[4] Analogies between Christ's work as savior and the physician's art of healing figured prominently in early Christian writing, always accompanied by an insistence on Christ's superiority to any human physician or material form of medicine. "There is only one physician," proclaimed Ignatius, bishop of Antioch, in the early second century, "first subject to suffering and then beyond it, Jesus Christ our Lord."[5] For Ignatius and other early Christians, the spiritual healing performed by Christ brought believers into a state of ultimate well-being, beyond suffering and death. In addition, it often protected and delivered them from sickness and vulnerability to sin and evil in this life.

To prepare and equip themselves as fit vessels for the healing power of Christ, many early Christians took pains to purify their bodies. Thus, an early second-century sermon instructed Christians to "guard the flesh" in order to "receive the Spirit." Although controversy and diversity of opinion existed on the exact relationship between Christ's spirit and the physical bodies of his believers, many early Christians seem to have believed that the spirit of Christ was manifest in their bodies. An early second-century sermon proclaimed, "This flesh is a copy of the Spirit." The wonders of this replication of Christ were beyond description: "So great is the life and immortality which the flesh is able to receive, if the Holy Spirit is closely joined with it, that no one is able to proclaim or to tell 'what things the Lord has prepared' for his chosen ones."[6]

As Christianity spread into different parts of the ancient world, belief in the healing power of Christ came to expression in numerous ways. In Syria and Egypt, holy men withdrew from society to fight demons and prepare their bodies for Christ and attracted streams of visitors to their outposts eager to be cleansed and healed. In urban environments, Christians banded together for worship services that incorporated exorcism and healing along with other practices that strengthened individuals through union with Christ and with one another as members of his collective body in this world. Urban Christians exercised their faith through missionary outreach, often to the sick and poor, as did Christian traders traveling across the seas and along the roads and rivers of the ancient world. Especially around Constantinople, but in other cities as well, this outreach led to the emergence of a holistic system of religiously based health care, in which churches and monastic communities provided nursing care and medical services as well as religious rituals through which people found repentance for their sins and absorbed the protective, cleansing, and transforming vitality of Christ.

Imperial Context

Christianity's early success can be understood partly in terms of its relationship to the greatest imperial and colonial system the world had ever known. In many places, Christianity took root amid the dislocations and brutalities associated with imperial warfare, taxation, and military rule. The new religion developed partly as an antidote to the sufferings caused by these difficulties.

In addition to the actual rise in sickness, injury, and death caused by crowding, war, and poverty, the dislocations caused by loss of village networks and weakening of kinship ties thrust people into situations of increased emotional isolation. As some scholars argued, these dislocations made people more sensitive to the precarious nature of individual existence, and hence more fearful of sickness and death.[7] In the urban environments where early Christianity developed, sickness and death emerged as central concerns reflective of the breakdown of traditional communities and the greater isolation felt by individuals.

In some respects, the radical altruism of Christian teaching ran counter to the hierarchical structures and brutalities of the Empire, and Christians stood up against them. In other respects, Christian leaders took cues from the imperial system, which drew people from different locales and cultures together, enabling them to see the world in universal and politically comprehensive terms. As a faith for people of various cultures organized around the authority of one god, Christianity resonated with and conformed to the imperial political order in which it grew. Thus, Christianity developed as part of a new world order, as well as an antidote to the dislocation, fear, and suffering produced by Roman imperialism.

While it attracted growing numbers of Gentile converts, the new religion emerged from within Judaism and often through Jewish communities dispersed in the ancient world. Jewish sensibilities stamped early Christianity, and Christian worship and theology derived foundational elements from Hebrew scripture. Although condemnations of Jewish religion and people also developed among early Christians—the second-century extremist Marcion even declared the God of the Old Testament evil, and the antagonist of Christ—in important respects, the underlying Jewish foundation of early Christianity worked against dualistic tendencies to separate spirituality from material life. Of course, dualistic tendencies influenced Jewish as well as Christian thought in late antiquity, but in many quarters, a strong Judaean tradition of commitment to the God of creation, history, and this-worldly law limited the influence of philosophical idealism.

The traumas experienced by first- and second-century Jews also shaped early Christianity. As historian Elaine Pagels argued, the Jewish communities in which Christianity developed cherished stories about ancestors who lived under God's protective watch, but that traditional sense of religious security was seriously shaken by the killing of tens of thousands of Jews in the Roman-Judaean war and the expulsion of survivors from Judaea. Heightened concerns about sickness and death in response to these traumas built on several centuries of Jewish vulnerability and efforts to come to terms with a world in which God seemed terribly remote. Apocalyptic writings composed over the preceding centuries revealed individual visions of cosmic catastrophe. The destruction of the Jerusalem temple in 70 CE fed expectations of such catastrophe, amplified anguish over the breakdown of religious tradition and collective solidarity, and intensified feelings of personal isolation.[8]

Jews were not the only ones besieged by anxiety, sickness, and disorder. Growing demand for magical spells and cures reflected the dislocation, confusion, and fear that pervaded the Mediterranean world in the first centuries after Jesus' death. A rich supply of religions flourished, reflecting the pluralism and eclecticism of urban life in late antiquity.

Amid this diversity and religious competition, and amid the breakdown of traditional communities, Christianity attracted people from a variety of different backgrounds and encompassed a variety of different influences. Jewish ideas about a God of justice and mercy who presided over creation mingled with Persian ideas about a contest between personified forces of good and evil, with Neoplatonic ideas about ideal reality and the immortality of the soul, with Egyptian ideas about immortality and bodily resurrection, and with Greco-

Roman ideas about sacrifice, stoicism, and individual virtue. People separated from more traditional, stable, and homogeneous societies absorbed new religious influences that contributed to the very tendencies toward individualism and introspection that opened them to new religious influences in the first place.[9] The preoccupation with sickness and death in early Christianity represented disconcerting tendencies toward individualism, as well as an enveloping sense of social and religious crisis that plagued Jews especially. For people drawn to Christianity, hopes of dispelling isolation, suffering, and fears of sickness and death coalesced around the person of Jesus and his victorious power of healing.

Christian Nursing

As a number of primary documents attest, care for the sick was a distinctive and remarkable characteristic of early Christian missionary outreach. Early Christians nursed the sick to emulate the healing ministry of Jesus, to express their faith in the ongoing healing power of Christ, and to distinguish Christian heroism in the face of sickness and death from pagan fear. Polycarp, bishop of Smyrna in the early second century, identified care of the sick as one of the chief tasks for which church elders were responsible. A guidebook for Christian communities written in Rome around 215 instructed bishops to pay house calls on sick members.

In their ministrations to the sick, Christians adopted a simple rite, based on descriptions of healings Jesus performed, of anointing the sick with oil "in the name of the Lord." Anointing the sick on the lips, ears, and eyes, where demons could enter, early Christians performed rites "to guard the flesh as a temple of God." A second-century sermon conveyed this sort of concern for protection: "While we still have time to be healed, let us place ourselves in the hands of God the Physician."[10]

The New Testament Letter of James strongly commended the ritual of anointing as an enactment of Christian faith. Known to Irenaeus in the second century, the Letter indicated that anointing the sick was an important task performed by church elders. "Is one of you ill?" demanded the writer. "Let him send for the elders of the church to pray over him and anoint him with oil in the name of the Lord; the prayer offered in faith will heal the sick man, the Lord will restore him to health, and if he has committed sins they will be forgiven. Therefore," the writer asserted, "confess your sins to one another, and pray for one another, that you may be healed" (James 5:14–16).

Not surprising, given their commitment to anointing and zealous charity on behalf of the sick, Christians in late antiquity expressed a high degree of interest in illness and employed relatively specialized medical knowledge in discussing it. According to the historian and linguist R. J. S. Barrett-Lennard, Egyptian papyri from the fourth century show that letters written by lay Christians mentioned illness more frequently than letters written by a similar cohort of pagans. In addition, Barrett-Lennard observed, "The range and breadth of terms" associated with illness, health, and healing in letters written by Christians "is striking and in sharp contrast to the generally straightforward terminology used by non-Christian writers." Despite the existence of pagan healing shrines and deities known from other sources, Barrett-Lennard observed further, the surviving pagan letters do not attribute specific concerns about illness and healing to pagan deities. In contrast, the surviving letters written by Christians explicitly refer to God and Christ as gods concerned about human illness and healing.[11]

Barrett-Lennard also found an emphasis on healing in some of the earliest documents associated with monasticism. Five letters to ascetic holy men in mid-fourth-century Egypt indicate that these men were famous for the healing effects of their prayers for the sick. Barrett-Lennard interpreted these letters as evidence that healing played a central role in the emergence of monasticism in Egypt, and that holy men in late antiquity carried forward the performance of healing earlier associated with Jesus and the apostles. Other scholars concur. Stanley Harakas noted that although holy men devoted themselves to ordeals of suffering to perfect themselves spiritually, they also took time to perform more mundane healings for people who sought them out. And they employed a wide variety of material means in these endeavors. "Aided and abetted by their holiness," Harakas wrote, holy men "used the panoply of prayer together with their medical skills, folk wisdom, and herbal lore to cure the ills of others," in effect affirming that outreach to the sick was an essential aspect of their holiness.[12]

Christian exorcism, healing, and concern for the poor and sick developed in a diversified market of religious and medical services. The healing powers of various religious deities, priestly officials, objects, shrines, and rituals were in great demand throughout the Mediterranean world in the early centuries after Jesus' death, and Christians competed well in this arena. Amid the eclectic assortment of healing agents offered by physicians, magicians, and priests of various sorts, Christian beliefs and practices proved relatively effective in combating disease, alleviating suffering, and imbuing believers with strength. The success of early Christianity had everything to do with its salutary, invigorating effects.

In a recent book comparing Christianity with other healing cults in the ancient Mediterranean world, Hector Avalos argued that the Jesus movement provided a health care system that was cheaper and more accessible than any- thing offered by competing groups. People who sought healing from other deities and miracle workers had to undergo more complicated, and often far more costly, procedures. For example, for curing malaria, priests of the goddess Gula demanded 7 twigs of tamarisk, 7 twigs of date palm, 7 bottles of wine, 7 bottles of beer, 7 bottles of milk, 7 bottles of honey, and 15 silver drinking vessels. Healing rites performed by the priests of Isis were also expensive, and her temples could be difficult to reach, especially for people who were sick and not able to travel easily. The temples of Asclepius were more numerous and open to anyone who could pay, and the priests of Asclepius sometimes traveled to the homes of the sick. But the healing rituals offered by the Ascle- pian system were not free, as they were in the Christian system, nor were they as simple to practice. Whereas healing rites at the temples of Asclepius, Isis, and other Hellenistic deities could involve much rigmarole and expense, fol- lowers of Jesus simply had to call on him and invoke his name. Without claim- ing that the healing power associated with Jesus was intrinsically greater than that of Isis, Asclepius, or any other god, Avalos argued that early Christianity won adherents because its health care system was cheaper, and more accessible and accommodating, than what other groups provided.[13]

Christian nursing was especially noticeable during epidemics. A mid-third- century letter from Dionysius, bishop of Alexandria, described the dedication to the sick and dead displayed by Christians during an epidemic and their fearlessness in the face of sickness and death. "Most of our brethren showed love and loyalty in not sparing themselves while helping one another," Dio- nysius reported, "tending to the sick with no thought of danger and gladly departing this life with them after becoming infected with their disease." While Christians ministered heroically, "the heathen were the exact opposite." Ac- cording to Dionysius, people without Christian faith "pushed away those with the first signs of the disease and fled from their dearest. They even threw them half dead into the roads and treated unburied corpses like refuse in hopes of avoiding the plague of death."[14]

Dionysius may have exaggerated the contrast between pagan cowardice and Christian compassion and fortitude. But whatever its embellishment, his account of fearless charity among Christians reflected understanding of how Christians were supposed to act. His account helped to shape Christianity's reputation, as did other, similar stories that depicted Christians not only as brave and compassionate, but in some instances at least, able to throw off disease. While Dionysius praised Christians for accepting their own sickness as nothing "but a discipline and testing," his observation that the plague spared

Christians more often, and "struck the heathen more heavily," certainly contributed to the idea that Christian faith could inoculate believers against disease and even death.[15]

A similar story from the early fourth century comes as an eye-witness account of the drought, famine, disease, and war that ravaged Caesarea and other cities in the eastern Empire during the reign of Maximin Daia. Eusebius, the bishop of Caesarea and celebrated father of church history, was graphic: "Moaning was heard everywhere, and funeral processions were seen in every lane, square, and street, with the usual flute playing and breast beating." In some places, he wrote, "naked bodies lay scattered about unburied for days." Among these, "some were eaten by dogs, for which reason the living began killing dogs, for fear they might go mad and start devouring people." In this hellish situation, "the zeal and piety of the Christians were obvious to all the heathen." According to Eusebius, Christians "tended to the dying and to their burial, countless numbers with no one to care for them." Christians also "gathered together from all parts of the city a multitude of those withered from famine and distributed bread to them all, so that that their deeds were on everyone's lips, and they glorified the God of the Christians."[16]

Despite the considerable political force exerted to suppress Christianity, sociologist Rodney Stark attributed its remarkable growth in the second and third centuries to the extreme altruism of Christians who attended the sick during epidemics. While pagans headed for the hills, if they were able, Christians exhibited heroic willingness to care and die for others. This altruism, combined with reports of marvelous immunity to disease among some Christian nurses, explained how the rate of conversion could outpace the rate of Christian death and apostasy, at a time when severe (albeit sporadically enforced) penalties existed for practicing Christianity. Stark argued further that the intellectual explanations and theological comforts of paganism paled beside those Christianity offered. Christians attracted converts through their personalized view of reality that conceptualized epidemics as punishments for sin, offered salvation from sin, and described the Kingdom of God as a stable, just, and healthy realm awaiting the faithful beyond the present world of misery. This engaging and ultimately hopeful vision, coupled with the efforts Christians made to reach out to the sick and gather supportive people and resources around them, gave Christians the edge, when it came to strength and survival, over pagans who lacked such support.[17]

The disastrous epidemics of the second and third centuries, by Stark's estimate, demolished a quarter to a third of both urban and rural populations in the Mediterranean world. As well as providing Christians opportunities to prove their bravery in the face of death, these epidemics provided opportunities to proclaim the superiority of the Christian God. Christianity won out over paganism, according to Stark, not simply because Constantine embraced and legalized it, but because its approach to life (and death) was both admirable and effective. In addition to displaying heroic and compassionate virtue, Christians improved the survival odds of the people they nursed, who might otherwise have been left to themselves, without water or food or any emotional support. With survivors prone to convert, Christians might actually have been more immune to disease than pagans, as well as better equipped to cope with fear and suffering when they did fall ill, which also contributed to their higher rate of survival. Had these "crises *not occurred*," Stark argued, "Christians would have been deprived of major, possibly crucial opportunities." These epidemics helped defeat paganism, according to Stark, because paganism exposed "its relative inability to confront these crises socially or spiritually—an inability suddenly revealed by the example of the upstart challenger."[18]

Writing just before his death in the early second century, Ignatius celebrated the strength and well-being of those who "belong entirely to God." For the persecuted bishop of Antioch, participation in the vitality of Christ was not an exercise in passivity, but an all-out engagement in spiritual warfare. And Ignatius welcomed the opportunity to prove his faith. Sent to Rome to be executed during the reign of Trajan, he represented himself as a hero, bound "in chains for the sake of the Name." Approaching death in the coliseum, he exhilarated, "Now at last I am beginning to be a disciple." He dared the minions of evil to take him on: "Fire and cross and battles with wild beasts, mutilation, mangling, wrenching of bones, hacking of limbs, the crushing of my whole body, cruel tortures of the devil—let these come upon me, only let me reach Jesus Christ!"[19]

Early Christian Medicine

While the epidemics that ravaged ancient cities offered Christians many opportunities to exercise their healing faith, the legalization of Christianity expedited new levels of institutional organization for health care, especially in Constantinople, the new capital of the Roman Empire. Rulers seated there lost control of the western provinces of the Empire at the end of the fourth century, but the city remained the center of Eastern Christendom until its surrender to Ottoman Turks in the fifteenth century. Christian hospitals developed in this region as a result of a combination of factors, including relatively cordial ties between medicine and Christianity and activism on the part of Christian physicians.

According to historian Timothy Miller, the origins of the modern hospital can be traced to these early Christian institutions. Hospitals developed in the East as prime manifestations of idealism about Christian society and as institutions second in religious importance only to churches. Hospitals where physicians treated the sick (as distinct from hospices devoted simply to palliative care) first emerged in late fourth-century Caesarea and Constantinople under the leadership of Basil and John Chrysostom, both of whom promoted care of the sick as an exemplary form of Christian philanthropy. Their hospitals provided models for hospitals in other cities, and later, for the development of Islamic medical care and medical training that, in the twelfth century, in turn inspired the crusading Knights of Saint John to develop new hospitals in Europe.[20]

Close connections between medicine and Christianity played an important role in the expansion of Christianity eastward from Antioch and Edessa into Persia and, beginning in the seventh century, into China. In 411 or 412, when the Syrian Rabbula became bishop of Edessa, the cosmopolitan city near where the Silk Road crossed the Euphrates, he "found Edessa crowded with churches" and "teem[ing] with heretics," according to historian Samuel Moffett. Rabbula responded to this chaotic situation by attacking the heretics and encouraging the construction of hospitals. During his two decades as bishop, Edessa became a center of orthodoxy, Christian medicine, and missionary outreach.[21]

Nestorian Christians poured into Edessa from Antioch in the fifth century, after the Council of Ephesus declared their leader Nestorius a heretic, despite the fact that his consideration of the human aspects of Christ and his mother were not as much of a departure from established doctrine as his detractors in Alexandria maintained. Nestorian Christians became merchants and missionaries along the Silk Road and established an important school in Nisibis, which became famous as a center for the study of religious literature and was also known, by the late sixth century, for its department of medicine.[22] According to Moffett, "It was from the Nestorians that the Arabs learned much of the Greek science and learning they were later to pass on to a Europe, which, overrun by barbarian invasions, was losing much of its ancient Greek heritage." Nestorian priests and merchants also took their learning to China, converting members of the Uighur tribe in the eighth century. One famous general in the Chinese army during the eighth century was a Nestorian priest known for healing and caring for the poor.[23]

Cooperation between Christians and medical practitioners was stronger and more persistent in the new city of Constantinople than in Rome, where the status of medicine associated with Hippocrates and Galen lost ground. In the Western Empire during the fourth and fifth centuries, physicians did not enjoy the same prestige they did in Constantinople and were more often denounced for ineptitude and greed. The besieging of Rome and other western cities by Germanic invaders beginning in the fifth century weakened the influence of Greek medicine, along with other aspects of Greek culture that had shaped the early development of Christianity. That influence became more tenuous with the expansion of Roman Christianity into northern Europe and its assimilation into more primitive cultures. In the East, by contrast, significant new advances in public support for medicine occurred. By the early sixth century, the government in Constantinople authorized the establishment of publicly supported institutions that combined Christian nursing with medical treatment of disease. These new institutions differed from older, publicly supported outpatient centers staffed by physicians by offering long-term care and specialized medical treatment.

Already in the third century, Origen had championed the idea that Christ was "the Great Physician," along with the idea that bishops and other representatives of Christ were "physicians of souls." The Cappadocian Fathers built on these ideas first articulated by Origen. Gregory of Nyssa referred to Christ as "the true doctor of the soul's suffering," and Gregory of Nazianzus elaborated on the metaphor of healing to conceptualize the incarnation of Christ and his saving power. In his biography of Basil, Gregory of Nazianzus recalled that the great man had based his approach to pastoral work on his understanding of medicine, noting that Basil had studied Hippocratic texts as part of his upper-class education in Greek philosophy and that he had considerable knowledge of herbal remedies as well. Basil personally visited the sick in his hospital, greeting them with a kiss and attending to their wounds and aliments, and for centuries afterward, monks emulated his humility and friendship for the sick.[24]

Following Origen, Basil argued that God gave medicine, as he did other arts, to help mankind and that Christians should be grateful for the remedies that medicine provided because they were gifts from God. On the other hand, God cured people without medicine, and monks would do best to eschew medicine and rely on God alone. In any event, overreliance on medicine and desperate efforts to cling to life should be renounced by all Christians: "Whatever requires an undue amount of thought or trouble or involves a large expenditure of effort and causes our whole life to revolve, as it were, around solicitude for the flesh must be avoided by Christians."[25] Thus, Basil urged Christians, "Take care never to provide the lower part of your nature with great power of dominion by adding weight to the flesh." He emphasized the need for asceticism, which gave more weight to the soul, and observed that when the soul was "developed to its proper stature by the practice of virtue, the body suffers a corresponding deterioration."[26]

Along with these guidelines for the proper use and understanding of medicine, Basil and other early Christians drew from their familiarity with medicine, and their understanding of recovery from sickness, to conceptualize the nature of Christ. Historian Michael Dornemann recently identified numerous passages in early Christian writings that developed the theme of Christ as the soul's physician and showed that Basil's reading in Hippocratic medical texts informed his ideas about how Christ worked to form an impression of spiritual purity and vitality on believers. In Hippocratic writing on "The Physician," for example, "It is recommended that the physician have a healthy appearance, since he can only care effectively for a sick person, if he himself makes a good impression." In his use of this enjoinder to explain the nature and power of the Incarnation, Basil explained that Christ's "divinity is undefiled and unspoiled, even if it exists in a material nature. It sets right the feeling of suffering, it itself is not filled with suffering."[27]

Healing as Counterweight to Philosophic Idealism

Missionary outreach to the sick contributed to the reputation and stability of the new religion and epidemics gave Christians opportunities to take the practical advantage as well as moral high ground in relation to paganism and demonstrate the salutary effects of their faith on a larger scale than would otherwise have been possible. At the same time, a number of churchmen worked to define Christianity against extreme forms of philosophic dualism that denied the body's importance as the site of spiritual transformation. Irenaeus, the second-century bishop of Lyons, faced escalating tendencies to separate Christianity from this-worldly concerns so important to its origins in Judaism, tendencies that redefined Christianity as a story about a redeemer who descended from the astral world to free souls from imprisonment in matter. In his influential work *Against Heresies* (c. 180–185), the bishop asserted that Jesus had not disobeyed Jewish scripture by healing on the Sabbath, but had acted out the true meaning of his healing work as the renewal of God's work of creation. In opposition to magicians whom he accused of playing tricks that did little to combat sickness in anything but the most ephemeral way, Irenaeus celebrated the effective and lasting healing power of Christ. "Those who are in truth His disciples, receiving grace from Him," the bishop wrote, "do in his name perform miracles, so as to promote the welfare of other men." Thus, Irenaeus viewed the real work of healing as an ongoing, essential part of Christian life and a fundamental aspect of the combat against Satan that was pulling the whole drama of human redemption forward.[28]

Healing practices contributed to the character of early Christianity in a variety of ways, not the least of which was in constraining the influence of more radical forms of idealism and cosmic dualism. For the churchmen whose writings established what came to be known as orthodox doctrine, the dangers of radical idealism commanded more attention than the dangers they perceived from opposite tendencies—to which they were far less susceptible themselves—to see Jesus as a man without divine nature. Indeed, the flowering of Christian thought from Irenaeus in the second century through the Cappadoccian fathers in the fourth century to Augustine in the early fifth, can be understood partly as an effort to carve out theological positions that resisted tendencies to entirely subsume the cosmic dualism of good and evil in a philosophical dualism of spirit and matter. If healing figured prominently in Christianity's popularity and success at a practical level, then at the philosophical level, commitment to the resurrection of the flesh and to the closely related symbolism of Christ the Physician figured prominently in efforts to distinguish Christian theology from extreme forms of philosophical idealism.

Many scholars identify the dualist views of spirit and matter in Christianity with Gnosticism, which they describe as a protean phenomenon in late antiquity, involving broad-ranging ideas about the nature of religious knowledge.[29] In one important study, Elaine Pagels characterized Gnosticism as an investment in the subjective and allegorical nature of religious truth that produced a profusion of interpretations dividing early Christianity into dozens of different sects.[30] Most would agree that Gnosticism was a heterogeneous and pervasive phenomenon in Greco-Roman culture. On the moderate end of the spectrum, Gnostic thought was simply a tendency to imagine the material world as a manifestation of spiritual forms and truths. On the other, more extreme end of the spectrum, organized sects emerged to facilitate the liberation of souls from the world of flesh that encrusted them. Gnostic sects emerged in full force during the second century, driving Irenaeus and others to great effort to preserve Christianity against what they viewed as despicable heresies. But Gnostic tendencies were present prior to the second century, often in milder and less organized forms that contributed to the cultural ethos out of which Christianity emerged.

Gnosticism is often associated with Neoplatonic thought and with the cosmic dualisms and depictions of salvation coming into Hellenistic culture from Persia and India. In their most extreme form in Christianity, Marcion and his followers in mid-second-century Rome contrasted the vengeful creator god of Jewish scripture with Christ, the true and loving redeemer of mankind. Marcion portrayed the Jewish god in terms of law, punishment, and warfare, in contrast to Christ, whom he identified with goodness, light, and love. For Marcion, salvation through Christ required renunciation of the Jewish god and the dark world of the flesh associated with him. Christ was the purely divine being who descended into this world to lift human souls up to the spiritual realm that was their true and eternal home.[31]

More subtle influences of Gnostic thought, or what Kingsley Barrett called pre-Gnosticism and proto-Gnosticism, colored the thought-world of the earliest Christian writers. Barrett and others pointed to the "affinity" to Gnosticism in the Gospel of John, written about 100, especially in the allusions to "the Gnostic myth of the descending and ascending redeemer-revealer that gives form to the language in John 8." John, of course, affirmed Jesus' connection to Moses, Abraham, and the God of Jewish scripture as well as the real suffering of Jesus and the resurrection of the flesh. But Gnostic influence is evident in the dualistic contrast John made Jesus draw between darkness and light: "Whoever follows me will never walk in darkness but will have the light of life" (John 8: 12). It may also be evident in Jesus' claim "I know where I have come from and where I am going" (8:14) and in his assertion "Before Abraham was, I am" (8:58).

According to Barrett, John's anti-Judaism is also a marker of Gnostic influence. "Your father is the devil," John has Jesus say to the Jews who question him (8: 44). In John's version of the Passion narrative, Pilate presents the Jews as having lost their commitment to the kingship of God: "We have no king but the emperor" (19:15). As Barrett argues, the mockery involved in John's story of Pilate giving Jesus the title "King of the Jews" (19:19) ultimately fell back on the Jews because of their failure to recognize Jesus as king.[32]

Dualistic philosophies had a spiritualizing effect on Christian interpretations of healing, even as Christian investment in healing worked against much stronger variants of those philosophies. John did not lose sight of Jesus' work as a healer, but he also interpreted healing as a symbol of eternal life. Thus, in response to charges of "breaking the Sabbath" and "claiming equality with God" (John 5:18), John quoted Jesus as saying, "In very truth I tell you, whoever heeds what I say and puts his trust in him who sent me has eternal life; he does not come to judgment, but has already passed from death to life" (5:24).

Written before the gospels, New Testament letters written by the apostle Paul also carried a spiritualizing influence, albeit of a milder and Jewish-friendly kind. Some Christians interpreted Paul's claim in I Corinthians 15:50 that "flesh and blood cannot inherit the Kingdom of God" as a Gnostic formula and used the passage as evidence of Paul's support for their denial of bodily salvation. Irenaeus countered that interpretation by arguing that Paul invoked "flesh and blood" as a metaphor for the immoral behavior of "living in a fleshy way." Paul was not referring, so Irenaeus argued, to eternal life as a disembodied state, but to the new spiritual bodies Christians would inherit in the life to come.[33]

Paul on the Human Embodiment of Christ

Saul of Tarsus, a vigorous Jewish opponent of the Jesus sect until his conversion sometime around 50 CE, did more than anyone to shape early Christian understanding of healing and its relation to baptism as a spiritual transformation that brought believers eternal life through union with Christ. As a Hellenistic thinker, he conceptualized healing as a spiritual salvation. As a Jew, he conceptualized healing as a communal as well as individual process, and one that involved moral behavior, sexual purity, and genuine vitality. Paul's letters to early Christian communities were widely read (and still are), and his ideas about baptism, resurrection, and Christian life influenced Christian thought and liturgy profoundly. His theology was radical in its emphasis on the necessity of spiritual control of the body, especially with regard to sex,[34] but still Jewish in its commitment to bodily life and conduct as the domain of God's creation. "By that baptism into his death we were buried with him," Paul reminded the Christian community in Rome, "in order that, as Christ was raised from the dead by the glorious power of the Father, so also we might set out on a new life" (Romans 6:4). Echoing Jewish belief that God intended human beings to return to a state of well-being and obedience to God like that once enjoyed in paradise, Paul made it clear that baptism was not a way to discount the human body, or transcend it, but rather the way to transform it. Thus, he called Christians in Rome to "yield your bodies to God as implements for doing right" (6:14). If "you once yielded your bodies to the service of impurity and lawlessness, making for moral anarchy, so now you must yield them to the service of righteousness, making for a holy life" (6:19).

Stories about Paul in the book of Acts indicate that he was both a recipient of Christ's healing power and, after his conversion and recovery from blindness, an exorcist and healer in his own right. In one story, Paul's awesome performance as a healer creates confusion about his identity, which he dispels by exposing his body to show himself as really human, not just apparently so. In the city of Lystra, on the mainland north of Cyprus, where Paul and his assistant, Barnabas, drew a large crowd, Paul looked a lame man in the eye and spoke to him in "a loud voice" (Acts 14:10), causing the man to spring to his feet. Amazed by this performance, the people shouted, "The gods have come down to us in human form!" In their excitement and confusion, the people "called Barnabas Zeus, and Paul they called Hermes, because he was the spokesman" (14:11–12). Alarmed at this pagan misreading, Paul and Barnabas "tore their clothes and rushed into the crowd shouting, 'Men, why are you doing this? We are human beings, just like you' " (14:14–15).

In his exhortations to the Colossians, Paul preached that becoming one with Christ required "putting off the body of the flesh" (Colossians 2:11), but most scholars agree that flesh in this context is a metaphor for hedonistic behavior, not a repudiation of the body as such.[35] In the same section of the Letter, Paul emphasized the embodied nature of Christian life. In Christ, he instructed, "the whole fullness of deity dwells bodily" (2:9). In his Letter to the Romans, Paul also focused on the body as the site of spiritual transformation: "If the Spirit of him who raised Jesus from the dead dwells in you, he who raised Christ from the dead will give life to your mortal bodies also through his Spirit that dwells in you" (Romans 8:11).

The intellectual historian Troels Engberg-Pedersen argued that Paul's understanding of Christian faith was informed by Stoic thought. Inspired by Aristotle's discussion of the connection between virtue and reason, Stoic philosophers from Chrysippean and Cicero to Seneca described the individual's encounter with reason as a potentially liberating change that resulted in effective participation in public life and active dedication to the common good. Paul substituted Christ for reason, Engberg-Pedersen argued, infusing Stoic commitment to ethical virtue with a new element of mystical experience that Paul identified with love.[36]

But at a more fundamental level than affinity with Stoicism, Paul's view of Christ was grounded in Jewish thought and practice. As a Jew, Paul viewed illness, infirmity, suffering, and death as God's punishments for sin and as occasions for repentance for sin. He also viewed wholeness, happiness, and spiritual healing as a new creation that restored the well-being Adam and Eve had enjoyed in paradise. Like other Hellenistic Jews, he drew from Greek philosophy to interpret Jewish thought in more individualistic, spiritual terms. If the new creation was spiritual and infused with promises of the soul's immortality derived from Hellenistic philosophy, it was still Jewish in its focus on the body as the site of the spirit's indwelling.

Paul understood Jesus in the context of Jewish scripture: as the Messiah foretold in scripture as well as the last and greatest in a long line of judges and prophets raised up to lead God's people to righteousness, well-being, and victory over the forces arrayed against them. As a Hellenistic thinker as well, Paul interpreted this victory in spiritual terms: it was a spiritual conquest over evil. Paul never repudiated the Law of Moses. As New Testament scholar John Gager argued, he simply did not expect Gentile Christians to become Jews. Both groups ("the Jew first and then the Greek"; Romans 1:16; 2:10) were heirs to

God's promise to Abraham. "In the end," as Gager explained Paul, "there are not two peoples of God but one. Jews and Gentiles—humanity in its entirety—form one corporate body, not identical with Israel and certainly not with any Christian church."[37]

Gager argued that Paul presented Jesus to non-Jews as the embodiment of Jewish scripture and ethical monotheism—for them. Paul's commitment to community life was essentially Jewish, as was his ethical monotheism, concern for the poor, and vision of human righteousness and well-being. His understanding of illness and disability as punishment for sin was Jewish, as was his interpretation of suffering as a means of repentance. In his Letter to the Romans, written partly to combat hostility to Jews in the community of Roman Christians, Paul made it clear that the eternal life obtainable through Jesus was an extension of God's covenant with Israel: "There will be anguish and distress for everyone who does evil, the Jew first and also the Greek, but glory and honor and peace for everyone who does good, the Jew first and also the Greek" (Romans 2:9–11).

Along similar lines, many early Christians understood Jesus as the fulfillment of Hebrew prophecy and developed ritual practices of transformation and healing that built on Jewish ideas about a covenant relationship with God and its implications for health and well-being. As the Epistle of Barnabas has Moses declare, "Set your hope on Jesus, who is about to be revealed to you in the flesh." When Moses spoke of the people's entrance "into the good land, a land flowing with milk and honey," Barnabas claimed, he uttered a parable about Jesus, who "made us men of another type," "as if he were creating us all over again."[38]

Although this commitment to being created anew defined early Christianity, the exact meaning of what that entailed prompted vigorous dispute. Spiritualized interpretations of new creation in Christ played an important role in promoting the divinity of Christ and explaining the nature of salvation, but in more dualistic and extreme forms, they threatened to undermine the investment in material creation inherited from Judaism. Paul and his followers offered interpretations of the new creation in Christ that were radical in their demands on believers, but still this-worldly in their emphasis on the body, the need for healing, and the importance of pure and righteous behavior. This investment in human bodies and behavior, and in their spiritual purification, represented an alternative to more extreme spiritualizing tendencies that interpreted the new creation in disembodied terms.

Paul's letters are like other examples of Jewish wisdom literature in incorporating idealistic philosophy into Judaean visions of God's relation to the world. As a genre, wisdom literature offered meditations on human experience and philosophic ideas about the soul's immortality that were current in the Hellenistic world and that helped to explain Jesus' apparently ignominious death. The intellectual background of wisdom culture helped Jesus' followers translate older connections between sin, misfortune, and disease on the one hand, and repentance, righteousness, and healing on the other, into the more individualistic culture of diaspora Judaism. Jews living outside of Palestine faced the challenge of retaining distinctively Jewish forms of obedience to God in multicultural, urban environments. Wisdom literature enabled Jews in different parts of the Mediterranean world to express their Judaism—and for some, their enthusiasm for Jesus—in Hellenistic form, by grafting ideals about the soul's immortality onto older Hebrew ideas about suffering, repentance, and healing.

The Wisdom of Solomon is one example of the Hellenistic Jewish literature that provided a new context for thinking about Jesus and his reputation as a healer. That text drew on the old idea that God punished his enemies with sickness and misfortune while protecting his people. As Solomon explained, "No healing was found for" the enemies of God, "but your children were not conquered even by the fangs of venomous serpents, for your mercy came to their help and healed them" (16:9–10). Of course, God's people were not exempt from chastisement: God allowed serpents to bite them in order "to remind them" of his word (16:11). Their faith quickened by this reminder, the people "were quickly delivered" from the effects of venom. As Solomon explained, in his philosophical way, it was "neither herb nor poultice cured them, but it was your word, O Lord, that heals all people." In addition to the relief it gave from bodily suffering, God's healing word gave his people safe passage through death: "For you have power over life and death; you lead mortals down to the gates of Hades and back again" (16:11–12). These passages reflect the infusion of Greek ideas about the immortality of the soul into more traditional Jewish thought about the material rewards of ethical righteousness. As the Wisdom of Solomon declared, "The righteous live forever, and their reward is with the Lord; the Most High takes care of them. Therefore they will receive a glorious crown and a beautiful diadem from the hand of the Lord" (5:15–16).

Baptism

The early Christian rite of baptism was an exalted form of healing. It was a rite of initiation in the mystery of Christ that gave people eternal life and fortified them against sickness and sin. As an initiation into the Christian community, baptism remade individuals into members of the living body of Christ.

As the ultimate healing ritual in early Christianity, baptism reenacted the death of Jesus, his resurrection, and triumph over evil. Preparations for baptism customarily took place during Lent, in emulation of the events leading up to the crucifixion of Jesus. Initiates received instruction in Christian beliefs and practices and underwent a series of preparatory exorcisms that involved anointing the bodily orifices with oil as an aid to expunging demonic influence and sealing the body against demonic penetration. This use of oil prior to baptism linked the rite to the more commonplace Christian practice of anointing sick people with oil, and to a more general understanding, derived from Judaism, of the need for purification from sin and protection against evil forces that made people vulnerable to sickness.

The culminating immersion in water was a test and ordeal. Once the preparatory catechisms and exorcisms were finished, initiates had to face death with nothing of their own but faith in Christ to bring them through. Stripped of all power and left vulnerable except for their reliance on Christ, initiates in some communities stripped to the skin (and loosed their hair if they were women) before stepping into the baptismal waters. In Syria, initiates wore white robes during their preparation for baptism and received crowns of green leaves for their head, in anticipation of the new life that awaited them, before entering the water. Most often performed at Easter, the completion of baptism marked the believer's transformation through the resurrected Christ. A common meal, celebrating the community's shared life in Christ, followed the initiation of new members, as it followed communal worship on other days.[39]

Baptismal waters were a burial chamber and drowning ordeal on one hand, and a quickening fluid that freshened and restored life on the other. Immersion in these waters encouraged visceral sensations of terror and hope and of change from one to the other. The story of Jonah's fall into the sea and into the belly of a whale was part of the background of Christian baptism, as was the story of the flood and God's preservation of Noah. These stories portrayed God's mercy in preserving his people from waters of death. Early Christian thought about baptism also drew from Judaean depictions of divine mercy, and indeed of God himself as living water.

Along this line, the late first- or early second-century Letter of Barnabas presented Christian baptism as the fulfillment of scriptural prophecies regarding the living waters of God. Pressing the claim that Jesus was the embodiment of Jewish hope, Barnabas quoted Jeremiah 2:13, claiming that the prophet's words had come true with respect to Jews who resisted Christianity: "This people has done two evil things: they have abandoned me, the fountain of life, and they have dug for themselves a pit of death." Then, quoting Isaiah 33:16–17 and Psalm 1:3, "His water will never fail; you will see the King in glory," Barnabas claimed that the prophet Isaiah foretold the arrival of Christ as the savior who would enable his people to see the King in glory and enjoy the water of God: "And the one who does these things will be like the tree that is planted by the streams of water, which will yield its fruit in its season and whose leaf will not wither, and whatever he does will prosper." Thus, Barnabus understood baptism as the regaining of paradise, with "a river flowing on the right hand, and beautiful trees were rising from it, and whoever eats from them will live forever." As the Letter insisted, this promise of health, fertility, and prosperity required suffering: baptism signified "the water and the cross together. For this is what he means: blessed are those who, having set their hope on the cross, descended into the water."[40]

Early Christian baptism drew from the Jewish rite of purification by immersion in water, or *tebilah*, originally performed outside the temple in Jerusalem during holy days. Even before 70 CE, when the destruction of the temple put an end to that practice, Jews built immersion pools, or *mikvehs*, in their homes and synagogues as expressions of commitment to ethical obedience to God in everyday life. Baptism developed along these lines as a ritual bath that cleansed believers from sin and restored a right relationship with God. However, immersion in a mikveh could be repeated as the need for purification required, whereas Christian baptism was supposed to be a once-in-a-lifetime event.[41]

Baptism represented full admission into a covenant relationship with God. It also involved identification with Christ, receipt of his healing and death-defying power, and membership in a community identified with his living, resurrected body. As practiced earlier by John, the baptizer of Jesus, baptism brought people into the Kingdom of God. John (and perhaps Jesus) may have participated in, or least been familiar with, the Essene community, an apocalyptic Jewish sect whose library at Qumran, known as the Dead Sea Scrolls, was unearthed in the twentieth century. The Essenes performed a purifying rite of initiation closely associated with a sacred, communal meal. Along with other apocalyptic sects in first-century Judaism, the Essenes espoused a theology of the Two Ways, one of moral perfection heralding the messianic age of redemption, and the other of unrighteousness and sin. The early Christian rite of baptism developed along similar lines, as an initiation into a Way of purity and righteousness that followers identified with the Kingdom of God.

Healing as Victory over Evil

If baptism was the ultimate healing rite of early Christianity, the performance of exorcism was an act of discipleship that displayed the power of Christ in a dramatic way. As a means of expelling sin and evil from others and healing them in the name of Christ, it was also a means of Christian outreach. Casting out demons was a trademark of early Christianity, and Christians acquired reputations as exorcists in atmospheres charged with sensitivity to demons and their malevolent powers. In exorcism as well as martyrdom, Christians defined who they were, and how powerful they were, by confronting the spiritual forces of evil. And in exorcism as in martyrdom, Christian victory over evil had invigorating effects. Exorcists identified, confronted, and defeated demons perceived to torment, debilitate, and intimidate people, much as martyrs showed the world that Christ could not be destroyed by persecuting his representatives.

The early church historian S. V. MacCasland identified exorcism, more than teaching or preaching, as "perhaps the outstanding mark of discipleship in the early church."[42] The well-known historian of late Roman culture, Ramsey MacMullen, also affirmed the importance of exorcism in second- and third-century Christianity, and described it as a "shoot-out" with "nasty, lower powers" that inhabited their victims, causing all kinds of affliction. "The manhandling of demons—humiliating them, making them howl, beg for mercy, tell their secrets, and depart in a hurry," MacMullen wrote, "served a purpose quite essential to the Christian definition of monotheism: it made physically (or dramatically) visible the superiority of the Christian's patron power over all others." This type of commanding spiritual power harked back to Jesus, who confronted and expelled demons by the spirit or finger of God, and to the heroic saints of ancient Israel, whose decisive action against enemies without, and corruption within, exhibited divine inspiration. "In a tradition that reached back to its very roots," MacMullen observed, "Christianity in the person of its most electric figures lit up the dualism they preached" through "confrontation with the enemy."[43]

In fourth-century Egypt, the holy man Antony (251–356) emerged as one of the most dazzling of these figures. He fought heroic battles against demons and conducted healing power for countless pilgrims who visited him. A virtuous man beloved in his village but beset by terrible demons, Antony first struck out for the tombs outside his village, then moved further away to an abandoned fortress in the mountains. According to his biographer, Athanasius, bishop of Alexandria (296–373), Antony intended to purify himself so completely that Christ would work within him to defeat every malevolent spirit who tormented him, or even came his way. In the tombs, "he yelled out: 'Here I am—Antony! I do not run from your blows." In answer to his calls, demons in the form of "lions, bears, leopards, bulls, and serpents, asps, scorpions, and wolves" came out to fight him. In his mountain fortress, visitors listened to him sing out, "Let God arise, and let his enemies be scattered; and let them that hate him flee before him." When friends broke through the door of his fortress, eager to see and emulate him, "Antony came forth as though from some shrine" in a state of "utter equilibrium." Looking stronger in body, not weaker, from his ascetic discipline and battles against demons, Antony had become a perfect vessel of Christ. "Through him the Lord healed many of those present who suffered from bodily aliments; others he purged of demons, and to Antony he gave grace in speech."[44]

Athanasius presented Antony as an exemplar of Christian orthodoxy, and thus as a living representative of the doctrine affirmed at the Council of Nicaea in 325 that Christ was both man and God, and that Christ extended his divine power, which was his by nature as God's Son, through his adopted saints and their healing work. Opponents of this doctrine included followers of Arius (250–336), the excommunicated priest of Alexandria, who argued instead that Christ was a man named as God's son because of the works he performed. In lifting up Antony as evidence against Arianism, Athanasius emphasized the power Christ worked through Antony to combat evil, defeat demons, and cure sickness. In other words, the whole purpose of Antony's retreat from society and as an ascetic disciple was not to raise himself to Christ, but to become so empty of passion that the divine power of Christ would flow through him.

Despite the dramatic performances of Christian healers, the attractive resonance between Christianity and medicine and the good reputation Christians acquired as caretakers of the sick, political legitimacy, demographic growth, and institutional organization brought new problems to Christianity. The expectation of transformation through baptism apparently left some converts expecting more, perhaps because fourth-century Gentile Christians were not all as philosophical as the church fathers, or as steeped in Jewish scripture, with its reverence for the created world and love for material images of redemption, as earlier Christians had been. Ambrose, the fourth-century bishop of Milan, imagined that the concrete presentation of God's living water in the baptismal rite might leave his catechumens wondering, "Is this all?" Such anxiety, coupled with efforts on the part of Christian leaders to winnow the field of all miracles except Christian ones, led to new ways of eliciting the healing power of Christ.[45] Yearning for healing in Europe, Asia, and Africa led to the veneration of healing saints whose lives (and deaths) represented the spiritual purity and proximity to Christ to which many believers aspired. Relics, images, and stories of these saints renewed and revitalized the tradition of miraculous healing associated with Jesus and his disciples.

3

Healing in Medieval Christianity

In *The History of the Franks* (c. 592), Gregory of Tours described a
healer outside of Nice with "iron chains wound round his body, next
to the skin," and "a hair-shirt on top." For most of the year, the
healer, Hospicius, "ate nothing but dry bread and a few dates."
(During Lent, he made broth from "Egyptian herbs," to which, Gregory observed, "hermits are greatly addicted.") "Through the agency
of this holy man," according to Gregory, "the Lord deigned to perform remarkable miracles," including the restoration of hearing and
speech to a young man struck deaf and dumb during a fever. That
young man had been on his way to Rome, accompanied by a deacon, hoping that a visit to the tombs of the apostles would produce a
cure. Along the way, the deacon stopped in to see Hospicius after
leaving the young man, who was consumed with fever and "a tremendous ringing in his ears," at a nearby inn. "Hospicius felt miraculous powers rising in him through the Spirit of our Lord" and
instructed the deacon to bring the stricken fellow straight to his hut.
Hastening to the inn, the deacon "seized" the young man by the
arm "and rushed him off to the Saint," who treated the patient vigorously, as Gregory described:

> Hospicius laid his hand on the man's hair and pulled his
> head in through the window. He took some oil, consecrated
> it, held the man's tongue tight in his left hand and poured
> the oil down his throat and over the top of his head. "In the

name of my Lord Jesus Christ," he said, "may your ears be unsealed and your mouth opened, by that miraculous power which once cast out the evil spirit from the man who was deaf and dumb." As he said this, he asked the man what his name was. "I am called so-and-so," he answered, enunciating the words clearly. When the deacon saw what had happened, he said: "I thank you from the bottom of my heart, Jesus Christ, for having deigned to reveal such a miracle by the hand of your servant. I was on my way to Peter, I was going to Paul and Lawrence, and all the others who have glorified Rome with their blood. I have found them all here, in this very spot I have discovered them."[1]

This passage serves as a good point of departure for thinking about healing in medieval Christianity, for comparing it to earlier forms of healing associated with Jesus, and for identifying differences between East and West. With respect to the past, Gregory presented Hospicius as a direct spiritual descendent of the founders of Christianity, linking his performance as a local saint in sixth-century Gaul to cures performed by Jesus, the apostles, and the holy men of early Christianity. Thus, in casting out the demon causing the young man's loss of hearing and speech, Hospicius replicated one of the cures ascribed to Jesus in the gospels (Mark 7:31–37; cf. Matthew 15:29–31) and carried forward the rite of exorcism that was such a conspicuous part of early Christianity. In using oil as part of a simple but forceful procedure to expel demons, Hospicius followed in the path of bishops, deacons, and lay exorcists in early churches who used oil to exorcise and heal the sick, and also emulated the disciples who, under commission from Jesus, "cast out many demons, and anointed with oil many who were sick and cured them" (Mark 6:13; cf. Matthew 10:1; Luke 9:1). Indeed, the point of Gregory's story was that the people of Gaul did not have to travel to the tombs of the apostles in Rome to be cured. They had saints of their own through whom the healing power of Christ flowed in much the same way it had five centuries earlier.

But if medieval saints carried forward the healing work performed by Jesus, his disciples, and the holy men of late antiquity, some changes had occurred. Like the renowned fourth-century Saint Antony, Hospicius healed visitors at a primitive outpost away from town. But whereas Antony retreated from cosmopolitan Alexandria to engage in fantastic battles with demons in the form of vipers and wild beasts, Hospicius was a country saint who defeated a demon by exerting muscular force over another man. In the rough-and-ready form of Christian healing Gregory described, the deacon "seized" the young man and "rushed" him to Hospicius, who pulled the young man in through the window of his hut by the hair, grabbed his tongue "tight," and forced him to swallow holy oil. Although Anthanasius depicted Antony as combative in asserting his power over evil and New Testament writers portrayed Jesus as confrontational with demons, no one suggested that either Jesus or Antony manhandled patients the way Hospicius did.

The changes Christianity underwent as it spread into Europe during the early medieval period had everything to do with its popularity outside the urban centers of the Mediterranean world and with its accommodation to the heroes, customs, and beliefs of Germanic, Frankish, Celtic, Scandinavian, and Slavic tribes. In its medieval European rustication, Christianity became less sophisticated and less philosophical than it had been among Jews and Gentiles in Hellenistic culture. But if Christianity lost some of its intellectual complexity in early medieval Europe, its pragmatic side flourished. In an age replete with violence, bloodshed, blindness, crippled limbs, and festering sores, Christianity advanced in Europe during the Middle Ages as a popular aid to human recovery, strength, and vitality.

The Healing Powers of Saints

Christian healing expanded in Africa, Asia, and Europe through devotion to the miraculous powers of the saints and their relics. As the persecution of Christians, and the birth of new martyrs, slowed in the fourth century, missionaries eagerly dug up the graves of old martyrs and transported their bones to new places where Christianity was becoming more firmly established. Describing this process, Darrel W. Amundsen wrote that, for many new converts, "the bones of holy men and their relics became the very core of Christianity, taking the place of theological subtleties that they could not hope to understand."[2]

Many Christians revered the bones and even the dust of saints because of the healing miracles attributed to them. For example, Bede, the eighth-century chronicler of English history, described postmortem healings performed by Oswald, "the most Christian king of Northumbrians," who fell valiantly fighting another tribe and their pagan king in 642. Hopeful Christians sought cures by traveling to the spot where Oswald was slain and by ingesting dirt brought home from there. "Many people took away the very dust from the place where his body fell, and put it in water, from which sick folk who drank it received great benefit," Bede wrote. "This practice became so popular that, as the earth was gradually removed, a pit was left in which a man could stand."[3] Similar tonics made from the detritus of saints' remains were highly touted. Afflicted with dysentery, Gregory of Tours found relief from a draught made of scrapings from St. Martin's bones.[4]

Christians moved relics from one site to another, often with great fanfare and elaborate accounts of the saint's life and miracles. The translation of relics from one shrine to another figured prominently in the development of a market economy in medieval Europe, contributing to the buildup of numerous goods and services around and along the way to shrines and, as the wealth associated with religious life accumulated, to new and sometimes fabulous productions of sight and sound. As Barbara Abou-El-Haj explained in her study of art devoted to the relics of medieval European saints, "What pilgrims could not see had to be dramatically visualized, in architectural settings and in heavenly visions, as well as in acoustically and visually orchestrated liturgies."[5] Medieval liturgies, feasts, and pilgrimages carried forward the earlier Christian tradition of manifesting the healing power of God in real time, preserving important continuities with the origins of Christianity while at the same time accommodating new peoples and cultures and facilitating the growth of new forms of material culture and aesthetic expression devoted to religion.

Medieval Christians venerated saints for a variety of reasons, including victory in battle, revenge, happiness, repentance, goodness and purity, fear of hell, and desire for eternal life in heaven. But by far the most common reason was hope of a cure. In his analysis of three thousand miracles reported at twelfth- and thirteenth-century English and French shrines, Ronald Finucane found that 90 percent of them involved healing.[6]

Belief in the healing miracles of the saints coexisted with and contributed to other aspects of medieval life. Shrines dedicated to the bones of saints became centers of community life, and local religious authorities built, rebuilt, or redesigned churches and altars to house them. Monks imported relics for their monasteries, refurbished chapels for them, and, under the auspices of the saints, expanded the facilities of their monasteries to include pharmacies and health care clinics for pilgrims. Shrines and monasteries became destinations, resting places, and ports of call for pilgrims drawn to their relics from a distance. They also served local people, providing welfare services and business opportunities, as well as liturgical ceremonies. As commercial traffic and marketing developed around these religious and health care centers, especially in the West after the tenth century, the entrepreneurial ethos of medieval Christian healing contributed to Christianity's development as a pragmatic religious tradition committed to empirical effects and therapeutic outcomes.

The Superiority of Christian Miracles

Prior to the twelfth century, when universities emerged as relatively independent centers of study and expertise in the West, medicine developed in a kind
of symbiosis with Christianity and, to a considerable extent, within the context
of monastic life. In the West, where Greek medicine was less well known than
in the East, monks often treated sickness and injury with the help of simple
handbooks based on Galenic medicine, along with herbal remedies and healing
practices drawn from tribal custom. But if medicine complemented Christian
faith in many situations, Christian writers constantly found it necessary to
stipulate that faith was better.

An avid proponent of Christianity's superior efficacy over ordinary medicine, Gregory of Tours gloried in examples of how the power of the saints
triumphed after the efforts of doctors had failed. With an ominous reminder
that a saint's "power is shown just as much by the punishment meted out to
fools as it is by the grace accorded to those who have been cured," he warned
against "skeptics, who, after witnessing a God-sent miracle, would have recourse to earthly remedies." A case in point was Leunast, the archdeacon of
Bourges during the late sixth century, who was afflicted with cataracts. Having
"sought the help of a number of doctors" to no avail, Leunast traveled to the
shrine of St. Martin and stayed there for weeks, praying and fasting until the
saint's feast-day arrived and his vision began to clear. Not satisfied with this
miracle, however, the man sought remedy from a Jew, "who bled his shoulders
with cupping-glasses, the effect of which was supposed to be that his sight
would improve." But at the moment the blood was removed, full blindness
returned. Hoping for forgiveness and relief, the archdeacon repaired to St.
Martin's for another long stay, but his prayers were spurned; he had dared to
seek improvement on a miracle from the "earthly remedies" of a Jew.[7]

Although Gregory insisted on the superiority of miracles over medicine
and the superiority of Christian faith over Jewish art, he did not exclude these
inferior elements from Christian life or discount their subordinate benefits.
As something of a medical authority himself, Gregory employed medical and
pharmacological handbooks derived from Greek texts. In subordinating respect
for medicine to faith in Christ, he was like Pope Gregory I (d. 604), who
vigorously championed the healing miracles of the saints but also retained a
physician from Alexandria as part of his household.[8]

As historian Valerie Flint showed, medieval Christians often described
Christ and his saints as superior physicians, and medical procedures also
proved to be useful models for describing how Christian miracles worked.

Thus, Sulpicius Severus described the expertise with salves demonstrated by an angel who successfully treated St. Martin's wounds. St. Simon of Montfort prescribed surgery to a monk in a dream, and then pricked the monk's foot, which cured him and left noxious fluid on his bed. The Virgin Mother reached her hand into the mouth of a mute in a thirteenth-century English vision and enabled him to speak by manipulating his tongue.[9]

Granting medicine a place below the miracles performed by saints, some Christians invoked its secondary legitimacy to discredit pagan magic. Caesarius of Arles condemned the harm done by devilish charms, lamenting that misguided souls do not seek "the church's medicine"—or even "the simple skill of doctors!"[10]

Although churchmen often acknowledged that medicine had a place in Christian life, they took a harder line against practices that seemed to undermine Christian doctrine and authority. As the vita of Eligius, the seventh-century bishop of Noyon, warned, "No pretext, no illness, nothing whatsoever can permit of the presumption of your approaching or questioning lot casters or seers or soothsayers or enchanters. Such wickedness will instantly deprive you of baptismal grace." Eligius also cautioned the sick against the common practice of setting "devilish charms at springs or trees or crossroads" and advised them instead to "trust in God's mercy alone and receive the sacrament of the body and blood of Christ in faith and reverence." A sick Christian might "ask some holy oil of his church and have his body anointed in the name of Christ" but should never turn to material elements, incantations, or wonder-workers not authorized by the church.[11]

While threatening dire consequences to Christians tempted to engage in activities that subverted Christian authority, Eligius acknowledged a similarity between crossroads charms and holy oil by warning against the former as a prohibited form of spiritual intervention. In similar claims to Christianity's greater strength and higher ranking against pagan forces, some missionaries chopped down holy trees and demolished heathen shrines, leaving this destruction to carry the message. Others who championed the miraculous power of Christianity took shrewd advantage of their competition by refurbishing older temples as churches, constructing churches from the wood of holy trees, erecting Christian shrines next to recognized holy places, and even converting the waters of pagan springs to baptismal use.

Along with these replacements, the material manifestations of Christian belief and practice proliferated. Bede attributed the rains that ended a drought in seventh-century Sussex to a mass conversion of pagans. Charlemagne found it necessary to command eighth-century Christians to stop ringing baptismal bells for the purpose of averting hail. A tenth-century codex from Winchester explained that "thunder at the third hour" of the night signified "the anger of the Lord, or his judgment made manifest in the world," whereas thunder at daybreak signified "that a people is being converted to faith in Christ."[12]

It is easy to dismiss medieval enthusiasm for miracles as an expression of the irrational mentality of ignorant people, and more than a few historians have done precisely that. The famous eighteenth-century historian Edward Gibbon even blamed the collapse of the Roman Empire on the intellectual and moral weakness of Christianity, which he saw reflected in superstitious devotion to miracles, among other things.[13] But miracles figured importantly in Christianity from the start, and the most learned Christians accepted miracles, especially miracles of healing, as an essential aspect of Christian life and a sign of the power of Christian faith. As Christianity spread through Europe with fairly lax theological control and ecclesiastical oversight, this aspect of Christianity flowered everywhere and even, critics charged, ran rampant.

In its competition with the pre-Christian beliefs and practices of European groups, Christianity entered into, and helped to develop, a religious world that was imaginative, florid, and pragmatic. Enthusiasm for miracles stimulated material and aesthetic expressions of Christianity, enriching its sights and sounds and contributing to countless and sometimes magnificent productions of religious art. Enthusiasm for miracles also reflected serious interest in the practical benefits of religion as well as reverence for the wonders of nature. As historian Miri Rubin observed about medieval thought generally, "The miraculous was widely perceived as part of nature."[14] To some extent, then, the profusion of miracles in medieval culture reflected fascination with nature and its hospitality to miraculous displays of beauty and power.

As miracle traditions became more expansive and elaborate through contact with tribal religions, they also supported a vigorously pragmatic approach to the natural world. The medieval eye for material benefits of healing contributed to the development of market economies and artistic production and also helped stimulate the empirical observations and cause-and-effect logic of proto-scientific thinking. Competitive efforts to capture the practical benefits of nature's miracles for Christianity contributed to the incorporation of pre-Christian traditions under the aegis of Christianity and eased the accommodation of many practical forms of medicine into this religious world.[15]

The writings of the twelfth-century German Benedictine Hildegard of Bingen illustrate the proto-scientific thinking associated with belief that God's hand could be discerned in nature. Hildegard compiled two medical works: *Causes and Cures*, a depiction and explanation of the origins and remedies of numerous diseases, and *Physica*, a nine-book pharmacopoeia. These works show familiarity with contemporary Latin medical texts based on Greek medicine along with extensive knowledge of herbs and their medicinal uses and pioneering attention to gynecological processes and problems. Hildegard's medical writings are also shot through with metaphysical descriptions of the sources and processes of disease and weakness, vitality and healing.

Causes and Cures opens with a depiction of God's creation of the world as a well-ordered, hierarchical system, balanced in terms of the four elements: fire, air, water, and earth. In humanity, God's highest creation, these elements were manifest as heat, breath, blood, and flesh—the humors of classical medicine. The harmony and vitality of the material world, including the human body, reflected God's design in creating the world and the perpetual infusion of "greenness" (*viriditas*), which Hildegard identified with the Holy Spirit. But the Fall profoundly disturbed this order. Sin disrupted the order and balance of creation, blocked some of this greenness and countered it with poison, and made the descendants of Adam and Eve vulnerable to all kinds of affliction. In depicting the common effects of sin in the human body, Hildegard cited the production of phlegm, the humor associated with torpor and darkness, which led to many kinds of disease: "For if man had remained in paradise, he would not have had the *flegmata* within his body, from which many evils proceed, but his flesh would have been whole and without dark humor." More specifically, "tasting evil" produced the "smoky moisture" that caused "sores and openings" in the body, which in turn produced phlegm. The flegmata that resulted from tasting evil caused all sorts of problems, including making blood change "into the poison of semen, out of which the sons of man are begotten."[16]

If Hildegard was atypical in the wide range of her practical and theological interests and remarkable in many of her expressions, especially in her delightful concept of veriditas, she was much like her contemporaries in embracing the material world as the domain of divine creation, where the signs of God's will, law, and stratagems could be discerned. As she explained in the *Physica*, "In the beginning, every creature God made was good." But after the Fall, when the devil beguiled Adam and Eve into disobedience through his serpent, "seeds of cruel and poisonous vermin rose up for this revenge, revealing infernal punishments with their death-bearing cruelty." God provided many natural antidotes for these ills, although considerable knowledge was required to employ them. For example, "If a person becomes leprous from lust or intemperance, he should cook agrimony, and a third part hyssop, and twice as much asarum as there is of the other two in a cauldron. He should make a bath from these, and mix in menstrual blood, as much as he can get, and get into the bath." Afterward, he should apply a salve of "goose fat, twice as much chicken fat, and a bit of chicken dung," and then rest. Repeated performances of this procedure, the recipe promised, would produce a cure.[17]

Use of the drafts and unguents prescribed in Hildegard's *Physica* contin-ued for several centuries, and the Renaissance humanist Johannes Trithemius commended her knowledge of "the many wonders and secrets of nature."[18] The influence of her medical writings derived both from the wealth of empir-ical description and practical instruction they provided and from the encom-passing theological vision they conveyed. As respect for Christian theology encouraged her to look for antidotes for illness in God's creation, so experi-mentation and examination of nature inspired her theology. The idea of cause and effect held this world together: both divine will and human sin set off chain reactions in nature and the human body; health and sickness were pro-duced by metaphysical causes. Close observations and careful classifications of nature were expressions of reverence for God as well as means of domes-ticating nature and remedying human illness and pain.

They also coexisted happily with belief in miracles. And the profusion of miracles in medieval Christendom obviously reflected Christianity's new lo-cales and the diverse cultures onto which it was grafted. In the West, this hybridization of Christian and pre-Christian traditions was more unchecked than in the East, where orthodox expectations about religious experience were well articulated and highly conservative, and where governmental, ecclesiasti-cal, and private philanthropies were better coordinated.

Orthodox Medicine and Philanthropy

Commitment to a holistic Christian society was strong in the East. Beginning in the fourth century, Eastern bishops urged citizens to construct a virtuous society, dedicated to the common good and to the welfare of the sick and poor. "Eastern bishops came to see the practice of philanthropia," according to his-torian Timothy Miller, "as a force which aimed at transforming the pagan world, represented by the ancient polis, into a truly Christian society, a heavenly city."[19] In recasting the ancient Greek ideal of a strong, unified, and virtuous polis in Christian terms, Eastern churchmen supported the interdependence of church and Empire and the emperor's obligation to act as God's emissary, at the same time emphasizing man's free will and potential for deification. In some contrast, Augustine and other churchmen affiliated with Rome empha-sized the innate sinfulness of human beings and the need for obedience to rulers authorized by God to control and punish human behavior. For reasons both theological and practical, churchmen in the West were less idealistic about Christian society, more pessimistic about human nature.[20]

As a result of more holistic and optimistic thinking about Christian society,

Christian healing in the East was more systematically organized and more fully integrated with medicine than in the West. The organized promotion of Christian healing in the East was limited, however, by waves of invasion by Persians, Arabs, Bulgars, and Slavs beginning in the seventh century. Also, emperors found it necessary to restrain Christian altruism even in the early years of visionary expansion. Thus, John Chrysostum's idealistic plan to build a hospital for lepers outside the city gates cost him his job as bishop of Constantinople in the early sixth century. And emperors did not often live up to the expectations of the religious idealists over whom they ruled.[21]

Although it was imperfectly realized, Eastern churchmen held a comprehensive vision of Christian philanthropy and civic life in which medicine played an important role. Because a number of prominent physicians in Asia Minor came from aristocratic backgrounds, medicine enjoyed a social prestige that it lacked in the West, where "great families," according to Miller, "on the whole rejected medicine as an acceptable career." In the East, state-supported institutions incorporated medicine under the aegis of Christianity, and the ideal of a holistic society characterized by Christian philanthropy persisted even as the strength of the Eastern Empire diminished. "In the new world which followed the Persian and Arab invasions of the seventh century," Miller wrote, "Eastern bishops continued to view medicine and the Christian institutions which dispensed it as ideal vehicles to express the central Christian virtue of charity."[22]

During the fifth century, Christian leaders established hospitals in a number of cities, primarily as institutions for the poor. In the mid-sixth century, Emperor Justinian assigned the supervision of hospitals and physicians to bishops, and strengthened the connection between Christianity and medicine by attracting wealthy Christians to hospitals as patients and donors as well as by locating medicine firmly within the ecclesiastical domain. This consolidation of medical operations under Christian auspices helped to diminish suspicions about medicine's reputation as a pagan art, a reputation especially strong in Constantinople, where Asclepian temples supported prominent physicians.

Justinian's bureaucratic move also facilitated the development of medical specialties, medical libraries, and the development of hospitals as teaching institutions. His system for administering hospitals did not last, and relentless warfare and increasing political and military weakness continued to undermine the strength of all Byzantine institutions. But the ideal of a heavenly society on earth, characterized by Christian arts and philanthropy, figured importantly in the expansion of Byzantine culture in the Slavic regions to the north beginning in the sixth century, and in maintaining Constantinople as a stronghold of Byzantine culture even during Latin occupation in the thirteenth century and during increasingly hostile relations with the Ottoman Empire in the fourteenth.[23]

According to historian Demetrios Constantelos, the Byzantine Empire supported a variety of health care institutions, including "general hospitals, leprosaria, maternity clinics, opthalmological dispensaries, and foundling institutions." In these institutions, efforts to preserve life and relieve suffering were remarkably sophisticated and included surgical procedures in urology, orthopedics, and obstetrics and considerable understanding of hygiene and physiology. And these institutions exerted wide influence. According to Constantelos, "Byzantine medicine and organization of medical institutions were spread among the Serbs, Roumanians, the Slavs in general, the Arabs, the Armenians, and the Italians."[24]

Icons as Agents of Healing

The fast-growing popularity of pictorial representations of Christ and his saints in seventh-century Byzantium fed a demand for religious healing in an era of tumultuous change. Amid the incursions of Islam on one hand and the prevalence of indigenous healers on the other, icons became increasingly popular as stand-ins for Christian holy men and as accessible, alternative means of enlisting the same kind of healing power that holy men offered. No less important, veneration of the Theotokos, or Mother of God, and her icons was enormously popular as a means of receiving divine energies and salutary effects. The artistic style of icons changed in response to the growing demand for their use as vehicles of healing power. Flatter and more solemn, austere, and commanding depictions of Christ and his saints replaced the more naturalistic depictions characteristic of earlier, Hellenistic icons, thus reflecting the growing authority of these images of sacred persons and devotion to their healing energies.[25]

In a study of Byzantine icons, historian Leslie Brubaker explained the meaning of visual perception in Byzantine culture in relation to religious experience. Examining a sermon preached by the patriarch Photios at the completion of the mosaic of the Virgin and Christ child in the apse of Hagia Sophia in 867, Brubaker called attention to Photios's enthusiasm for "the painter's skill, which is a reflection of inspiration from above," and to his interesting claim that the painter "exactly established the natural (life-like) imitation." Brubaker explained that, by "life-like," Photios did not mean realistic in the modern sense of photographic likeness, but rather that the artist represented real persons in a compelling way. In orthodox understanding, icons conveyed energies emanating from sacred persons and produced tears, repentance, and healing in receptive believers. In the context of this understanding of the spiritual power of icons, emotional responsiveness to these images developed as a central part of Orthodox worship. As John of Damascus explained in the eighth century, "The honor given to the image is transferred to its prototype."[26]

Against popular practice and monastic support, Emperor Leo III condemned the veneration of icons in the eighth century, and Leo V and his successor, Theophilus, took up the iconoclast cause again in the ninth century. To these emperors, the adoration of icons seemed corrupt and pagan compared to the pure faith of Muhammad, which exerted pressure on Orthodox thinking, as did spiritual purists within eastern Christianity. Against the Orthodox doctrine forged at the Council of Chalcedon in 451 that Christ was one person "in two natures," some Christians in the East maintained that Christ had only one divine nature (monophysis), or alternatively, that Christ took on flesh, but that his flesh was incorruptible. These non-Chalcedonian views led to the separation of "Oriental" churches in Egypt, Syria, Persia, and India. In these Oriental churches, resistance to the idea that divinity could be manifest in material form worked against the practice of venerating icons, but that practice never disappeared. In Byzantine (Greek) Orthodoxy, the demand for icons as the organizing and most essential part of worship, both at home and in church, persistently overrode the drive for a more purely transcendent understanding of God.[27]

Empress Theodora, wife of Theophilus, along with many of the monks and people of Byzantium, supported the veneration of icons. The Second Council of Nicaea in 787 officially reinstated the practice, affirming that real communication took place between worshipper and icon, and that icons brought worshippers face-to-face with Christ and his saints and in direct contact with their healing and purifying energies. The Council declared, and later theologians affirmed, "When we honor and venerate an icon, we receive sanctification."[28]

Iconoclasts had objected to icons on the grounds that they were idols. In defense, icon-loving theologians argued that idols were fraudulent images without prototypes, and thus not to be confused with icons. Iconophiles linked icons to the Incarnation, arguing that God's manifestation in material form sanctioned the veneration of icons, and that rejection of icons amounted to denial of the Incarnation. Thus, Orthodox theologians defended the veneration of icons as a fundamental expression of the doctrine of incarnation, which they interpreted to emphasize the image of God in man and man's potential perfection and deification.[29]

Carried in ritual processions and enshrined in churches on freestanding pillars, many smaller framed icons were touched and kissed so often that they had to be covered in precious metals and jewels—both as an expression of reverence and for protection against erosion. On church walls, large, colorful cartoons of the Trinity, Theotokos, and saints surrounded worshippers, inviting communion. Painters facilitated this communion by directing the eyes and body language of these wall icons toward the center of the church, where worshippers stood, hopeful of receiving and experiencing divine energies.

Healing in the Context of Monastic Life

As the primary institutions where the practice of medicine and its confluence with miracles developed, medieval monasteries housed herb gardens, apothecaries, and infirmaries for sick or elderly residents. In larger monasteries, guesthouses served as hotels for patrons, nobility, and wealthy visitors, many of whom sought strength and healing from the herbal medicines available at the monasteries, as well as from relics, prayers, and liturgies. At larger monasteries, a monk appointed almoner dispensed food and clothes to poor pilgrims who sometimes gathered in throngs, especially on feast days. In some monastic houses, the almoner supervised the sheltering of poor pilgrims; in others, the infirmarian assumed that duty as part of his general responsibility for care of the sick. The cellarer also played an important role in this regular work of hospitality and care for the poor and sick. The Rule of Benedict, which governed the routine of daily life in many western European monasteries from the sixth century on, instructed the cellarer to "take the greatest care of the sick, of children, of guests, and of the poor, knowing without doubt that he will have to render account for all these on the Day of Judgment."[30]

A ninth-century plan for an abbey dedicated to St. Gall set forth a picture of monastic life that included a community hospital.[31] According to the plan, one whole section of the monastic compound was given over to the sick. A physician's house, including a pharmacy, was part of the plan, along with a separate building for bloodletting and a kitchen, bathhouse, cloister, chapel, herb garden, and infirmary, all dedicated to care of the sick. This abbey of St. Gall was never built, but its plan for full-scale treatment of the sick is a good picture of medieval ideas about health care and reflects the widespread acceptance of medicine as an appropriate part of monastic life.

In Eastern Christianity, healing shrines and hospitals were often built alongside each other, and cooperation between the two was fairly routine. Summarizing this cooperation, Stanley Harakas wrote that "some patients would go to the hospital first, where physicians might refer them to the saints; others would go to the church first and then, at the urging of the saints, to the hospital." But rivalry between medicine and Christianity also existed in the East, as it did in the West, despite the respect often accorded physician-priests in Greek Christianity. Beginning in the seventh century, as pressures mounted against the Byzantine Empire, physicians lost status, hospitals became poorer or disappeared entirely, and healing cults associated with particular saints grew to overshadow medicine and take up the slack resulting from medicine's decline.[32]

Monastic commitment to charity allowed monks and nuns to pursue medical knowledge and skill, and commitment to the superior power of Christ and his saints worked to confine this pursuit within the framework of religious life. By the early twelfth century, Catholic monks had become so proficient and specialized in the medical arts that church councils banned them from practicing medicine for gain and pursuing medical studies outside of religious centers and outside the context of religious charity. But these proclamations never questioned the role of monks as apothecaries in a religious setting, or the place of monasteries as centers of skilled nursing and medicinal treatment.[33]

Asceticism played an essential role in legitimating monks and nuns as religious healers and medical practitioners. In the early development of monastic life, severe restrictions on food, sleep, sex, and comfort separated pious individuals from ordinary human society in ways that enabled them to represent divine power. As Peter Brown pointed out, ascetics often acquired tremendous social authority because the deprivation and self-discipline that separated them from ordinary mortals imbued them with a kind of transcendent objectivity and the appearance of being agents of divine power. Even if they lived in deliberate isolation as hermits, as Hospicius did on the outskirts of sixth-century Nice, religious ascetics were often public leaders who resolved disputes, expelled demons, and treated the sick and disabled.[34]

Monastic communities, where pious individuals gathered to pursue ascetic life together, functioned similarly. As assistants to the saints, and holy people in their own right, monks and nuns served as agents of divine power. At the same time, the protective and empowering cloak of asceticism enabled them to acquire medical knowledge and skill with relative impunity. In many instances, medical expertise enhanced their social authority and reputation for sanctity.

Of course, a variety of other social and religious forces complicated the authority that monastic communities and their residents exerted. Tribalism, warfare, the waxing and waning of ecclesiastical oversight, and, in the West from the eleventh century, the growth of urbanization, market economies, and more secular institutions like guilds and universities distorted, corrupted, and advanced monastic life. Still, monasteries and their residents competed successfully in this complicated, developing world, thanks in no small part to the relics they housed and celebrated and to the artistic projects, hospitality, and health care services associated with those relics. In fact, from the eleventh century on, many Christians in western Europe complained that monasteries competed all too well for wealth and power. Alliances between noble families and monastic houses turned some of those houses into luxury hotels for wealthy visitors and pious enclaves for noble sons and for women with dowries sufficient for their comfortable upkeep. Such straying from the asceticism originally associated with Christian monasticism prompted considerable ridicule, and also reform. In the twelfth and thirteenth centuries, new mendicant communities of Dominicans, Franciscans, lay sisters (beguines), and others emerged to restore the asceticism of primitive Christianity to religious life. Not coincidentally, their renewed commitments to Christian asceticism involved renewed commitments to Christian charity and outreach to the poor and sick.[35]

In addition to stimulating the development of market economies through the erection of buildings and the promotion of goods and services associated with their veneration, relics also stimulated a demand for miracles that drew Christianity further into the entrepreneurial ethos of emerging market economies. In the ancient world, the simplicity and inexpensiveness of Christian practice contributed to Christianity's successful competition with other healing cults. In medieval Europe, in some contrast, the lavishness of Christian belief and expression contributed to its growth and popularity. But as asceticism also flourished, reformers constantly criticized the wealth of churches and the mercenary attitudes of priests. The conflicts between advocates of Christian materialism and advocates of Christian poverty were, at least to some extent, conflicts about what kinds of empirical manifestations of Christian faith were valid and most compelling. Both sides embraced Christianity as a religion of empirical manifestations and effects and, most emphatically, as a religion of healing. And both sides found new ways of attending to the suffering bodies of their fellow human beings through devotion to Christ and his saints, however much they disagreed about the social implications of Christianity with respect to authority, hierarchy, wealth, and status.

Penance as a Form of Healing

Along with investment in healing miracles as prime manifestations of the divine power of Christ and his saints, the notion of penance as a regimen analogous to medical treatment dates to antiquity. Basil compared physicians who "exhort their patients to give heed to themselves and neglect nothing which pertains to their cure" to biblical demands for repentance. Thus, as "the physician of our souls," scripture "restores to health a soul afflicted by sin with this brief remedy: 'Give heed, therefore, to thyself,' that you may be given assistance toward your recovery proportioned to the gravity of your transgression." As a physician himself as well as a priest, Basil prescribed repentance as the medicine for sin and recommended measured forms of repentance, much as a physician would apply certain doses of medicine at his disposal. Sin was always to be taken seriously, Basil preached, but if the "fault is light and supportable, the penance done for it should be equally so."[36]

Irish missionaries eager to establish centers of monastic discipline in Europe played important roles in the further development of an ingeniously calibrated system of penance that extended some of the purifying benefits of ascetic practice to ordinary Christians unable or unwilling to take up the rigors of monastic life. Missionaries introduced Christianity to Ireland in the fourth and fifth centuries, where they promoted a vigorous form of asceticism inspired by the desert monks of North Africa. Far removed from Roman authority, Irish monasteries grew as centers of religious life for particular clans and the people and territory those clans controlled. In this highly decentralized religious environment, the arm of the Roman Church was exceedingly weak, and Christian authority in Ireland was invested almost entirely in ascetics and the monasteries associated with them. Along with their role as builders of local religious centers, Irish ascetics were famous as pilgrims whose wanderings to liberate themselves from worldly ties coincided with the impulse to evangelize. These charismatic preachers and healers drew many people to monasteries that offered liturgies, instruction in Christianity, and health care.[37]

Beginning in the 590s, Irish *peregrini* (wandering holy men) traveled to the European mainland. Columbanus, the most famous of these, led the way in establishing new monasteries and contributing to the vitality of older ones, thus stimulating the development of Christianity as a local religion, especially in Gaul. Because the power of their sanctity was so well-suited to the development of local authority, Irish peregrini and the monasteries they established attracted Frankish nobles whose patronage contributed to the erosion of the strict ascetic ideal exemplified by Columbanus and his followers. Less ironic, Irish monasticism and its influence in Europe contributed to the development of the medieval system of penance, which systematized the therapeutic principle that particular sins, like particular diseases, required particular cures.

The *Penitential* handbook attributed to Columbanus begins with the assertion that, just as physicians apply a range of different antidotes in their treatment of different ailments, so penance should be meted out in specific forms in treatment of particular sins. Thus, physicians "heal wounds in one manner, sicknesses in another, boils in another, bruises in another, eye diseases in another, fractures in another, burns in another." By implication, "so also should spiritual doctors treat with diverse kinds of cures the wounds of souls."[38]

Though designed originally for monastics, this way of diagnosing and treating sin came to be applied to infractions of secular law as well as to the more strictly spiritual lapses of ordinary people. As a form of discipline that covered almost anything, the penitential system had a regulating effect on medieval religious and social life. The original intent of this highly rationalized approach to treating sin had been to support asceticism and enable pious in-dividuals to conform themselves to God's will more perfectly, but the system of penance had the eventual effect of allowing forgiveness to be construed as a matter of duty and external behavior, or even payment in lieu of that duty, rather than of genuine transformation or redirection of will. This mechanical approach to repentance was one of the main abuses that reformers in the sixteenth century objected to in the Catholic Church.[39]

Baptism as a Protective Seal

Whatever Christian missionaries intended as they made their way through marauding bands of Vandals, Goths, Celts, Slavs, and Finns, baptism became part and parcel of the bloody business of warlord uprisings, tribal conflict, and reform by military conquest. In the profoundly violent context of early medieval conversions, baptism came less to represent the culmination of an extended process of individual transformation and more one of collective solidarity—or collective surrender or hope of miraculous aid in battle. For example, in 587, King Recared in Spain sent word to the people of Narbonne to follow him in conversion to the Catholic faith. Having staged a contest between Arian and Catholic bishops for his allegiance, Recared sided with the Catholics on account of their miracles, which better abetted victory in battle.[40] A century and a half later, in 745, Pope Zachary made an equally strategic appeal to the advantages of Catholicism when he offered miraculous aid to the Franks if they agreed to the reforms laid out by his Anglo-Saxon missionary Boniface: "If your priests are pure and clean of all unchastity and blood-guiltiness, as the sacred canons teach and as our brother Boniface preaches in our stead, and if you are in all things obedient to him, no people can stand before you, but all pagans shall fall before your face and you shall remain victors."[41]

Once essential preparation for baptism, catechism increasingly came to be postponed until afterward. In southern Gaul in the fifth century, and more widely by the eighth and ninth centuries, the rite of baptism became detached from catechesis and confirmation of faith.[42] The shortage of bishops in the hinterlands and the uneven transmission of Catholic doctrine by rustic priests helped justify this separation. So did the growing popularity of infant baptism among parents eager to secure a place for their children in heaven and to open the way for their children to receive blessings on earth from the saints.

In its early Christian origins, baptism conducted initiates through a life-and-death confrontation with evil, with victory through participation in the agency of Christ. As the expectations about baptism as a revelatory event and triumphal experience of spiritual healing diminished and preparations for it became simpler and less exhaustive, its relationship to healing changed. In his history of medieval baptism, Peter Cramer described how the once momentous rite of initiation into Christianity became increasingly formulaic. The popularity of infant baptism contributed to a leakage of ethical engagement, Cramer argued, even though infant baptism carried profound meaning of its own and was not without ethical impact. As a symbol of both the vulnerability of human creatures and the purity of the Christ child, the baby represented the fears and hopes of the community, bonding people to each other, and to Christ, through the baby's presence as a ritual object. But in Cramer's analysis, these new dimensions of meaning did not fully offset the tendency to regard baptism as an external operation. Combined with the decline in catechesis, numerous gaps and variations in doctrinal knowledge, and the increasing use of adult baptism as a signifier of surrender or fortified strength in battle, infant baptism also came to reflect a new element of passivity in the ritual process of initiation into Christian life and a widening gap between laity and priests. In Cramer's view, baptism became less an ethical transformation of the participant's will and more a mechanical procedure. To quote Cramer, "The balance which the Fathers had seen in the sacrament between the voluntary and the involuntary, between the individual 'turning' towards Truth, and the Truth to which the soul turned had been upset by the spectacle of a child, perhaps no more than a few weeks old." Instead of providing a ritual map for a transformation of will, baptism collapsed into a "magical-medicinal cure" that "ignores the willing subject." In this regard, the baby offered for baptism served as "an exact symbol of his parents' sense of passive weakness—and fear—before the prospect of Judgement."[43]

Without denying the importance of fear as a factor in early medieval Christianity, or the illiteracy and general mayhem that made metaphysical analysis hard to sustain, we might just as well say that, in simplifying the baptismal rite for use by groups of converts and parents of babies, medieval Europeans retained at least part of its meaning as a rite of liberating purification that imbued participants with the feeling of vitality, a sense of personal integrity, and courage in the face of death. No less important, the pared-down and more expedient medieval rite fit well into the larger world of religious imagination shaping Western culture, making Christian healing more widely available than ever before.

Exorcism

Although Christ and his saints continued to disarm demons at a remarkable rate, neither the number nor the strength of these villains seemed to decline. As the protective seal of baptism became more widespread, Christ met new demons and acquired new spiritual helpers in his battles against them. As part of its adaptation to Indo-European cultures, Christianity assimilated a new host of fairly specific deities and spirits. Some of these became angels in the service of Christ, such as the dragon-slayer Michael, who originated in the East as an angelic warrior prince opposed to the forces of evil and who to some extent replaced the Germanic war god, Woden.[44] Others became demons that brought pestilence and torment to mankind and frequently presented themselves to be vanquished by Christ and his saints.

If swelling ranks of angels and demons made purists uncomfortable, they also enabled Christianity to elaborate on its long-standing tendency to personalize good and evil. The tendency to anthropomorphize evil and become fascinated with personal relationships between people and demons or Satan contributed to the witch hunts of the late Middle Ages and early modern period. It also became a means of exploring and describing subjectivity and its torments and modes of relief. Along with the penitential system, with its classifications of sin and calibrations of remedies, fascination with the personal relationships between demons and their victims opened human subjectivity to new inspection and analysis and perhaps laid some of the preliminary groundwork for modern psychological thinking.

In the later Middle Ages, attacks by demons became occasions for describing their human victims in vivid and relatively specific detail. By contrast, in descriptions of exorcisms performed by earlier saints—like the one attributed to Hospicius, who used exorcism to cure the young man of deafness and dumbness—the personalities and physical characteristics of the afflicting demon and his human victim were not relevant or well described. By the twelfth century, exorcisms appeared less frequently among cures attributed to saints but with more elaborate description. In his analysis of three thousand miracles recorded in thirteenth- and fourteenth-century England and France, Finucane observed that "the intrusion of demons was quite limited. They were normally only associated with mental aberrations, when the victim was said to have become possessed, and they seldom appeared in other forms of illness."⁴⁵ At the same time, analysis of saints' lives in an overlapping period shows a high percentage of elite Christians whose reputations for supernatural power involved well-differentiated "struggles with demons."⁴⁶

A good example of this more focused interest in demon-infested subjectivity comes from the letters and vita of Hildegard of Bingen, who, after great effort, cured a noblewoman tormented by a vicious evil spirit. Apparently, Sigewize liked to preach, but her excited sermons were perceived as confused and morally dangerous. After pilgrimages and other means failed to yield relief, either for her or those around her, Sigewize insisted that Hildegard, whom she called "crumpleface," was the only one who could effect a cure. Thus called upon, Hildegard diplomatically orchestrated a liturgical event involving seven priests who endeavored to bring Sigewize to her senses through "fasting, scourging, prayers, alms and the command of God himself." When all that failed, Hildegard brought Sigewize to her own cloister, where she and her sisters "never slackened" in their efforts to cure the troublemaker—"not for terror, nor for the disorder with which the demon confused those who pressed upon it for its sins, nor for the mocking and filthy words with which it sought to overcome us, nor for its terrible breath." Finally, on Maundy Thursday, as a priest was exorcising the baptismal font, Sigewize "emitted a blast from the terrible spirit that oppressed her." Hildegard met the blast with a vision of God confronting the Devil and, when she described this, "the wicked spirit emerged, together with a terrible voiding from the woman's private parts." As a result of Hildegard's inspired leadership and steadfast commitment to a cure, Sigewize "was freed and remained sound in mind and body for the rest of her life."⁴⁷

The difference between this exorcism and the one performed by Hospicius in the sixth century suggests how perceptions of exorcism had changed. Hildegard's treatment was more subtle than that of Hospicius, and that greater subtlety was not simply the result of Hildegard's extraordinary intelligence. Sigewize demanded more cunning treatment, in contrast to Hospicius's nameless patient, whose communication with his saint and consciousness of what was happening inside him played no part in the story of his cure. Hospicius's cure was physical: the saint seized the patient's hair and tongue and made the demon leave by pouring oil on the patient's head and down his throat. By contrast, Hildegard healed by inserting her interpretations of God and the Devil into Sigewize's subjectivity. Without relinquishing any faith in God's miraculous activity, or in the cause-and-effect agency of metaphysical forces, Hildegard employed elements of empirical observation and strategic analysis that pointed in the direction of psychological thinking.

The Eucharist

Healing was part of the Eucharist from the beginning. Early Christians anticipated bodily resurrection through participation in fellowship with Christ during the Eucharistic meal, and physical healings in the course of the meal were not unusual. Originating as a common meal of fellowship and discussion celebrating the communal union in Christ, the Eucharist evolved, toward the end of the first century, from a full meal into a symbolic one. Small doses of bread and wine came to represent the body and blood of Jesus, and consuming them brought participation in the death and resurrection of Christ and in the body of believers on earth. As Christian populations mushroomed in the late fourth century, the Eucharist became more of a dramatic spectacle, often accompanied by music, processions, and ritual vestments for the priests who officiated. According to historian Paul Bradshaw, Christians "were no longer an elite group of highly committed believers, but a much larger mass of nominal converts, many of whom lacked a deep understanding of the Christian faith." The frequency of lay participation in the Eucharist declined significantly, and churchmen instructed people to regard the Eucharistic elements with fear and awe. As part of this change, healings increasingly occurred in response to the Eucharistic elements, and those elements took on some of the same functions that saints and their relics performed.[48]

During the controversy over icons in the eighth century, iconoclasts argued that the bread and wine in the Eucharist were sacred images of the body and blood of Christ and the only images appropriate for veneration. The iconophiles rejected this view, defending the veneration of pictorial representations of the Trinity, Theotokos, and saints, with the argument that the Eucharist was not an image or symbol of Christ, but the live presence of his divine humanity. As historian John Meyendorff explained, the Eucharist was "a mystery to be received as food and drink, and not to be 'seen' through physical eyes," as icons were. Orthodox priests uncovered the Eucharist elements only during consecration and communion. Kept hidden behind a protective screen, they epitomized the divine mystery of the Incarnation. In Byzantine theology, the substance of the elements did not change during communion; rather, the humanity of participants changed. In the fourteenth century, defending the Orthodox understanding of the mystery of the Eucharist and the deification of believers, Gregory of Palamas wrote that Christ took on "everything human" to "penetrate through the whole of us." In the Eucharist, which epitomized this penetration, "we receive God Himself in our souls—the Body and Blood of God, and the soul, mind, and will of God—no less than His humanity."[49]

In the West, discussion and controversy went on for centuries about the nature of the Eucharistic elements and their transformation. In the thirteenth century, representatives of the Roman Church argued that, while the "accidental" or apparent attributes of bread and wine stayed the same, their essential substance changed into the body and blood of Christ through the words of the liturgy. Although it did not become official Catholic doctrine until the Council of Trent in the sixteenth century, this theory of transubstantiation was influential in the West long before that and reflected characteristically Western concerns for rational explanation and fascination with the relationship between appearance and reality. Such rational explanations of the Eucharistic miracle did little to discourage expectations of miraculous healings through the Eucharistic elements, even as they also prompted criticism, among reformers, of priestly exploitation of popular desires for magical healing.

The Eucharist also became the centerpiece of clerical efforts to stabilize and centralize ecclesiastical authority. As interest in the healing power of the Eucharistic elements increased in the West, celebrants advertised this power through linkages with Mary, at the same time enlisting her to glorify the Eucharist. The thirteenth-century Franciscan cardinal Bonaventure reported approvingly that some recipients smelled the honey of the Eucharist made by "our bee the Virgin Mary." Linkages with the Mother of Christ also stimulated visions of the Eucharist as an infant child, and some Christians even saw the child bleeding on the altar. As elaborate processions developed to carry the Eucharist to the sick, people congregated along the way for healing and other blessings. Beginning with the devotions of thirteenth-century Cistercian beguines, the feast of Corpus Christi developed in Liège and spread to other parts of Europe and England. During this summer feast, clergy led the Eucharist parade through the streets, accompanied by musical instruments, wagon tableaus, and, of course, expectations of healing. Historian Miri Rubin recounted, "The host was so powerful that it could even cure by proxy; a woman was cured by an abbot who had touched the host earlier in the day" and "not through any other meritorious act." Many feared misuse of the Eucharist as a cause of sickness, misfortune, and death. Priests took elaborate precautions against dropping or spilling the elements and even worried that magicians might get hold of them.[50]

Exploring Human Suffering

Even as the healings attributed to the Eucharist in the West seemed to be more mechanical (and thus tarnished, in the eyes of critics, by similarities to magic), they also reflected new interest in the suffering humanity of Christ and in the mystical relationship between his suffering and that of ordinary people. In some contrast to Basil in the fourth century, who understood Christ's healing power in terms of his transcendence of suffering and ability to stamp a divine impression of health on believers through his perfect fusion of humanity and divinity, medieval Christians venerated the wounds of Christ and the flow of blood, wine, tears, and milk associated with them. Images of the suffering Christ may have developed first in the East, where emphasis on the mystery of the Incarnation and mystical ideas about the deification of humanity were long-standing traditions.[51] As they developed in the West, images of Jesus suffering were often feminized, exuding weakness rather than strength, and sometimes milk as well as blood.

Especially in the lives and writings of female saints, some of the most graphic accounts of religious suffering from the late Middle Ages identified the physical sufferings of female saints with those of Christ and celebrated the saint's deification through her emulation of Christ's suffering. As historian Caroline Walker Bynum showed, numerous mystics of the late medieval period viewed suffering as the ultimate form of religious service, enabling them to become like Christ and, like him, to heal others. Thus, after a period of withdrawal, the fourteenth-century Dominican St. Catherine of Siena emerged as a tireless activist committed to caring for the sick and feeding the hungry. Her renunciation of all ordinary pleasure and inability to eat ordinary food brought her to "the Fountain of Life," where "she fastened her lips upon that sacred wound, and still more eagerly the mouth of her soul, and there she slaked her thirst." Catherine participated in the sufferings of Christ as a prerequisite for her own religious sustenance and for becoming a vehicle of sustenance for others. "We must attach ourselves to the breast of Christ crucified, which is the source of charity, and by means of that flesh we draw milk," she wrote to an abbess in Florence. "The means is Christ's humanity which suffered pain, and we cannot without pain get that milk that comes from charity."[52]

The humanity of Jesus came to the fore in Catherine's writings and in other writings describing the lives and visions of late medieval women mystics. Through suffering, the humanity of the saint and the humanity of Jesus coincided, body to body and soul to Spirit, each contributing to a mystical relationship that revealed the other's humanity. This interest in suffering as an interpersonal phenomenon encouraged new outpourings of Christian service to the sick and poor. For many pious Christians, care of the sick and poor provided religious contexts in which mystical experience of the sufferings of Jesus might occur.

In the late eleventh and early twelfth centuries, groups of lay mendicants, inspired by stories about the lives of Jesus and his disciples, and by a general spirit of ecclesiastical reform, dedicated themselves to radical poverty, to helping the poor, and to healing and care of the sick. They sought an alternative to priesthood and monastic life, which they criticized for being enmeshed in feudal wealth and authority and for being far removed from the poverty and spiritual authority manifest in Jesus and his disciples. Some of these *paupers Christi* became incorporated in new religious orders, most notably of Franciscans and Dominicans, which became officially recognized by and established in the Roman Church. Numerous other communities and associations of pious women and men followed the *vita apostolica* without being officially sanctioned (or constrained). Especially in towns and cities, which were centers of increasing poverty and disease as well as population, unofficial congregations of religious women, the beguines, dedicated themselves to hospital work and other forms of public health care. As fervent lay women from a variety of social backgrounds who embraced poverty and banded together in unofficial, urban religious communities, beguines were often perceived as a danger to the Church. Yet these lay mystics did as much as anyone to establish Christian support for hospitals and other forms of public health care in late medieval cities.[53]

Both the Crusades and the growth of urban populations inspired many expressions of religious charity. The military orders of Knights Templar, Lazarus, and Hospitallers sponsored a range of health care services in the Holy Land and in major European cities. Franciscans and other new religious orders established and managed hospitals, and many paupers Christi worked in hospitals and almshouses managed by municipal and religious authorities. The epidemics of plague that devastated many cities in the fourteenth century led to new outpourings of religious activism. Referred to by various names—Beghards, Lollards, Cellites, beguines—new waves of paupers Christi emerged to devote themselves to the care and burial of plague victims.[54]

This outpouring of religious service to the sick and poor in late medieval Europe, along with the exploration of human suffering as a subjective experience, coincided with urban growth and expanding market economies. Impatience with the corruption, impurity, and laxity of the Catholic Church and desire to recover the early Christian spirit of asceticism and charity led to groundswells of religious fervor and asceticism, especially among women.

Franciscans, Dominicans, beguines, and other religious groups carried forward, with renewed commitment, the tradition of healing and care for the sick that harked back to the ministry of Jesus and, during the intervening centuries, had made Christianity a popular success. But even as these zealous souls rededicated themselves to a central and well-established aspect of Christianity, they also led the way in important new developments in the expression and analysis of religious experience.

Like other important developments in medieval Christianity, their exploration of human suffering occurred in a world full of empirical signs of Christ and his saints. In some respects, their tendency to view suffering and its relief as a spiritual transaction—described in terms of infusions of metaphysical power—simply encouraged suffering and obscured understanding of its psychological working. In other, perhaps more revolutionary and important respects, observations and expectations of the empirical effects of divine power led to ways of articulating and mapping human suffering that led eventually to better understanding of the emotional and psychological aspects of human experience and to more general understanding of how religion often worked as an antidote for pain and means of combating illness and stress. No less important, the pragmatic and empirical aspects of medieval Christianity contributed to the development of hospitals and other health care facilities and to the growth of religious groups committed to care of the sick who continued to advance expectations of Christianity as a religion of healing.

4

Healing in Early Modern Christianity

The sixteenth century witnessed a peculiar kind of religious unrest in which belief in the existence of spiritual realities fell under widespread scrutiny, even as the material manifestations of those realities, and testimonies to them, multiplied. Efforts to purify Christianity were not new, but the effort to rid it of superstition had never gone so far or been so widespread. The attack against superstition signaled an unsettling distrust of received tradition. At the same time, it triggered new enthusiasm for divine revelation and authentic signs of Christ and coincided with new prophecies and new claims about miracles, witchcraft, and demons. The clamor for religious purity characteristic of early modern reformers coincided with growing unease about religious authority. And their concern about religious truth coincided with growing concern about the proper reach of human knowledge and power. Demands for religious purity and truth mounted with the invention of the printing press, civil unrest, expanding market economies, the growth of urban centers, and the exploration of the globe.

On one hand, the religious splendor and evangelical fervor of Catholic Christianity had never been greater. The growing prosperity of the middle class, the wealth of chantries (endowments for masses and prayers) and guilds affiliated with saints, the popularity of devotion to Mary and the Eucharist issued in a profusion of religious art. In Zurich, for example, the number of commissions for church art increased by a factor of 100 between 1500 and 1518.[1] The boundaries of world Christianity had shrunk considerably between 1350 and 1500 as a result of the expansion of the Ottoman Empire in Western Asia and North Africa and the disappearance of Christian communities in China, Central Asia, Scandinavia, and Greenland. The tide reversed dramatically in the sixteenth century, with Franciscans, Dominicans, Jesuits, and other Catholics planting new missions in China, Japan, India, Ceylon, the East Indies, and the Americas.[2]

On the other hand, amid lavish and expansive religious expression, mockery of religious gullibility and resistance to clerical authority also flourished. The Dutch critic Desiderius Erasmus (c. 1466–1536) likened the practice of appealing to particular saints to address particular problems—St. Apollo for toothache, St. Roch for plague, St. Christopher for protection against sudden death, for example—to the worship of pagan gods. And with more revolutionary implications, lay people published pamphlets mocking the clergy and condemning the cult of saints and images as "tricks" for deceiving them and keeping them subservient to the church.[3]

In many places, this anger against the Catholic Church and the cult of saints was violent and revolutionary, but it was not a secular uprising. Participants demanded a return to the primitive Christianity described in the New Testament and to direct communion with Christ. In northern Germany, where Martin Luther (1483–1546) rose to fame in the early sixteenth century, apocalyptic rhetoric, street dramas, pamphlets, and woodcuts described a world upheaval in which Christ appeared to unmask princes and prelates as swine. In bursts of religious emotion, ordinary people—peasants, laborers, and women—acted as persons possessed by the Holy Spirit. As historian Peter Matheson described radical religious activity in the streets of northern Germany in the early sixteenth century, "the divine" appeared "more intimate" and "the human more earthy. Every city becomes Jerusalem. The time is now and the place is here!" Capturing this conflation of divine and mundane realities, one woodcut depicted John the Baptist "welcoming Christ, but the river is not the Jordan; it is the River Pegnitz, with Nuremberg in the background."[4]

Sectarians caught up in signs of the end of time engaged in laying on of hands, anointing, and other performances designed to manifest God's living spirit and healing power.[5] Luther and other more restrained reformers resisted such dramatic, incendiary performances, but they, too, sought healing in Christ. People who clamored for reform wanted the whole earth purified and their own humanity sanctified and perfected. Many radicals wanted to see Christ himself and witness miracles of healing performed in the Holy Spirit; other reform-minded Christians wanted to live in full consciousness of God without the distraction of saints or priestly rigmarole. These Christians tended to view sickness as a means God used to draw attention to him and away from worldly preoccupations.

Condemnations of the Cult of Saints and Their Healing Powers

With varying degrees of thoroughness and radicalism, vocal minorities of theologians and lay people challenged the validity of healing miracles promoted by, and benefiting, the Catholic Church. One of the clearest and most influential expositors of this challenge, the French reformer John Calvin (1509–1564) condemned petitions to the saints for healing miracles as misguided and sinful and laid out a framework for Christian living that focused on worship of a transcendent God. Through his writings and governorship of the city of Geneva, Calvin's directions for Christian living played a major role in early modern debates about miracles and in the emergence of new ideas about Christian health, medicine, and science.

In his effort to restore Christian life to its original strength and simplicity, Calvin turned to the New Testament letters of Paul for judgment on what constituted Christian life and ministry. But even as he held to Paul's authority, Calvin brushed aside the apostle's reference to healing as one of the gifts that Christian saints could claim. Calvin acknowledged that, in addition to the chief offices of proclaiming the gospel and administering the sacraments, Paul "lists others, as powers, the gift of healing, interpretation, government, and caring for the poor." But Calvin thought healing and interpretation were no longer relevant: "Two of these, I omit as being temporary, for it is not worthwhile to tarry over them. But two of them are permanent: government and caring for the poor."[6]

In this sweeping, almost offhand dismissal, the reformer removed healing from the list of Christian ministries, not even stopping to argue the point. He recognized the continuing importance of government and charity as proper offices of the church, assigning elders to "the censure of morals and the exercise of discipline" and deacons to care of the poor.[7] But healing and interpretation were in a different category entirely. They were extraordinary gifts of the spirit bestowed on Christ's earliest followers to reflect the momentous events of his actual appearance on earth, not ongoing practices of Christian life. Claims to make them so were false and harmful to the Christian religion. Over the centuries, Calvin believed, superstitious stories about the healing powers of saints had crept in to corrupt Christianity, as had fantastic, so-called prophecies and other distortions of gospel teaching.

As much as anything, Calvin insisted, Christians needed to eradicate "perverse worship." With regard to God's judgment of priestly rituals, "Those who expect his approval for their paltry observances contrived by men's will" were deceiving themselves. Priestly rites were nothing more than "a sham obedience which is paid actually to men." As for the expectation of miracles from saints and their relics—and all other beliefs and practices not justified by scripture— "There religion (if it still deserves to be called religion) is defiled with more, and more senseless, superstitions than ever any paganism was."[8]

Along with the German reformer Martin Luther, the Swiss reformer Huldrych Zwingli (1484–1531), and other theologians critical of corruption and confusion in the Catholic Church, Calvin took a dim view of many of the beliefs and practices associated with miracles of healing and with the cult of saints that figured so prominently in popular religious life and brought enormous wealth to the church. Luther condemned efforts to manipulate God through petitions to healing saints and expressed outrage at the materialism of the church and at the expenditure of resources on lavish shows of piety that would be better spent on relief for the poor. But his understanding of the relationship between material and spiritual reality was not as radical as that of Calvin and the Swiss reformers, who emphasized the absolute spiritual transcendence of God. Luther argued that God always met people in their humanity, through material forms of worship and piety, and in conformity with external authority; preachers in the Reformed tradition rejected the idea that the infinite spirit of God was present in any finite, material form.[9]

Calvin acknowledged that miracles accompanied the world-changing revelations God made through Moses and Jesus, but he emphasized that these miracles were not part of the natural scheme of things. Although most Christians assumed they *were* part of nature, Calvin rejected that assumption. As historian Carlos Eire explained, "Calvin's denial of miracles in the material sphere is the capstone of his metaphysical assumptions. Uneasy with any intermingling of spiritual and material, he takes the miraculous out of the ordinary and moves it into the realm of revelation." To expect miracles of healing as part of Christian faith would be to seek God in creation, and that, for Calvin, was the essence of idolatry.[10]

But for all his criticism of the superstition, priestly corruption, and disrespect for God associated with miracles of healing, Calvin was sensitive to the *fear* of illness, pain, accident, and death that beset humanity and appreciative of Christianity's power to assuage it. As one of his comprehensive surveys of human vulnerability made clear, human beings stood in desperate need of healing and protection. "Innumerable are the evils that beset human life," he lamented, "innumerable, too, the deaths that threaten it." With regard to the body alone, "a man cannot go about unburdened by many forms of his own destruction, and without drawing out a life enveloped, as it were, with death." In whatever direction we turn, disaster and death lie at hand:

> Embark upon a ship, you are one step away from death. Mount a horse, if one foot slips, your life is imperiled. Go through the city streets, you are subject to as many dangers as there are tiles on the roofs. If there is a weapon in your hand or a friend's, harm awaits. All the fierce animals you see are armed for your destruction. But if you try to shut yourself up in a walled garden, seemingly delightful, there a serpent sometimes lies hidden. Your house, continually in danger of fire, threatens in the daytime to impoverish you, at night even to collapse upon you. Your field, since it is exposed to hail, frost, drought, and other calamities, threatens you with barrenness, and hence, famine. I pass over poisonings, ambushes, robberies, open violence, which in part besiege us at home, in part dog us abroad. Amid these tribulations must not man be most miserable, since, but half alive in life, he weakly draws his anxious and languid breath, as if he had a sword perpetually hanging over his neck?[11]

In this masterful piece of religious rhetoric, Calvin catalogued the potential dangers in ordinary life to point to the insecurity at the core of human existence. According to some interpreters, his ability to describe the tortured nature of the human condition came from personal experience; his biographer William Bouwsma called Calvin "a singularly anxious man and, as a reformer, fearful and troubled."[12] Others have taken Calvin's claim to religious assurance more seriously and perceived more equanimity and modest self-confidence in the man. Whether or not Calvin was a worrier, as Bouwsma claimed, he was a spokesman for the cultural dilemmas of his time with a blueprint for resolving them. His theology reflected desire for absolute truth in an age beset by religious turmoil.

The recovery, translation, and wider dissemination of a variety of ancient texts—religious, philosophical, and scientific—contributed to the creativity and thirst for cultural renewal of the early modern period. Erasmus anticipated a new era of Christian philosophy, and his vision inspired Calvin, as did his commitment to the study of biblical and patristic sources in their original languages as a guide to religious reform.[13] With respect to the cult of saints, Calvin went further than Erasmus, who deplored the commercialism, superstition, and grotesqueness often associated with it, but still venerated Mary and believed that prayers to St. Genevieve had saved his life when he was stricken with fever. Calvin and others in the Reformed camp also went further than Luther in their insistence on the absolute transcendence of God, expressed in the principle that finite nature could not contain the infinity of God.[14]

Calvin argued that human misery devolved from the "contagion" of Adam's sin, which "infected" all humanity and "was conveyed in a perpetual stream from the ancestors into their descendants." Even so, God's will lay behind every single disease and misfortune and every particular instance of healing and prosperity. Christians should pray not to force God's hand but to align themselves with his will. Like Job, they might find their prayers answered with further difficulty instead. God used illness to punish individuals for sin, Calvin argued, and to teach them to rely on and seek comfort from him. The greatest benefit a person could receive in this life was not freedom from suffering, but the assurance of God's love that enabled fearless acceptance of suffering and death. Thus, Calvin saw relief from sin as man's most fundamental need, and the gift of faith, which included assurance of acceptance by Christ and trust in divine providence, as the sole means to obtaining it: "When that light of divine providence has once shone upon a godly man, he is then relieved and set free not only from the extreme anxiety and fear that were pressing him before, but from every care." Invoking the Psalms, he assured his readers that, once "received into God's safekeeping and entrusted to the care of his angels," they would "not fear the terror of night, nor the flying arrow by day, nor the pestilence that stalks in darkness, nor the destruction that wastes at midday."[15]

If suffering could be weathered gracefully in this life, it might be expunged in the next. Assurance of God's love carried the expectation of eternal life and the resurrection of a perfectly healthy spiritual body. This expectation of immortal health was inspired by faith but also rooted in "knowledge of ourselves," Calvin believed, derived from "considering what we were given at creation." Alluding to the perfection of Adam and Eve described in Genesis as well as to a more innate sense of "how great our natural excellence would be if only it had remained unblemished," Calvin hoped that "the great nobility of our race" might "not be buried beneath our own dullness of wit," and that "we may press on to the appointed goal of blessed immortality." Immorality was both a "restoration" of God's creation and a process of being "engrafted" into Christ now, as Paul had explained, so that "we grow into one body with him." Thus, God made the eternal health of bodily resurrection incipient among those to whom he gave "the sole remedy for their deadly disease—the preaching of his Word."[16]

If full health in this life was the very image of resurrection in heaven, no one should ever take pride in health now, or think of it as a sure sign of salvation. Indeed, Calvin urged just the opposite: concentration on one's vulnerability to sickness, misfortune, and distress. Thus, suffering was medicine administered by God "lest, swollen with other good things—either of the soul or of the body, or of fortune—we grow haughty, the Lord himself, according as he sees it expedient, confronts us and subjects and restrains our unrestrained flesh with the remedy of the cross." With an eye on eternal life, God applied the medicine of suffering "in accordance with what is healthful for each man. For not all of us suffer in equal degree from the same diseases, or, on that account, need the same harsh cure."[17]

With regard to the healing miracles ascribed to Jesus in the New Testament, Calvin explained them as manifestations of Christ's divine glory, not events that Christians should expect to see continued through history. Christ's human form did not reveal his divinity; his miracles did. The miracles that he and his apostles performed illustrated the momentous world change brought about by his appearance on earth. These miracles ended with the deaths of the apostles who witnessed and conveyed his glory.[18]

With respect to the living power of Christ in the Eucharist, Calvin believed that communion with Christ was real—not just symbolic—but that this communion was real for Christians in other parts of their lives as well, and that participation in the Eucharist was not essential for salvation. He regarded the sacrament of the Eucharist as vital to the health of the church and as an important aid to Christian life, but rejected the adoration of the elements associated with Catholic piety, along with belief in their agency as means of physical healing. Christ's real flesh and blood was present in the Eucharist, Calvin believed, but in a spiritual and celestial form that should not be equated with the material elements of bread and wine.[19]

Modernizing the Cure of Souls

Following Luther, Calvin objected to the penitential system developed in medieval Christianity for two main reasons: first, because only God had the power to forgive sins, not priests or any of their external devices, and second, because the sins committed by every individual were innumerable and never could be exhausted by a piecemeal approach. Rather than seek particular remedies for particular sins as participants in the penitential system did, Calvin focused on the underlying contagion of which particular sins were symptoms. This contagion, though common to all humanity, came to expression differently in each individual, and God administered particular sufferings accordingly. Thus, although Calvin rejected the penitential system, he reaffirmed the ideas underlying it: that souls were diseased and needed to be cured, that Christ was the soul's physician, and that the right treatment for sin varied from one person to another: "The heavenly physician treats some more gently but cleanses others by harsher remedies, while he wills to provide for the health of all, he yet leaves no one free and untouched, because he knows that all, to a man, are diseased."[20]

Calvin was certainly not the first Christian to inspect his conscience and find it deeply contaminated with sin; in this and many other ways, he followed Augustine. Nor was he the first to dwell on the terrors of suffering and death; plenty of medieval Christians did that. What made Calvin an important herald of modern religious faith was his insistence that Christians should plumb these terrors for themselves and discern their therapeutic purpose. In making self-discovery of sin and its consequences a requirement of faith, he went beyond Augustine to mandate self-scrutiny and conviction of sin as a spiritual discipline for every Christian. He also went beyond Augustine in making this discipline a tortured kind of consolation and sign of salvation. And finally, he began to transform the fears of hell that had figured prominently in religious life since the plagues of the fourteenth century into a more self-conscious anxiety about ordinary human existence. Without relinquishing belief that death would be followed by eternal punishment or reward, he dwelt on the terrors that underlay ordinary life, eliding them with damnation, and making damnation a palpable reality that could be, and should be, experienced now.

Building on Luther's reformulation, Calvin rejected the Scholastic idea that priests held "keys" to absolution that believers could rely on for both immediate relief and eternal salvation. After the Fourth Lateran Council of 1215 made confession an annual requirement of every Catholic, theologians took up the question of how to deal with believers who went to priests to confess their sins because they feared the punishment in store for them. The sorrow expressed by these believers, however genuine, dwelt more on the feared consequences of sin than on remorse for the sin itself. As part of their authority, priests held keys of absolution that could turn a Christian's confessional fear of punishment (attrition) into the sorrow for sin itself (contrition) that absolution required.[21]

With Luther, Calvin removed the priest and his sacramental powers from the process of absolution and made Christ the exclusive priest in that process, and the believer's faith, created and conducted through Christ, the sole agency. Calvin drew Christ deeper into the human psyche and, in doing so, made religion less a matter of engagement in the objective rites of a collective culture and more an interior drama of emotional and intellectual struggle. Like so many other aspects of his reform agenda, Calvin's approach to penance was a pared-down, refocused, and modern version of received tradition. He hoped to reveal the full spectacle of God's work in creation, history, and individual human life by returning to the essentials of Christian life, stripping away the obstacles, corruptions, and misunderstandings that he perceived to encumber the church. But for all his respect for scripture and early Christian life, Calvin's effort to heighten awareness of the awful glory of divine providence was not simply an attempt to recover the piety of the past. He sensed a gathering momentum driving Christianity forward as well as the need to restore its ancient purity. This sense of being at a great turning point in the unfolding history of divine providence coincided with new interest in getting to the bottom of the human psyche, new appreciation for the problem of human suffering, and new understanding of what the cure of souls entailed.

"Sicklied o'er with the pale cast of thought"

Acceptance, welcome, and even cultivation of suffering had long been part of Christian life. Christian heroes proved their faith through martyrdom in the early church, and ascetic deprivation and self-inflicted discomfort commanded respect as a path of sanctity throughout early and medieval Christianity. In the late medieval period, mystics developed this tradition of Christian suffering further by employing fasting and other forms of pain and deprivation to celebrate the humanity of Jesus and to identify their own humanity with his.[22] In its attention to ordinary human existence, Calvin's focus on the redemptive role of suffering in human life grew out of this rich tradition of Christian respect for suffering, and especially out of the latent humanism in medieval Christianity. At the same time, however, Calvin's emphasis on God's absolute transcendence led him away from devotion to suffering as a means of establishing a personal relationship with God. His distaste for any effort to force God's hand led him to focus instead on the sufferings God administered in the ordinary course of life. Rather than celebrating the mystical fusion between the believer's suffering and the suffering humanity of Jesus, as late medieval ascetics did, Calvin urged attention to God's strategic purpose in administering suffering as means of teaching, testing, and drawing men and women toward him.

If Calvin's recommendation of self-analysis ran easily to morbid introspection, he was not the only one of his era captivated by self-discovery, or the only writer to describe it as an endlessly engrossing process. In some respects, as Peter Kaufman pointed out, Calvin's preoccupation with dark causes, purposes, and stratagems was not unlike that of Hamlet. Constant brooding over the assassination of his father, Claudius the king, and his mother's hasty re-marriage to the assassin made Hamlet "sicklied o'er with the pale cast of thought" (3.1.85). Hamlet's plight is less the result of original sin than of the machinations of a ruthless king and mother, and as Kaufman acknowledged, "*Hamlet* is not camouflaged Calvinism. No amount of interpretative acrobatics will make either Hamlet or Shakespeare a pietist." Yet, systematic interrogation of intention and feeling makes Hamlet and Calvin similar. Shakespeare's prince moves toward a form of self-understanding not unlike Calvin's belief in divine providence and acceptance of its determinative role in individual life. "There's a divinity that shapes our ends," Hamlet confesses in the play's last act, "Rough-hew them how we will" (5.2.10–11). Hamlet's brooding also carries an element of therapeutic value that enables him, finally, to accept his situation for what it is, and to be a better king for it. For Hamlet as well as for Calvin, introspection had practical benefit insofar as it led to acceptance of God's will and to a clearer understanding of relationships to other people, surrounding forces, and events.[23]

Just as early modern Christians expressed political unrest in religious terms, they also tended to think about human subjectivity that way. Investigations of fear, anxiety, and depression proceeded mainly through theological reflection and pastoral guidance, through prayer and Bible study, and by listening to preachers apply scripture to contemporary life. Scientific approaches to human psychology had yet to be born, and medical treatment of mental disorder was gruesome. Physicians treated insanity with incarceration, purgation, and experimental remedies; in seventeenth-century France, at least one physician used the new technique of blood transfusion to inject lamb's blood into the veins of mental patients.[24]

In seventeenth-century England, the medical establishment and its allies in the Anglican Church tried to link sanity with religious moderation and control, denouncing religious enthusiasts for attempting to treat mental disorder, and even targeting extreme religious piety as a mental disorder. But religious enthusiasts had the practical edge, especially when it came to healing: "The claims of the spiritual physicians and the complaints of their enemies agreed on one thing," historian Michael MacDonald observed, "religious healing was often effective and very popular." The Puritan preacher Richard Baxter described a constant stream of melancholics seeking his guidance as a physician of the soul and keeping him from other work, and he expressed annoyance that Catholic priests and radical sectarians appeared equally busy. Fervent sectarian prayer, song, exorcism, and belief in the efficacy of the Holy Spirit were hard to compete with. The most effective prescriptions the medical establishment had to offer were reason, moderation, and self-discipline, which they, too, often conceptualized in religious terms as expressions of Christian virtue.[25]

Despite the attractions of religious enthusiasm, religious moderation gained increasing respect as a regimen conducive to good health. Robert Burton's *Anatomy of Melancholy*, first published in 1621, praised emotional restraint and self-discipline as Christian expressions of health and criticized religious fervor as unhealthy. Much quoted and plagiarized during the seventeenth and eighteenth centuries, Burton's brilliant, learned, voluminous, and bombastic work made Christian government of despair the key to good health and social purpose. According to Burton (1576–1639), religiously inspired melancholy was humanity's most destructive enemy: "It more besots and infatuates men," he claimed, "than wars, plagues, sicknesses, dearth, famine, and all the rest." Attempting to pin the malady down, he defined religious melancholy as a subspecies of love melancholy, and observed that, in religious cases, the object of maddening devotion was God. Thus, Burton made overheated devotion to God the cause of humanity's most devastating ills. Distinguishing between religion run wild and frenzied and religion that was balanced and rational, he condemned priestly superstition as a prime instigator of the former.[26]

Although some cases of religious melancholy were "begun first from some great loss, grievous accident, disaster, seeing others in like case, or any such terrible object," many others "proceeded from too much fasting, meditation, precise life, [and] contemplation of God's judgments." To remedy the affliction, Burton advised, sufferers should quit the habits, company, or situations associated with religious distress, seek comfort in cheerful friends and productive work, and "observe this short precept, give not way to solitariness and idleness."[27]

In some respects, Burton summarized classic and medieval ideas about religious melancholy. He repeated Augustine's argument for rational and industrious forms of penance that kept believers from sinking deeper into sin and noted that Plato and other ancient writers had recognized religious melancholy as a serious affliction and viewed it as a branch of love melancholy. In identifying excessive and compulsive engagement in religious practice as a cause of melancholy and offering constructive remedies for it, Burton followed the penitential tradition in medieval Christianity, which warned against overscrupulosity and provided treatments for it. Other aspects of Burton's discussion, however, are suggestively modern. In applying the format of anatomy to analysis of melancholy, and thus laying out melancholy as if it were an object for dissection, Burton anticipated some of the insights associated with clinical, scientific studies of depression.

Anatomy became the centerpiece of early modern medicine thanks to the rediscovery of medical texts attributed to the Greek physician Galen, which ignited interest in dissection and anatomy at medical universities in Renaissance Italy. Handbooks containing basic aspects of Galenic medicine had been widely used in medieval Europe, but they contained only abbreviated translations or paraphrases of ancient texts. The rediscovery of classical texts, many of which had been preserved in Arabic, stimulated new discoveries in medicine as well as the reintroduction of ancient ideas. Once Galenic medicine became better known, criticism of it developed, along with new applications. Major corrections of Galenic anatomical theory began with the dissection work of Andreas Vesalius in Padua in the 1530s and culminated with the publication of William Harvey's work on the heart and circulation of blood in 1628. These advances attracted considerable attention and made anatomy the focal point of early modern medicine.[28]

Burton built on current fascination with anatomy, making it the governing metaphor for his analysis of mental illness, suggesting how enthusiasm for objectivity, empirical observation, and dissection could be applied to human subjectivity, opening it to closer inspection and more extensive rational analysis than before.[29] His insight into the relationship between melancholy and unrealized expectation was equally prescient. To "build castles in the air," he suggested, was to invite despair. As the poem he wrote for the front of the posthumous 1652 edition of his book indicated, fantasy led sometimes to ecstasy, and sometimes to defeat and terror. Melancholy could be discerned in the swings of fantasy, driving the sweetest expectations as well as the bitterest despair:

> Methinks I hear, methinks I see,
> Sweet music, wondrous melody,
> Towns, palaces, and cities fine;
> Here now, then there; the world is mine,
> Rare beauties, gallant ladies shine,
> Whate'er is lovely or divine.
>   All other joys to this are folly,
>   None so sweet as melancholy.
> Methinks I hear, methinks I see
> Ghosts, goblins, fiends; my fantasy
> Presents a thousand ugly shapes,
> Headless bears, black men, and apes,
> Doleful outcries, and fearful sights,
> My sad and dismal soul affrights.

> All my griefs to this are jolly,
> None so damn'd as melancholy.[30]

Burton never suggested that believing in Christ or bodily resurrection might be like building castles in the air. Nor did he come right out and say that oscillation between fears of hell and hopes of heaven was typical of religious melancholy. But he did expose the nervous energy underlying many forms of religious expectation in his day. Like Calvin, he encouraged Christian hope of salvation as a rational prospect attended by steady enterprise and the comforts of friends and family. Like Calvin, he was also preoccupied with the myriad ways in which this acceptance and sense of assurance about life could unravel, and sensitivity to the diseased and rotten nature of human life overtake the mind.

The modern attitude to Christian health represented by Calvin and Burton emphasized the vulnerability of human nature and the fine line between realism and despair. In this context, the healing power of religious faith became more of an antidote for the human condition and less a treatment for specific diseases and misfortunes. In some respects, the understandings of Christian healing exemplified by Calvin and Burton represented a return to conceptions held by early church fathers of Christ as the Great Physician and to Paul's conception of new life in Christ. At the same time, however, the religious thinking of Calvin and Burton contained new tendencies to downplay miracles and remove epiphanies of divine immanence from the material world, making God's activity in the world less immediate, more predictable, and subject to systematic investigation and experimentation.

Like Jews and Christians in the ancient world, Calvin and other Protestant reformers rejected magical forms of healing while asserting the therapeutic power of true religious faith. But in denouncing belief in ongoing miracles and equating it with belief in magic, Calvin and other reformers winnowed the field of divine activity in the world as it had never been winnowed before. Ancient and medieval Christians had rejected magic as inferior to Christian practice—if not downright evil—but generally acknowledged its existence and power. In the sixteenth and seventeenth centuries, skepticism about the existence of magic coincided with skepticism about miracles, and these tendencies to disbelief invited skepticism about the spirit world, and even about the existence of God. In his treatise on witchcraft, the Anglican clergyman Thomas Glanvill (1626–1680) claimed, "Those that dare not bluntly say, There is no God, content themselves (for a fair step and Introduction) to deny there are Spirits or Witches."[31] Not surprisingly, fear of such slippery slopes triggered defensive reactions.

Scholars interpret the witchcraft trials of the late medieval and early modern period in just these terms. Belief in demons and their ability to influence people, animals, and natural events intensified during this time, as people suspected of familiarity with Satan were rounded up, questioned, tortured, and executed. As the historian of witchcraft theory, Walter Stephens, showed, the judges at witchcraft trials were not the "fanatics or obscurantist crackpots" they are often made out to be, but men who "participated in the most vital, wide-ranging, and up-to-date philosophical and scientific debates." In the context of these debates, Stephens argued, witchcraft theory evolved as a way "to defend God and the world of spirit." During witchcraft trials, judges constantly asked indirect questions designed to extract descriptions from accused people about their interactions with the Devil. In Stephens's interpretation, the judges' interest in confirming the reality of the spirit world drove their need to know that the Devil appeared in material form, and this need drove their questioning and exertion of pressure on accused people to make confessions. Like other defenders of Christianity of their time, the judges resisted skepticism "because they had internalized it, and it riddles their texts with clashing logic and rhetoric." Stephens concluded, "Witchcraft theory was an impassioned protest that 'these things cannot be imaginary!' "[32]

While confessions extracted from people accused of witchcraft shored up faith in the invisible world, reformers were challenging many assumptions about that world and its role in human health and healing. Through their insistence on the believer's direct and immediate relationship to God, reformers criticized the materialism of Christian art and ritual, the lore associated with saints and their healing powers, and the validity of devotional practices surrounding sickness, death, and healing. In lieu of these materialistic expressions of Christianity, reformers urged people to focus on the transcendence of God and to trust in God alone for the antidote of transforming grace that would combat the sickness of sin and the fear of illness and death that resulted from sin.

Catholic Reforms

The hostilities that flared up between Protestants and Catholics obscured the many commonalities they shared and the larger trends affecting them both. Christians loyal to Catholicism participated in some of the same religious trends as Protestants, including, in some cases, criticism of the cult of saints and its investment in miracles of healing. As many scholars now emphasize, Protestant criticism of the elaborate ritualism, wealth, and corruption associated with Catholic piety and the Roman Church developed out of medieval Catholic reform movements, and some aspects of Protestant insistence on absolute dependence on God developed out of medieval mysticism.

Early modern Catholics appreciated their indebtedness to medieval Christianity better than Protestants did. But they also engaged in novel enterprises of self-examination and in new investigations of the structures and maladies of nature similar, in some respects, to those that engaged Protestants. At the Council of Trent, convened from 1545 to 1563, the Roman Church defended its sacraments and priesthood against Protestant attack and defined its relation to the world in a way that made the church a guardian and promoter of traditional Christian philosophy, liturgy, art, and social service. But although early modern Catholics felt a stronger sense of continuity with medieval Christianity than Protestants did, they also participated in the underlying shift toward more analytical approaches to Christian subjectivity and toward modern conceptions of faith as an antidote to the underlying malady of the human condition.

Ignatius of Loyola (1491–1556), the Spanish founder of the Society of Jesus, developed a program of spiritual introspection that transformed the meaning of penance along some of the same lines as Calvin's theology. His handbook of *Spiritual Exercises*, first printed in 1548 as a practical manual for mentors and confessors, bore more similarity to medieval penitentials than anything Calvin ever wrote, and he retained more of the old language from the cure of souls tradition than Calvin's writing. But in laying out a program of spiritual discipline that linked the process of redemption to self-discovery and self-understanding, Ignatius transformed the medieval commitment to spiritual purification into an interior process of self-analysis and self-development, much as Calvin had. As one commentator explained, Ignatius wrote the *Exercises* to help the individual "make a determinative choice about the future" and "to enable one to make that choice with objectivity and freedom of spirit and under the most immediate inspiration of God." The manual stated its purpose as enabling the "seeking and finding God's will in the ordering of our life for the salvation of our soul." Like Calvin, Ignatius emphasized the immediate personal relationship between the believer and God, making contrition an intrinsic part of this relationship, much as Luther and Calvin had, rather than something externally applied to the believer's soul or mediated through the saints.[33]

Ignatius, Luther, and Calvin were spokesmen for the growing momentum of commitment to religious reform that crested in the sixteenth century but had been building for several centuries before. Four centuries before Calvin, the Cistercian Bernard of Clairvaux (1090–1153) condemned what he perceived to be the rampant avarice and overall moral decline of the priesthood, complaining that in his own day, wooden priests with golden chalices had replaced the golden priests and wooden chalices of old.[34] Bernard inspired many later reformers; historians Jill Raitt and Dennis Tamburello showed that Calvin drew his understanding of pure mystical union with Christ from Bernard's writings.[35]

More than Calvin, however, Bernard urged devotion to the humanity of Jesus and Mary and encouraged its practice through care of the sick. His descriptions of the mystical love that joined humanity with God were widely influential, inspiring Marie d'Oigines (d. 1213), Beatrice of Nazareth (d. 1268), Hadewijch of Antwerp (d. c. late thirteenth century), and many other beguines in the Rhineland and Netherlands. Bernard's eloquence about the humanity of Jesus and Mary, the transformational power of suffering, and the importance of suffering as a means of salvation and union with God figured importantly in the flowering of lay mysticism and its stimulation of new initiatives in urban health care in medieval Europe.

The beguines' desire for unfettered union with God influenced the Dominican Meister Eckhart (d. 1327), who preached to beguines and was also inspired by them to equate union with God and spiritual freedom: "For God the Soul is the free and open way, into which he can plunge from out of his furthest depths; and for the soul, in return, God is the way of freedom, towards the depths of the Divine Being, which nothing can attain save the depths of the soul." Eckhart, in turn, influenced mendicant Friends of God in the fourteenth century, including John Tauler and Henry Suso, as well as the Brethren (and Sisters) of the Common Life, who practiced the *devotio moderna* of introspective meditation in the Netherlands and northeastern Germany during the fifteenth century. The most influential example of the new devotion, *The Imitation of Christ*, often credited to Thomas à Kempis (1380–1471), focused on the Eucharist as a celebration of the coinciding divinity and suffering humanity of Christ. This spiritual classic harked back to the spirituality of Bernard and the beguines, to their celebration of the humanity of Jesus, and to their sensitivity to suffering as the point where divine and human meet. The author of *The Imitation* speaks to Christ: "Ah, Lord God, how deeply the points of the thorns extend into thy most holy head: how cruelly they tore the tender skin of Thy flesh with the bones and nerves; so that from the wounds they made streams of blood flow down Thy neck, down Thy eyes, down Thy ears and face."[36]

With his sweeping denunciation of works as means to grace, Luther resisted the suffering some mystics cultivated as a method of absolution and means of participation in God. Yet Luther's equation between freedom from the law and complete faith in Christ grew out of this late medieval tradition of German mysticism. Like Thomas à Kempis, Meister Eckhart, and the beguines,

Luther understood absolution as the freeing of conscience through Christ. And he insisted on complete union: "It is necessary that Christ and my conscience be made one unique body, so that nothing offers itself to my view but Christ crucified and risen."[37] Luther's awe at the idea that finite, material humanity was capable of bearing the infinite divinity of God and his exhilarating sense of inner freedom from obedience to religious laws and works represent important elements of continuity that link Protestant and Catholic reformers and connect early modern religious sensibilities with medieval mysticism.

Luther's theology also resonated with religious sensibilities developed in Catholic religious art. Similarities to Luther's realism, his embrace of family life as the proper context for religious development, his emotional expressiveness, and his attunement to Christ's suffering can all be found in the works of the great Catholic painters and engravers of the Northern Renaissance. The Flemish painter Jan van Eyck (b. before 1395–d. 1441) used the new technique of oil painting to represent religious subjects with a new kind of realism. Van Eyck's pupil Roger van der Weyden (1399/1400–1464) depicted the holy family and other religious subjects in domestic settings. The German artists Mathias Grünewald (b. after 1454–d. 1528) and Albrecht Dürer (1471–1528) rendered the sorrows of Christ and his followers with emotional intensity and realistic concern for detail in ways similar to Luther's expressions in preaching and writing.

Both Protestants and Catholics participated in the developing interest in emotional feeling and human subjectivity characteristic of early modern European culture. These concerns influenced conceptions of Christian healing, contributing to more psychological interpretations of sin and salvation, as well as to controversies about miracles and their relationship to nature. The shift toward modern, secular ideas about nature and material reality had profound impact, in turn, on Christian health care.

Health Care and Hospitals

As with so many aspects of Christian healing in early modern culture, elements of continuity with past tradition coexisted with an underlying shift toward self-analysis that drew some energy away from public expressions of Christian healing. In Protestant regions especially, the shift toward more private forms of religious expression diminished religious support for public health care, whereas medicine and Catholic devotions often intermixed and donors invested wealth in acts of penance and hope of accruing spiritual merit. Protestants withdrew support from many hospitals where service to the sick and dying was intertwined with veneration of healing saints, and where care of the sick and dying was celebrated as meritorious work conducive to salvation. The decline in institutional support for public health care under Protestant regimes was especially calamitous in England, where Henry VIII confiscated church properties, including some hospitals and many pilgrimage shrines, in an effort to sever England's ties to Rome. "In some cities and towns," according to two leading authorities on the history of English hospitals, "the Reformation wrought havoc on the facilities provided by hospitals for the sick and poor." Outcries were raised, and not without effect, as some Protestant spokesmen saw the abandonment of the sick and poor as an affront to God: "For Christ's sake, ye rulers," complained Henry Brinklow in 1542, "look upon your hospitals, whether the poor have their right there or no. I hear that the masters of your hospitals be so fat that the poor be kept lean and bare enough; the cry of the people is heard unto the Lord, tho ye will not hear." Thanks to pressure like this, some hospitals survived and others were created. In London, where most of England's poor lived, Henry dissolved five hospitals, but several continued to operate and two others became established by 1560, one during Edward VI's reign and another by authority of the Catholic Queen Mary.[38]

Catholics persisted in religious commitment to public health care as Protestants backed away. Catholic religious orders continued their long-standing traditions of support for hospitals in many regions of Europe. And pious lay people, especially women, continued to engage in hospital work as a means of enacting devotion to Christ. While Protestants focused on the home as a center of worship, Christian education, and social welfare, Catholics inherited a historic commitment to care for the poor and sick that stretched back through medieval reform movements, through centuries of monastic investment in medicine and poor relief, and, before that, to the healing works of ascetics and apostles of early Christianity, and ultimately to Jesus himself. Thus, Catholics had strong historical ties, not only to institutions established and managed by the church to provide poor relief and care for the sick, but also to a spiritual tradition characterized by public devotion to human suffering.

Luther's emphasis on the family as the proper context of Christian life made care for the sick an essential part of Christian family life. His respect for the home as a health care center coincided with, and helped stimulate, a proliferation of manuals of home remedies and herbal medicine that the new printing technology made possible. Eventually, Lutheran appreciation of medicine and encouragement of good health contributed to strong commitments to public hospitals, but this development did not occur until the nineteenth century. During the seventeenth and eighteenth centuries, Lutheran churches ceded many of their welfare services to the state. As part of a general trend among Lutherans toward highly individualized piety, Luther's emphasis on active service to others came to be defined more in terms of interpersonal compassion than commitment to public welfare.

During the nineteenth century, reformers within the Lutheran fold reacted against the insularity of their own religious tradition. Partly inspired (and perhaps shamed) by Roman Catholic charity, Lutheran commitment to public service and social welfare grew, especially through the deaconess movement, which enlisted women in organized outreach to the poor and sick. Deaconesses contributed to the establishment of many Lutheran hospitals in Europe and the United States during the nineteenth and early twentieth centuries. Like Luther himself, later deaconesses believed in Christianity's compatibility with medical treatment and good health care while also affirming that sickness often served as the occasion for grace, redemption, and union with Christ.[39]

Luther's emphasis on the importance of biblical study influenced his understanding of the role of illness and suffering in Christian life and contributed to his positive view of human health and medicine. In the Old Testament especially, he found affirmations of the goodness of God's creation, and of human sexuality as part of that creation, that, to his mind, challenged monastic ideals of celibacy and withdrawal from the world. Biblical praise for God's concern for material and social existence influenced his understanding of the difficulties and sufferings of human existence as well as its comforts and rightful pleasures. Illness and suffering were meaningful occasions for faith and redemption, but this did not mean that Christians should cultivate personal suffering, as some medieval mystics did, or that physicians and medicines should be rejected: "God created medicine," Luther reminded, "and provided us with intelligence to guard and take care of the body so that we can live in good health."[40]

Although Protestant commitment to introspection and distrust of works as means of salvation contributed to a diminishment of public health care, Protestant emphasis on the home as a center of religious life compensated somewhat for this loss by promoting the responsibilities of households (especially of wives who managed them) to attend the sick and care for the poor and infirm. The English diary written at the turn of the seventeenth century by Margaret Hoby (1570/1571–1633) reveals that pious wives who managed big households during Elizabeth's reign served as primary health care providers for the families, laborers, and servants attached to the household. An earnest Puritan anxious about her own spiritual state, Hoby understood that her good work as a midwife, herbalist, and visiting nurse would not earn her own salvation. Nevertheless, she took some comfort in the thought that her skillful and effective work as a health care practitioner might be a hopeful sign of her salvation, as well as an instrument of divine grace for others. In any event, she never questioned her duty to treat wounds, nurse the sick, or assist in child-birth.[41]

Although important continuities exist between Margaret Hoby's commitment to caring for the sick and that of Catholic women in her own time and in the past, she had little interest in celebrating or even recognizing these continuities, at least partly because of her exaggerated sense of the discontinuities between Protestantism and "papism." Exaggeration aside, a real difference can be discerned between her sense of moral obligation to care for the people attached to her household and Catholic investment in care for the sick as a means of union with the sufferings of Christ. Many Catholics saw the sufferings of the poor as real extensions of the sufferings of Christ, and their own compassion as objectively fused with his; Hoby did not blur realities this way. Still essential to her vocation as a Christian, Hoby's commitment to the sick was moral but not mystical. At least in her diary, she never identified her own sufferings (which were many and onerous) with the sufferings of the people she cared for, and she never identified either with the sufferings of Christ.

This deeply pious woman was never possessed by Christ, or at least never suggested anything like that in her diary. If she longed for a transformation in identity, that longing took her into a process of self-examination that never reached any kind of satisfaction or emotional closure during the years she wrote in her diary. In this regard, Hoby's diary represents the sense of insufficiency and vulnerability at the core of human existence that Calvin expounded on so forcefully.

Hoby followed Luther, Calvin, and other reformers in concentrating on awareness of her dependence and responsibility to God and on God's use of suffering as means of instruction. Her concentration on the moral and psychological impact of suffering was typical of the investment in subjectivity characteristic of modern culture. The Protestant cult of self-analysis in which Hoby participated laid important groundwork for modern psychological thinking. Of course, religious contributions were not exclusively Protestant, nor as much of a departure from medieval culture as reformers said. Thus, Protestants figured prominently in a larger movement of religious and social reform in Western culture that included Catholics too. And early modern Christians drew from a variety of sources in their constructions of human subjectivity, including the explorations of human emotion undertaken by medieval mystics as well as the rich traditions of Christian philosophy, biblical commentary, and visual and performing arts.

Early Modern Medicine

The fluid and often fruitful interplay between miracle and medicine did not disappear. But as religious attacks on magic escalated in the early modern era and expanded to include many events that had previously been classified as miracles, healers who invoked spiritual powers were sometimes accused of witchcraft. In other instances, they were denounced as charlatans with no real power at all. "Scientific" studies of nature became increasingly popular and increasingly dissociated from religious faith as universities developed apart from ecclesiastical control and as physicians established medical guilds to license practitioners and regulate medical practice. The emerging medical establishment condemned reliance on folk remedies prescribed by "cunning men" and "wise women."

The fledgling medical establishment exercised only limited authority, however. Although ambitious in purpose and intolerant of unlicensed practitioners, the Royal College of Medicine included only thirty-eight physicians commissioned to supervise medicine in London in 1589, when the population of the city was around 120,000. During the sixteenth and seventeenth centuries, historian Keith Thomas calculated, "the ratio of the London population to its resident members and licentiates can never have been less than five thousand to one and was usually very much greater."[42] Moreover, the remedies prescribed by licensed physicians were, by today's standards, as unscientific as many of those prescribed by cunning men and wise women, and often considerably less helpful. Physicians routinely prescribed vomiting, leeching, blistering, emetics, and doses of minerals for a variety of ills, and often stuck to their medical theories however excruciating or unfortunate the outcome.

Despite the best efforts of physicians to set medicine apart, the relationship between medicine and religion stayed murky. Patients and folk practitioners often did not distinguish medical prescriptions from magical, symbolic, supernatural remedies, although by the seventeenth century, as Thomas observed, "the medical use of toads, pigeons, gold-rings or snake-skins had come to be justified by reference to their supposedly inherent natural properties." But the distinction between natural and spiritual properties was deliberately confused by "Neoplatonist intellectuals" who believed that intellectual forces permeated the material world and recommended the recitation of words or incantations for their natural therapeutic effect. Some people distinguished medicine from magic by the absence of charms or incantations in medicine. Thus, in defending herself from witchcraft in 1592, Joan Warden claimed that she never used charms, but only "ointments and herbs to cure many diseases." But that distinction did not stick well either, for even physicians invoked God's help and virtually everyone believed that recourse to prayer was appropriate in times of need.[43]

In other words, the state of medical and scientific knowledge in early modern Europe, England, and America was as fluid, controversial, and confusing as the state of religion. Great claims to advancement were made (and continue to be made in retrospect) about both science and religion in this period. A tendency to denigrate old institutions and overestimate the originality of new efforts typified the rhetoric of early modern religious reform. A remarkably similar tendency typified medical and scientific rhetoric as well and, until quite recently, persisted among historians of early modern science.

Historian Mary Lindemann argued that claims for the revolutionary nature of early modern science and its radical discontinuity with the past are better understood as enthusiastic efforts to promote science than as fair and balanced assessments of historical process. Science enthusiasts often claimed the sixteenth and seventeenth centuries as the dawn of a new era. And more than a few observers likened the bold new spirit in science to that in religion. Even in his own day, admirers referred to the Swiss scientist Theophrastus Bombastus von Hohenheim (1493–1541), better known as Paracelsus, as "the Luther of the physicians." Although Paracelsus did not subscribe to Luther's theology, his attacks on established medical authority reminded people of Luther's attacks on clerical authority. Paracelsus denounced the Galenic theory of disease and its attribution of disease to imbalances in bodily humors. He proposed instead that diseases were external entities, ultimately spiritual in nature, which invaded the body from outside.[44]

By the early seventeenth century, philosophers of science were condemning the classical theories of ancient Greek medicine for their ignorance of empirical reality and dependence on abstract theories. In a sarcastic characterization of how scientists in his own day still proceeded according to the outmoded classical method, Francis Bacon complained in 1623, "We create worlds. We prescribe laws to Nature and lord it over her." In this wrongheaded, outmoded approach to science, "We impose the seal of our image on the creatures and works of God, we do not diligently seek to discover the seal of God on things." In denouncing theories about nature that derived from philosophic speculation and setting the revolutionary nature of modern experimental science and its inductive methodology over against them, Bacon sounded a bit like Luther, who complained that Scholastic theologians looked at life through preformed categories of thought. Luther sought to replace Scholasticism with real-life experience. "It is not by understanding, reading, or speculation that one becomes a theologian," he preached, "but through living, dying, and being damned." Similarly, Bacon believed that scientists had finally begun to renounce the idealistic methods of their predecessors. Those methods had led to arbitrary and inaccurate pictures of reality derived from abstract theories. In welcome contrast, the new science took up the patient and far more significant work of discovering "the seal of God on things."[45]

Empirical observations of nature were hardly new, however, but in fact fundamental to Hippocratic and Galenic theories of medicine, as well as to the healing practices of many wise women and cunning men. In the ancient texts attributed to Hippocrates and Galen, writers instructed physicians to attend to the whole body's response to disease, to the individual nature of illness, and to external indicators of ill health, such as pallor and flushed skin. As Lindemann argued, the scientific theories of the sixteenth, seventeenth, and eighteenth centuries did not constitute a radical break with long-standing respect for material evidence, and temptations to see early modern medicine as constituting a great surge forward in medicine's triumphal story of progress ought to be resisted. Thus, Paracelsus was not truly the harbinger of modern ideas about disease that some have claimed him to be. If his theory of diseases as external entities seems to anticipate modern ideas about infection, his conception of them as spiritual entities descended from the stars places his theories in an entirely different realm from biological science, which views disease-causing microbes as products of natural selection and adaptation. Similarly, Bacon's glee in discerning "the seal of God on things" resonates more with medieval idealism about nature and with the religious empiricism of Hildegard of Bingen than with biological theories of evolution.

As Lindemann argued, the idea of a great "Scientific Revolution" dividing the intellectual outlook of the seventeenth century from that of the past is really a myth: "No sharp schism characterized epistemology then, and men like William Harvey and Isaac Newton were as much heirs of an older world as founders of a new one. Likewise, the often postulated breakthrough toward clinical and scientific medicine that purportedly happened in the late eighteenth century was not . . . a sudden rupture, but the result of multifarious conditions and forces, some of which can be easily traced to medieval precedents."[46]

But if the history of early modern science is more continuous with the past than many of its promoters have claimed, the *rhetoric* of revolutionary reform and radical progress captured people's attention alongside the rhetoric of religious reform. The claims of sweeping breakthroughs to truth that characterized both religious and scientific expression in the early modern period compensated for a loss of certainty about received tradition and justified rejection of traditional authority and clerical control. The new sensibility at play in early modern culture had much to do with hunger for truth, order, and clarity. Early modern quests for authenticity in religion and objectivity in science signaled the emergence of a new ethos that combined earnest introspection with outward exploration of the material world. This shift in worldview was incomplete and compromised at every turn. Yet, even in its partial and confusing effects, the sense of change was widespread.

Just as important, enthusiasm for early modern science laid the groundwork for a later time when scientific thinking would dominate assumptions about reality and challenge all metaphysical ideas about nature. With few exceptions, neither the religious nor the scientific reformers of the early modern era anticipated the divide that would later open between religion and science and the assault on religion that would follow.

The Modernization of Christian Healing

The demand for religious healing did not diminish in early modern culture. Christian practices continued to be effective in treating all kinds of infirmities, illnesses, and complaints. Christian healing also flourished in modern culture in a more targeted way as a means of helping people cope with increased concerns about melancholy and the emotional and intellectual stresses of life. The appeal to Christianity for physical healing never ceased, as evidenced by the emergence of many new shrines to the Blessed Virgin Mary, by continuing faith in the power of prayer in virtually all forms of Christianity, and by Pentecostalism's enormous and growing popularity in the twentieth and twenty-first centuries. But Marian devotion often reflects a blending of Catholicism and indigenous forms of healing that involves modern expressions of cultural and ethnic identity. And modern prayer and Pentecostal healing, though not entirely dissimilar to premodern forms of Christian healing, are often self-consciously personal in their focus on the power of faith and in their understanding of the coincidence between faith and the Holy Spirit. Whereas belief in the necessity of faith as the essence of Christian discipleship goes back to the gospels, the modern concept of faith healing implies that the believer's devotion, or will to believe, is essential to the agency through which healing occurs.

Similarly, Christians in ancient and medieval culture expected miracles to occur in nature and assumed that spiritual entities and their powers became manifest in dreams, visions, prayers, sacraments, comets, earthquakes, accidents, epidemics, and healing miracles. This way of thinking has never died out. But a competing, more dichotomous view of mind and nature has gained an increasing number of adherents and affected the development of both Christianity and medicine. In its dualism, this view had important antecedents in ancient and medieval distinctions between spirit and matter and in the philosophical idealism of Greek philosophy that carried Christian theology forward. But modern thinking about mind and nature increasingly emphasized the predominance of nature and, in a complete reversal of ancient and medieval understanding, even came to see mind as a product of nature.

Max Weber and numerous other scholars have argued that the understanding of God and nature represented by Calvin and other early moderns injected new elements of strategic thinking into Western culture and modern religious life.[47] Without exaggerating the change, it is fair to say that the shift they expressed toward a more psychological understanding of Christian faith meant that individuals shouldered more responsibility for God, and for managing life, than before. Religion became more detached from the collective fabric of social life. Early modern preoccupation with individual faith marked an important shift in focus that transformed Christianity from an enveloping religious culture into a more introverted and privatized personal commitment that could be transported anywhere.

As accepted parts of the fabric of reality, saints in late antiquity and medieval culture represented the objectivity of religious life and the collective solidarity associated with it. As masters of spiritual power and tangibly present intercessors and representatives of God, saints stood on the boundaries of human society between people and God. As exemplars of humanity united with God, they represented particular groups in society: residents of a particular village, women in childbirth, knights, cripples, lepers. Believers attributed superior knowledge and objective insight to saints because of their purity, transcendence, and partial detachment from ordinary life. In rejecting these icons of shared cultural reality, early modern reformers encouraged more private and introspective forms of faith that made room for the development of secular trends in public life. Saints and their healing powers did not disappear, but they often relocated in relatively private enclaves in larger, increasingly secular societies or in cultural outposts resisting secular trends.

In his analysis of sixteenth- and seventeenth-century England, John Sommerville argued that tendencies to more individualized and introspective forms of religion coincided with tendencies to secularize space, time, play, language, art, politics, technology, and work. Conceptualizing modernization in relation to two ideal types of culture, Sommerville wrote, "At one extreme we may imagine a people whose religious rituals are so woven into the fabric of their life that they could not separate religion from the rest of their activities." At the other extreme, "we may imagine a society in which religion is a matter of

conscious beliefs, important primarily for the times of one's most philosophical and poetic solitude."[48]

The modern, psychological turn in Christianity created new impetus and
opportunity for secular medicine. It also created new impetus and opportunity
for pragmatic, outcome-oriented social welfare services for the sick and poor.
New enthusiasm for naturalistic theories about the causes of disease led to
secular approaches to public health care that, in turn, helped to rationalize the
work of Christian charity and the long-standing Christian concern for care of
the sick. Modern concepts of Christian benevolence emerged alongside new
developments in medicine and strategic social planning and eventually led to
the creation of new hospitals and improvements in public health. At the same
time, works of benevolence helped modern Christians cope with the anxieties
of spiritual doubt and spiritual effort, even if they believed such works would
not earn them salvation.

Some might claim that both medical science and social welfare advanced
because Christianity retreated to a more private sphere; others would argue
that the healing traditions associated with ancient and medieval Christianity
do not come off badly in comparison with the inhumanities of managed care
and endemic poverty in the world today. However the pluses and minuses of
modernization are calculated, Christianity's long-standing investment in healing and attention to suffering persisted in the context of new discoveries in
scientific medicine and new approaches to health care, and also contributed to
those new discoveries and approaches. Long-standing connections between
Christianity, healing, and health care passed into the modern era, even as the
practice of each altered to reflect heightened concerns for religious authenticity
and scientific objectivity.

5

Healing in Western Christianity's Global Expansion

Beginning in the sixteenth century, Franciscan, Dominican, Jesuit, and other Catholic orders reintroduced Christianity in India, Persia, China, and Africa, where it had diminished or died out during the Middle Ages. They also brought Christianity to new regions in the Americas, Africa, and Asia, where it had been little if ever known. British, German, Dutch, and Danish Protestants began organizing mission societies in the seventeenth century, and by the middle of the nineteenth, Protestant missions were growing faster than any other branch of Christian missions. In Britain and America, support for foreign missions became a hallmark of evangelical religion, and the self-sacrificing benevolence demonstrated by missionaries was hugely admired, especially among evangelical women.[1]

Western missionary endeavors coincided with Western political and economic expansion. Initially, Western religious outreach developed in tandem with the imperialism of Spanish, Portuguese, British, French, Dutch, and German rulers eager to develop trade and win sovereignty over new lands and peoples. Later in the nineteenth century, the fast-growing global expansion of Protestant Christianity coincided with full-scale industrial development in western Europe and the United States and with aggressive effort on the part of Western businesses to extract minerals and develop agricultural resources in non-Western regions.

New and more proficient ways of seeing and manipulating the world often served Western business investments and colonial rule

over subject regions and populations, and the technologies enabling this Western expansion surpassed most technologies elsewhere. Guns and sailing ships,
then better guns and ships, steam engines, trains, electricity, photography, air-
planes, and telecommunications all increased the visibility of people, places,
and things and transformed human interaction, industry, transportation, and
the conduct of warfare and government. The implications of Western expansion were so profound and far-reaching that the whole fabric of life changed
nearly everywhere.

In the ancient world, Christianity expanded as the political power of the
Roman Empire waned; in the modern world, Christianity and Western might
expanded together. Moreover, the impact of Roman imperialism on indigenous
cultures in the ancient world was never as far-reaching or thoroughgoing as
that associated with modern Westernization. Indigenous cultural traditions
persisted in both medieval and modern conversions, but in modern conversions, especially after 1800, assault on the social and cosmological structures
of indigenous cultures was profound.

For all the maiming and killing and baptisms resulting from combat in
the Middle Ages, the changes involved in becoming Christian left many fundamental assumptions about the nature of the material world and the organization of society relatively undisturbed. In the modern period, by contrast,
Protestant iconoclasm, vigilance against superstition, and emphasis on the
moral importance of ordinary life supported the construction of political arenas
in which people worked out their own salvation (or damnation) in terms of
progress and social change. Among Americans, tendencies to equate religious
and political liberty worked to undermine traditional notions of social hierarchy
and religious authority.[2] And in many places, however inadvertently, missionaries stimulated revolutionary attitudes and contributed to the politicization of
religious life.

Medieval Christians found it comparatively easy to baptize the customs,
shrines, and deities of tribal peoples in Europe, but modern missionaries, especially Protestants, balked at such syncretism. In nineteenth-century India,
for example, Protestant missionaries required Brahmin converts to take the
Lord's Supper with people of lower caste, thus forcing the Brahmins to aban-
don their religious purity and identity.[3] In another instance of the stiff requirements involved in Protestant conversion, the American missionary Robert
Hume insisted in 1845 that people in India must "learn to reject" the *Vedas*
and *Puranas* and to regard those sacred texts "with scorn and contempt."[4]
Earlier Christian missionaries demanded religious change from people, but
for practical reasons they rarely, if ever, condemned the teachings of other
traditions in such a wholesale way. For example, the ancient *Acts of Thomas*

praised the asceticism, celibacy, compassion, and healing powers displayed by St. Thomas in his missionary journey to India and contrasted his virtues with the selfish way India's rulers behaved. But Thomas's virtues also coincided, to a considerable extent, with India's own religious ideals.[5] Exploiting such similarities, ancient and medieval missionaries often grafted Christian virtues onto indigenous ones, aiming to demonstrate the inferiority of other religions, not extinguish them.

Catholic missionaries adhered more closely to this older strategy than did Protestants. For instance, the Jesuit missionary to China Matteo Ricci (1552–1610) compiled a book of ink drawings to illustrate Bible stories that represented Christian ideas in terms of Chinese virtues. To explain the drawing of Peter walking on the Sea of Galilee, Ricci wrote, "A man who has strong faith in the Way can walk on the yielding water as if on solid rock." Ricci invoked the Daoist concept of the Way and Confucian concepts of heaven and the wise man to proclaim the miraculous power of Christian faith: "When the wise man follows heaven's decrees fire does not burn him, a sword does not cut him, water does not drown him."[6]

Protestant missionaries defined the boundaries between Christianity and other religions much more sharply. Even genial souls like the famed medical missionary Albert Schweitzer (1875–1965) were contemptuous of native traditions. Regarding the traditional practice of painting mothers and their newborn infants white to protect or disguise them from evil spirits, everyone knew Schweitzer was making fun of them when he reminded women who had just delivered babies in his hospital, "Take care you don't forget the painting!"[7] While earlier emissaries of Christianity in Africa may have objected to traditional forms of ritual practice, Schweitzer's complete disbelief in such practices was distinctly modern and, to many people, unacceptable. But in having to defend their traditions against skepticism about the spirit world, conservatives became modern, too.

However much spiritual healing altered in the process, its persistence among Christians in Africa, India, and elsewhere in the modernizing world was not simply a vestige of primitive belief, as Schweitzer and other Western missionaries thought. People everywhere—in New England and Paris as well as Maharashtra and French Equatorial Africa—were employing spiritual practices for protection against the stresses of modernization, in spite of the skepticism about spiritual healing associated with modern science. Religious healing did not decline as much as it might have in response to the increasing secularity of modern life, partly because practitioners invoked quasi-scientific language to promote religious healing and explain how it worked. And for people who wanted to be Christian without capitulating to Western culture, miracles of Christian healing provided a means of maintaining direct continuity with cultural tradition and indigenous religious practice on one hand and with the new spiritual authority of Christ on the other.

The Politicization of Christian Healing

Although Western missionaries challenged the most egregious forms of colonialist exploitation, in the case of Protestant evangelicals especially, modern assumptions about reality colored their conceptions of Christianity and Christian healing and allied them, in fundamental ways, with the forces of Westernization. Missionaries often believed that Christianity and Western civilization were closely related and that Christianity would make the global expansion of Western civilization beneficial to everyone. Although their ideas about miracles varied, Western missionaries shared similar ideas about the social implications of the healing power of salvation from sin and eternal life in Christ. They often emphasized Christianity's healing of social ills, whatever they thought about miraculous cures of physical illness. Thus, for most Western missionaries, Christian healing meant promoting social peace, softening the blows of Western military, political, and economic advance, challenging the worst brutalities of colonialism, and enabling personal responsibility, education, good health, and better standards of living.

Along with these expectations of Christianity's positive effect on society, missionaries believed that the absence of Christianity produced diseased social conditions. Writing from Burma in 1817, the renowned American missionary Ann Hasseltine Judson expressed a view of heathen life that was typical of Protestant missionaries in her generation: "a whole populous empire, rational and immortal like ourselves, sunk in the grossest idolatry, given up to follow the wicked inclinations of their depraved hearts; entirely destitute of any real principle, or the least spark of true benevolence."[8] Like other Protestant missionaries of her time, Judson understood the healing power of Christianity as a total renovation of person and society involving both individual salvation and the establishment of God's Kingdom on earth.

While missionaries cried out against human misery, their doctrinaire interpretations of Christianity often defined the means of relief rather narrowly and usually in ways that excluded indigenous forms of spiritual healing. Missionary disdain for traditional forms of healing practice meant that people around the world faced Christian attacks against their own traditions of religious healing even as the stresses of Westernization led them to demand more of those traditions.

Disputes among Western missionaries added to the competitiveness associated with religious healing and to its tendency to become politicized. Prior to ecumenical developments of the late twentieth century, Catholics undertook missionary work not only to exercise their faith in Christ and the Church, but also to get ahead of Protestants and establish a strong Catholic presence in the non-Western world. For their part, Protestant missionaries often disparaged Catholics as corrupt, predatory, and superstitious. Military hostilities between Catholic and Protestant states heightened this religious competition. As competing views of how to obtain salvation fueled the antagonism, mutual disrespect between Protestants and Catholics exacerbated the tensions associated with Western expansion, as did intramural rivalries among various Catholic religious orders and among the wide array of Protestant groups striving for converts. In southern Africa by 1860, for example, the sheer number of different mission societies complicated efforts made by each of them, as American Congregationalists and English Methodists competed with Scottish, Moravian, Rhenish, French, Dutch, and Norwegian missions and with the Berlin and Hanoverian societies, as well as with the Church of England and the Roman Catholic Church.[9]

Both Catholic and Protestant missionaries urged separation between Christian practice and heathen superstition, but Catholics tended to be more willing to accommodate native beliefs and practices and build on them toward Catholic ends. In general, Protestants were more focused than Catholics on demonstrations of individual responsibility as evidence of conversion, more insistent on separation from indigenous culture as the price of individual admission to church fellowship, and more confident of Christianity's compatibility with modern business, science, and education. In the nineteenth and early twentieth centuries, Protestants were more likely than Catholics to preach about the providential course of history they found described in the Bible and to dwell more on the overturning of earthly kingdoms in anticipation of the coming of God's Kingdom. After the Second Vatican Council in the 1960s, dialogue between Marxists and Christians prompted Catholic missionaries in Latin America and Africa to advocate a theology of liberation from colonial dominance and poverty and to forge ahead, especially in Latin America, in identifying Christian healing with social justice. For these Catholics and for numerous Protestants thinking along similar lines, political and economic oppression epitomized human sinfulness, and Christian movements that led people toward social justice epitomized redemption and Christ's healing power.

Tendencies to explain Christian theology in terms of social justice had important implications for conceptions of Christian healing. Advocates of social justice equated the healing power of Christ with the reconciliation that followed the defeat of sinful forces of oppression. This language of social justice harked back to the healing acts of Jesus as disclosures of the Kingdom of God and to his radical moral teaching and leadership of an egalitarian religious movement amid the brutality of the Roman Empire. But the modern gospel of political liberation was not simply a recapitulation of New Testament stories; it also reflected the politicization and secularization of modern Christian life. Jesus directly confronted demons in his effort to bring the Kingdom to earth; modern disciples of liberation confronted political and economic injustice and interpreted the demons Jesus faced as symbols of that injustice.

As one example of this modern interpretation of Christian healing, the Brazilian theologian Rubem Alves expressed the Christian hope of resurrection as a politics of liberation informed by a Marxist understanding of social process. In an influential book published in 1969, Alves argued that Christian hope combined with revolutionary consciousness would lead people toward utopias of social equality and collective well-being. Thus, Alves interpreted Christian resurrection in terms of "man's discovery of freedom through love and communion with his fellow man." Once people were free enough to experience the "vitality, enjoyment, pleasure, and joy" of communion with each other, he argued, they became more aware of how certain living conditions prevented that communion and more motivated to hope and work for better conditions for everyone. "One suffers because the explosion of joyful expectation created by the 'aperitif' is frustrated by the powers that keep man under repression," Alves wrote. "Man longs for more, for fulfillment, for the resurrection of the body, for the fullness of life of which our present situation is only an exhilarating foretaste."[10]

While Alves invoked the traditional language of Christianity to say that "the future of man is in the resurrection of the body," he also insisted that "the language of the community of faith definitely opposes the platonic negation of the body" and that "one does not find in this language, consequently, any place for transcendence beyond the world or beyond the body."[11] New Testament scholars might agree that Jesus affirmed the importance of the body and the in-breaking of God's Kingdom in the midst of earthly life. They might also agree that, almost from the beginning, Neoplatonic tendencies to separate mind from matter altered what may have been Jesus' more holistic Galilean worldview. But in overlooking the demons and spiritual powers that filled the world of Jesus, Alves promoted an interpretation of Christianity close to political ideology and removed from premodern views of reality.

New Indigenous Forms of Christian Healing

In some contrast to the de-emphasis on transcendence in some forms of social justice theology, many converts integrated Christianity with traditional values and customs with an ease that caught many Western missionaries by surprise, if they understood what was happening. These new indigenous forms of Christianity often revolved around healing and incorporated miracles of healing into modern forms of social consciousness. Christians in Africa, Latin America, eastern Europe, and Asia combined social visions of Christian healing with practices of spiritual healing derived, at least in part, from indigenous traditions. And investment in indigenous forms of spiritual healing stimulated new interest in the miracles of Jesus, Mary, and the apostles and saints.

As the historian and missionary theologian Andrew Walls observed about African Christianity, this-worldly emphases in African traditions influenced the development of Christianity, as did African practices of ancestor veneration. Walls acknowledged that Christian missionaries introduced major changes in African religious thought, such as new emphasis on God's presence and importance in everyday life and a simpler, more dualistic understanding of spiritual forces locked in combat between good and evil. Missionaries also introduced biblical stories about Israel, as well as about Christ as savior and inaugurator of a new Israel. These themes became intertwined with African symbols, stories, and healing practices to produce expressions of Christianity that differed from Western forms. This intertwining reflected Christianity's capacity for adaptation to different cultures as well as the continuing power of African traditions. Belief in God's incarnation in human form and the Bible's validity in many different languages encouraged such adaptation, Walls argued, and helped to explain the tendencies of Christian converts to recognize their own deities in biblical stories. Thus, "all over sub-Saharan Africa," Walls observed, "the Christian God is known by vernacular names. The relationship between Africa's old religion and its new one is cemented in the conventions of speech."[12]

Interplay between Christianity and indigenous religions occurred in the context of the revolutionary social and cultural changes Western expansion brought to virtually all regions of the world, including the development of market economies, the breakdown of traditional kinship structures, and the emergence of modern forms of individualism. People turned to religion to manage these forces. In many cases, religion served as a means of negotiating social change and exercising some control over it. In this context, healing came to the fore, both as a means of coping with the suffering produced by social change and as a means of constructing new visions of society that would enable people to be healthier and more productive.

A sense of living connection to the healing miracles of Jesus and the apostles has been vital to Christianity's reception in many places. The emergence of Pentecostalism as a worldwide movement affirmed that miracles of healing rained down on God's people in the midst of secularized societies. And in many parts of the world, the healing miracles celebrated by Pentecostals offered continuity with traditional forms of religious healing, even as they addressed modern forms of social stress and alienation. People highly conscious of the political and economic pressures of modernization, eager to bring elements of traditional religious healing forward to meet these pressures, embraced the healing miracles of Jesus and affirmed their reappearance in the modern world.

Before the development of Pentecostalism in the twentieth century, forces leading toward a modern revitalization of Christian healing were already in play. As early as the sixteenth century, encounters with Christian missionaries in colonial situations politicized religious life and led to new religious movements in which miracles of healing supported resistance against social injustice.

Missionary Influence in American Indian Religious Movements

The arrival of Jesuit, Franciscan, Recollet, and Ursuline missionaries in North America coincided with the rampant spread of a variety of deadly new diseases and contributed to the destruction of traditional structures of authority, kinship, economic production, and social interaction. Some American Indians feared Catholic priests as carriers of disease, and not without reason, as the arrival of one tended to accompany the onset of the other. As in the past, missionaries promoted Christianity as a religion in which human suffering carried redemptive value. But unlike the emissaries of Christianity in medieval Europe, those in sixteenth-century North America encountered tremendous anxiety about Christianity's malevolent power, as well as interest in its message of salvation and healing. Thus, even in the sixteenth century, when Catholic missionaries expressed beliefs about the reality of spiritual healing similar to those of the Native Americans they hoped to convert, the cultural disturbance associated with Christian conversion was profound.

The death toll among North American Indians from smallpox, influenza, measles, and other European diseases far exceeded deaths from battle or military conquest, and this drastic decline in native populations expedited conquest and also heightened anxiety about witchcraft.[13] In the territory French explorers claimed as New France, Huron and Iroquois Indians initially viewed Jesuits as healers, and Jesuit records from the 1630s include a number of accounts of healings attributed to priests and their sacred rites and objects. One priest's application of holy water caused a blind man to see, and another's presentation of a picture of Jesus cured a woman of severe abdominal pains. The Jesuits encouraged belief that baptism could heal and protect people from disease and went along with the idea that the sugar and raisins they dispensed had curative power. But the hope people initially invested in these priests and their rituals and material objects soon evaporated as epidemics of smallpox and other diseases took their toll, reducing the population of Huron and Iroquois by half between 1634 and 1645 and raising suspicion that Jesuits were witches who inflicted disease. Many Indians who had accepted baptism renounced it and returned to traditional healers. Meanwhile, Jesuits were attacked, threatened, and forced into hiding. One historian argued that the whole community of Jesuits in New France escaped massacre only because Huron and Iroquois entrepreneurs feared that such retaliation would diminish their trade with the French. In one incident, a young man attacked a priest entering his village and was about to dispatch him with a hatchet when a woman intervened and begged him to stop. The man let the priest go, took his crucifix, and then agreed to return it on the condition that Jesuits stop the smallpox.[14]

As the Jesuits quickly discovered, Huron and Iroquois took dreams very seriously, regarding them as messages from the spirit world. In ritual practices that affirmed the importance of individual experience for the group as well as for the individual dreamer, some dreams required communal guessing, ritual enactment, and gift giving. The Jesuits discouraged these dream rituals (unless visions of Mary and Jesus were involved), as they did healing dances and recourse to shamans for healing cures. But investment in all these practices intensified as suspicions about the Jesuits mounted. In one Huron village, a man dreamed that the Creator told him the Jesuits would not be satisfied until every Huron had died. After discussion in the village council, villagers gathered to guess the dream and to drink from a kettle of ritually purified water as an antidote to the baptismal rite that Jesuits performed. In a similar reflection of fear of Christianity, a report circulated about a Huron woman who had returned from the dead to warn that the French guarded heaven. Indians were not admitted to the privileges of heaven, the woman reported, but were held as prisoners of war there. The souls of Indians fortunate enough to have escaped baptism lived happily in another part of the spirit world.[15]

Kateri Tekakwitha (1656–1680) represents a more positive appreciation of Christianity that inspires both Jesuits and Native American Catholics today as a symbol of social unity as well as personal piety and healing power. Born of an Algonquin mother and Mohawk father, Kateri was crippled, disfigured, and partly blinded in an outbreak of smallpox that killed her parents when she was a child. Under the tutelage of Jesuits and hospital nuns, she converted to Catholicism and became an ascetic famous for flagellating herself, consuming sand and glass, walking barefoot in winter, and devoting herself to acts of charity. As historian Christopher Vecsey and others have pointed out, Kateri's celibacy, extreme piety, and willingness to suffer not only demonstrated her devotion to the Blessed Virgin of Catholic Christianity, but also carried forward an older Iroquois practice of young women withdrawing from society to gather the spiritual power of their virginity for the welfare of the community. In addition to revitalizing this traditional practice, Kateri came to be seen, in her disfigured and suffering body, as a powerful symbol of the plight of her people. In her application of suffering toward spiritual and charitable ends, she represented the heroism of her people, as well as the Virgin's powerful sorrow for the sufferings of her son.[16]

Since her beatification in 1980, Kateri "has virtually been adopted by all Native Americans throughout the country," according to Bishop Donald E. Pelotte. "There are very few reservations where they don't have her picture." While many await a final miracle to qualify her for official canonization as a saint, some claim that a miracle of a certain sort has already been achieved. "It is the spirit of unification that has been growing among the various Native American nations since Kateri's beatification," a spokesman for the Bureau of Catholic Indian Missions explained. "There has been 'a healing effect,'" according to Monsignor Lenz, "that has brought many tribes to work and pray together, despite past problems."[17]

Although many Native Americans embraced Christianity, others resisted it even as they borrowed elements for indigenous movements of religious and cultural revitalization. In what some historians view as a parallel tradition to Christianity, Iroquois people told the story of a great peacemaker, born to a virgin mother, who sailed across the lakes in a white stone canoe, bringing peace to the warring Iroquois tribes. Many Iroquois preferred this Christ-like hero of their own, named Dekanawidah, to the European God whose power they feared and whose people seemed as often vicious and harmful as not. The story of Dekanawidah developed in conjunction with a rite of condolence, in which clan leaders from different Iroquois tribes gathered after the death of a chief to express their solidarity and swear off blood revenge among them. This ceremony became the ritual centerpiece of the Iroquois confederacy, which maintained strong military and political forces in North America until the end of the French and Indian wars in 1763 and the War of American Independence, when the Americans defeated the Iroquois who fought with the British and absorbed considerable portions of Iroquois land.[18]

Despite their formidable presence in the seventeenth and eighteenth centuries, by the turn of the nineteenth century, the Iroquois had lost most of their farmland and hunting ground to the Americans, and their Confederacy lay in a shambles. Amid these demoralized, impoverished, and disease-stricken people, the prophet Handsome Lake (c. 1745–1815) emerged with visions of heaven and hell similar to those of American Protestants who had moved into Iroquois territory. Handsome Lake's visions reflect both the influence of Christianity and Western culture and resistance to them, as well as strong elements of continuity with indigenous tradition.

In his visions, Handsome Lake encountered two roads in the spirit world, one leading to the house where Indians who succumbed to the vices of the white man were punished for their sins, and the other to a land of abundant fields and streams where faithful Indians lived in robust health. On the road to the heavenly place, Handsome Lake met Jesus, who showed him his wounds. Jesus encouraged Handsome Lake on his way, saying he hoped the Iroquois people would treat their prophet better than Christians had treated him. Handsome Lake also received a set of moral commandments from the Creator, parallel to those Moses received, to guide his people along the right road. This Code of Handsome Lake known as *Gai'wiio* or "The Good Message," established behavioral guidelines similar to those promoted by Protestant evangelicals but distinctive in ways that facilitated independent identity.[19]

The religion of Handsome Lake is one example of traditional religion that incorporated certain aspects of Christian healing while recongizing the maintenance of traditional identity as a political necessity as well as religious good. Christian conceptions of sin and connections between sin and sickness on one hand, and renunciation of sin and recovery of health on the other, led to regimens for pulling communities together as well as explanations of what had gone wrong. If emphasis on sin blamed victims for their miseries, it also made them agents of their own fate, with power to set things right.

One of the most important of all North American Indian prophets was Wovoka (c. 1875–1932), a Paiute Indian from Nevada whose response to the predicament of Western Indians in the late nineteenth century led him to a new vision of heaven and earth related to Christianity. Like the religion of Handsome Lake, the Ghost Dance founded by Wovoka incorporated aspects of Christian healing within a new religious movement that encouraged Native identity in the context of Western culture. Along with a moral code similar to that of evangelical Protestantism, the Ghost Dance promoted images of community renewal that derived, in part, from biblical stories of God's restoration of health and fecundity to Israel in response to her repentance and faith. Known to the Presbyterian family for whom he worked as Jack Wilson, Wovoka was a healer and shaman known for his ability to control weather. In a revelation he experienced in 1889, Wovoka saw heaven revealed and Indians there restored to health. He saw whites in heaven, too, although his vision gave priority to Indians as resurrected saints. In a message of accommodation, he preached that Indians should get along with whites, and work for them. At the same time, he recognized both the spiritual status and the political rights of Indians and drew parallels between Native people in the West and Americans in the East, and between his authority and that of the President of the United States.

Wovoka traveled to disseminate his message and received Ute, Shoshone, Arapahoe, Cheyenne, Sioux, Bannock, and Mohave delegations at his home in Nevada. His services as a healer were constantly in demand and, in addition to his personal ministrations to the sick and wounded, he sent out paint, feathers, clothes, and other material objects imbued with protective and healing powers through the mails. Most important, he officiated at the ceremony from which his religious movement derived its name. In a circle dance, sometimes with himself seated at the center, some participants fell to the ground and experienced visions of their deceased relatives in heaven.

The Ghost Dance religion took on a more militant cast as it spread among Plains Indians known for their bravery in war, especially the Sioux. Many of these Indians were penned up on reservations and prey to a variety of ills, including malnutrition, tuberculosis, alcoholism, grief, and despair. When Sitting Bull and other war heroes on the Sioux reservation at Pine Ridge got involved, and some of the men took to wearing Ghost shirts depicting their visions, said to protect them from bullets, the U.S. Army became alarmed at the possibility of an armed uprising. In 1893, amid provocation and panic on both sides, the soldiers opened fire on an encampment of Sioux families at Wounded Knee, killing 146 Sioux, including forty-four women and eighteen small children. As a result of this tragedy, the Ghost Dance lost much of its appeal as a means of salvation.[20]

With different outcomes, Nick Black Elk (1866–1950) articulated a vision of world healing that inspired many different people across North America and beyond. An Oglala Sioux holy man and, during part of his life, a Roman Catholic catechist, Black Elk went further than earlier prophets in affirming Christian beliefs and in explaining Native American spirituality to a larger American and European audience. He developed the implications of Native American healing with reference to Christian expectations of world renewal, making Native people exemplars of spiritual life. Perhaps with images of Christ's suffering and that of earlier saints in mind, he suggested that the sufferings endured by Native Americans inspired religious feeling in others and called attention to the humanity of people in pain. For Black Elk, Native American spirituality amplified the meaning of Christianity and carried transformational, redemptive implications for the whole world.

In addition to his efforts to expand the meaning of Christianity in light of Native American experience, Black Elk lead the way in reconstructing traditional Oglala rites in response to the new demands for healing that reflected new social difficulties and political challenges. As a leader of the Sun Dance revival on the Pine Ridge Reservation, Black Elk helped to transform an outmoded ritual of empowerment for free-riding hunters and warriors into a more relevant ritual of healing for people caught up in the disempowerment and suffering of modern Indian life. In the Sun Dance that Black Elk helped to recreate, individuals found help with alcoholism and other forms of disease, failure, and misfortune. They also found well-being through identification with a traditional religious community, as did the family members and friends who gathered to support them. In its previous manifestation, the primary function of the Sun Dance was to imbue hunters and warriors with spiritual strength. But it had always involved healing, both in various forms of shamanic doctoring that took place during the summer gathering and in thanksgiving to the spirits for cures that had occurred during the year.

In the new Sun Dance that Black Elk helped to recreate, healing moved even more to the fore. The old association between valor in warfare and stoic endurance of ritually inflicted pain became recast in a modern ceremony of personal and cultural redemption that culminated in flesh cutting and piercing. Christianity contributed to this transformation, at least indirectly. Most of the participants in the new Sun Dance were baptized Christians who embraced Christian ideas about redemptive suffering, even as they also respected the existence and powers of traditional spirits.[21] Flesh cutting and piercing evoked the crucifixion of Christ as well as the bravery of Native people and created a tacit link between their sufferings and the redemptive suffering of Christ. At the same time, the Sun Dance maintained the integrity of the Oglala religion and its importance as a source of healing as well as of ethnic identity and pride.

With the help of American editors whose reputations rose with his, Black Elk conveyed his sense of the resonance between Christianity and Native American spirituality to a broader world. In a vision inspired both by the biblical book of Revelation and by traditional Native American visions of the spirit world, *Black Elk Speaks* described horses thundering in from four directions to signal the convergence of spiritual forces in response to the tragic defeats of the Sioux people. A subsequent work, *The Sacred Pipe*, laid out the meaning and therapeutic benefits of the seven rituals sacred to Oglala Sioux, much as a catechism might introduce readers to the seven sacraments of the Catholic Church. For example, the purifying and redemptive effects of the sweat lodge ceremony paralleled the mystical, transforming, and cleansing power of Christ in baptism, repentance, and the Eucharist. "When we use the water in the sweat lodge," Black Elk explained in *The Sacred Pipe*, "we should think of *Wakan-Tanka* who is always flowing, giving His power and life to everything; we should even be as water which is lower than all things, yet stronger even than the rocks."[22]

In prescribing the earth-oriented spirituality of Native Americans as a supplement to the truths of Christianity and an antidote for the ills associated with the arrogance, greed, and destructiveness of Western culture, Black Elk spoke both as a Christian thinker and as a spokesman for Native American spirituality. "We should understand well," Black Elk told his readers in the foreword to *The Sacred Pipe*, "that all things are the works of the Great Spirit." Christians had much to learn from Native Americans about this all-powerful, ever-present Creator, as well as having something to give, Black Elk asserted: "We should know that He is within all things: the trees, the grasses, the rivers, the mountains, and all the four-legged animals, and the winged peoples; and even more important, we should understand that He is also above all these things and peoples." Once people realized that the transcendent Creator described in the Bible was the same Great Spirit that Native peoples experienced in nature, they would live in better harmony with each other and with the earth: "When we do understand all this deeply in our hearts, then we will fear, and love, and know the Great Spirit, and then we will be and act and live as He intends."[23]

In these proclamations, Black Elk carried the ideas of earlier prophets to a new conclusion. Like Handsome Lake and Wovoka, he was sensitive to the political baggage associated with the religion of those who subjugated Indian people and ruined their cultures. Like Handsome Lake and Wovoka, he incorporated healing and redemptive elements of Christianity into a reconstruction of traditional religion geared to meet the challenge of modernization while preserving Native culture. But Black Elk went beyond other prophets in developing the resonance between the sufferings of his people and those of Christ, and in suggesting that the religious traditions of Native people might help save the whole world. He cast Native Americans as suffering messiahs in a cosmic drama of fall and redemption and as historical people whose understanding of the spiritual powers of nature was an antidote to the ills of a fallen world dominated by Western materialism. In this creative reinterpretation of Christian history, Black Elk extended the meaning of Christian healing to include environmental and political concerns, with the understanding that these concerns were as much a matter of salvation from sin for Euro-Americans as they were a means of justice, empowerment, and healing for Indians.

Revolutionary Impact in China

Another variant of Christianity, similar to the new religious movements led by Native prophets in North America but much more violent, emerged in nineteenth-century China. In South China, missionary preaching about the Kingdom of God stimulated a new form of Christianity that challenged political oppression and fused indigenous forms of religious healing with stories about the healing ministry of Jesus and his disciples. Like the Ghost Dance, this Chinese movement expressed resistance to political domination in thoroughly religious terms. But disavowed by Protestant missionaries, the Chinese movement was remembered, in the twentieth century, as a forerunner of the modern Chinese communist republic. The Communist interpretation underscored the revolutionary political energy of the movement as it obscured the religious medium through which that energy found expression.

In 1832, the first Chinese convert to Protestant Christianity, Liang Afa, hit on the idea of distributing tracts outside the gates to the city of Canton, where educated young men from all over the region passed by on their way to take qualifying exams for civil service. That year, Liang published his own account of Christianity, describing God's creation of the world, Noah's ark, the covenant between God and Israel, the life of Jesus, and John's vision in the Book of Revelation of the ultimate triumph of the Kingdom of God. In 1836, this book passed into the hands of Hong Xiuquan, a young man from Hua County who had just failed his qualifying exam for the second time. His hope of a prestigious career dashed, Hong accepted a copy of Liang's book from the American missionary Edwin Stevens. Stirred by reading it, Hong proclaimed himself the younger brother of Jesus and set off baptizing people and preaching about his Father's coming Kingdom.

The religion of God Worshippers founded by Hong Xiuquan mushroomed into a mass movement after 1842, at the end of the Opium War, which had destabilized the Qing Dynasty and opened Chinese ports to British and other foreign ships. Amid the unsettling infusion of Western influence, Hong's movement developed into an organized political and military force that took hold of China's economic heartland with ruthless force. In 1853, a new dynasty calling itself the Taiping, or Heavenly Kingdom, established its Heavenly Capital, Tianjing, in the city formerly known as Nanjing. Millions of people died in this revolution.

In the Taiping Rebellion, religious healing demonstrated the spiritual authority of Taiping leaders, the benefits bestowed on supporters, and the cultural continuity between the new Taiping movement and charismatic religious figures of the past. At the same time, in his role as the son of God described in the Bible, Hong offered something new and revolutionary. For Hong, as for Jesus, healing miracles signaled the dawning of God's Kingdom on earth. Hong was renowned for performing miraculous cures, and many of his disciples established their authority through exorcism, charismatic healing, and spirit possession. Although these performances drew from the indigenous Chinese tradition of Daoism, especially from Daoist religious dance, spirit possession, and prayers to the stars, belief in Jesus and Hong as sons of the one and only God of heaven had a chilling effect on reverence for Daoist deities. Much as Handsome Lake directed his reformist ire toward healing shamans, the God Worshippers of China destroyed Daoist temples and performed exorcisms that cast out Daoist deities as malevolent demons.[24]

The Heavenly Kingdom was relatively short-lived and finally destroyed by Qing troops in 1864. But theories about its emergence and long-term influence have often been proposed. Followers of Mao Zedong interpreted the movement as a harbinger of their own revolution and downplayed its religious elements. Western scholars have seen the Taiping as an entry point for the influence of Christian millennialism into Chinese political ideology and viewed this influence as part of a failed history of missions to China or, less judgmentally, as a Chinese reconstruction of Christian themes with far-reaching political consequences.[25]

Echoes of the iconoclasm and revolutionary political force of the Protestant Reformation in Europe reverberated in the Taiping Rebellion. At the same time, Taiping rejection of traditional religion and commitment to the establishment of a heavenly kingdom on earth foreshadowed the religious iconoclasm and political utopianism of the People's Republic of China. Thus, in certain respects, the Protestant understanding of Christian healing as a total renovation of society played a crucial role in the development of a form of political modernization in China unlike those in the West.

Spiritual Healing in Africa

Western Christianity's global expansion led to entirely different outcomes in Africa, partly because of Christianity's deeper and more extensive connections

there, and partly because African leaders did not have the government bureauc-
racy, military establishment, or widespread cultural control and prestige that
enabled Chinese leaders to resist modern Western influence. Numerous prophetic and healing movements emerged in Africa in response to colonization
and missionary influence. And like new religious movements in North America and China, many of these African movements fused hopeful anticipation
of the coming of God's Kingdom with indigenous forms of healing that resonated powerfully with biblical stories about the healing work of Jesus and his
disciples.

To take one important example, the Liberian William Wade Harris (c.
1865–1924?) embarked in 1913 on a missionary trip to the Ivory Coast, where
the French colonial government was completing its pacification of tribal
groups. In a vision, the Angel Gabriel declared Harris to be a son and prophet
of God charged with the mission of bringing the gospel to people who had yet
to hear it. In response to this call, Harris dressed in a white robe with black
bands and traveled from village to village, Bible in hand, singing and dancing
to the accompaniment of a gourd rattle to ward off evil spirits. He admonished
people to give up their old gods and reliance on traditional healers and baptized
more than a hundred thousand people before being expelled from the Ivory
Coast in 1914 by French officials who feared that he was working to overturn
the government-imposed head tax. European missionaries questioned the legitimacy of the baptisms Harris performed but remained grateful for the role
he played in bringing so many natives into their churches. As the only European churches in the colony in 1914, Catholic institutions were the immediate
beneficiaries of his work. But when the first Protestant missionaries arrived in
1924, it seemed to them that many "Harrist Protestants" had been waiting for
them and their Bible-centered teaching and worship. Appreciation of Harris's
role as a latter-day John the Baptist even prompted Methodists to date the origin
of their mission to 1914, before any Methodists arrived.[26]

In addition to its contributions to the growth of Catholic and Protestant
churches in West Africa, Harris's missionary activity led to the creation of a
number of indigenous churches that combined traditional and Christian practice in deliberate efforts to help members successfully negotiate the transition
to modernity. The Harrist Church, one of the largest of these, focused on the
removal of witchcraft and its ill effects, as well as on education, moral development, and the resolution of problems entailed in making adjustments to
modern society. In the mid-twentieth century, the most prominent healer in
the Harrist Church, Albert Atcho (c. 1900–1980?), took the synthesis of traditional and Christian practices further. After two decades of work as a member
of a family of traditional healers, Atcho joined the Harrist Church in 1940 and,

as a result of his success as a healer among people of different faiths, drew many new members into the church. In the 1950s and 1960s, he developed a healing center in the village of Bregbo and also treated patients at a nearby mental hospital, where some received a combination of traditional and Western therapies.[27]

Atcho's center in Bregbo delivered health care to thousands of people. Some people received treatment as outpatients; those suffering more serious illness often arrived with their families, who took up residence and contributed to the village economy. At Bregbo, Atcho and his assistants viewed the whole process of healing in religious terms. They required every patient to make a full confession of sin prior to treatment, which entailed drinking and washing with a mixture of water and herbs blessed by Atcho. Patients often returned home with bottles of this holy water to protect them from sin.[28]

As many social historians have pointed out, Christianity functioned as an agent of social change in Africa, a medium through which Africans negotiated the transition from tribal economies and cultures of collective solidarity based on lineage or territory to more modern social structures. Although the meaning of Christian symbols, messages, and practices varied in particulars from place to place and person to person, they served as a kind of common currency in this process of social change.[29] As it did in many places where people negotiated the challenges of modernization, religion served as a medium for expressions of political protest and concerns for social justice. African churches broke away from missionary control to affirm African leadership and incorporate traditional practices of religious healing of which Western missionaries disapproved. These independent churches supported African religious leadership and African interpretations of Christianity. Like the Pentecostal churches that developed later, these "spiritual" churches emphasized the need to relinquish pre-Christian beliefs and practice in favor of a life of Christian faith. As numerous scholars have shown, they also appealed to traditional concerns for spirit healing, divination, and relief from witchcraft in describing Christianity's superior power and moral purity.[30]

Protestant missionaries' lack of interest in healing miracles contributed to the dissatisfaction many converts felt with missionary churches. Along with the frustration of having to submit to missionary authority, that dissatisfaction led to the formation of independent, African-led churches that incorporated spiritual healing and ancestor veneration as part of Christian practice. In the twentieth century, African interest in spiritual healing played a defining role in the growth of African Catholicism as well as in the growth of Pentecostalism.[31]

Early in the century, German Trappists, German Jesuits, and Irish Carmelites imported Marian devotions, established healing shrines modeled after the famous grotto at Lourdes, and encouraged prayer to Mary and other saints for blessings. In the Makoni district of Manicaland in eastern Zimbabwe, Marian devotion caught on among large numbers of people when Patrick Kwesha and other African religious leaders reconceptualized it as a powerful response to witchcraft, which many Africans perceived as increasingly rampant. Kwesha transported biblical images of Israel and the Kingdom of God into a new regional and cultural context and moved traditional European associations between the industry of bees and Mary into an African framework, envisioning Mary as the queen of spirits who could combat the evil forces ruining God's creation. It was Kwesha's dream to create a "Lourdes of Africa" entirely "conducted by African priests, brothers and sisters." He hoped that Mary's new "apostles" would "swarm over the whole of Manyikaland, as the bees, banishing all the heathenism, protestantism and superstition, and establish a pure and holy kingdom of God and glory of Mary." In this kingdom on earth, "our God may be called God of Manyikaland as He was called God of Israel, and Our Lady be called queen of Manyikaland as she is called queen of angels and saints."[32]

By the end of the twentieth century, African Catholics and Pentecostals had largely replaced the independent healing churches of previous generations. In a study of religious change in Manicaland, the ethnohistorian Terence Ranger contrasted Anglican "coolness" to spiritual healing with the development of African forms of Catholicism that centered on the healing and consoling powers of the Blessed Virgin Mary. Coupled with epidemics of influenza, measles, and whooping cough, the pervasiveness of malaria, and high rates of syphilis in the region, Catholic embrace of Marian miracles led to many conversions in the mid-twentieth century.[33]

Political Healing in South Africa

While Marian devotion and Pentecostal commitment to the gifts of the Spirit fused with traditional African practices of spirit healing and contributed to the development of African religious leadership, more straightforwardly political interpretations of Christian healing also emerged, especially in South Africa, where the social interpretation of Christian healing as a total renovation of society developed more completely than perhaps anywhere else. Between the Dutch Reformed Protestants who invoked Christianity to justify apartheid rule and the Africans encouraged by Christian principles to overthrow it, the Republic of South Africa has been an important arena in which the political implications of Christianity have been strongly argued and disputed. In the late twenieth century, the interpretation of Christianity as a means of redressing the injustices of colonial rule often won out, in part because of the way African leaders conceptualized justice in relation to Christian healing. For Nelson Mandela (1918–), Desmond Tutu (1931–), and other African Christians active in South Africa at the end of the twentieth century, apartheid was an intolerable disease that had to be eradicated and a collective sin that required repentance.

The politics of reconciliation promoted by Mandela and Tutu resulted from a long and painful process of religious and political development in which the politicization of Christian healing reached a certain point of culmination. In the nineteenth century, southern Africa was among the most highly saturated areas of Christian missionary activity in the world, with numerous stations occupied by European and American missionaries representing various denominations. In the early twentieth century, the religious scene became increasingly complicated as numerous prophets emerged to establish churches independent of white missionary control, many of which were intent on healing, especially through combat against witchcraft and evil spirits. As alternative, indigenous expressions of Christianity, these independent churches exerted pressure on European and American missionaries and the institutions those missionaries supervised, and on the theology they taught, as did the increasingly draconian laws against black enterprise, property ownership, education, and freedom in South Africa, where apartheid was officially established in 1948.[34] Escalating violence on the part of the state stimulated new forms of black resistance. It also coincided with indigenous efforts to incorporate traditional forms of religious healing into Christianity, along with a good deal of theological reflection on the part of both white and black opponents of apartheid about how best to resist it. Debate among the opponents of apartheid carried discussion of the meaning of Christian healing to a whole new level.

Mvumbi Lutuli (1898–1967) embodied the Christian humanitarianism of the first generation of black leaders explicitly committed to political resistance against apartheid, most if not all of whom had been educated at Protestant missionary-supported schools. A graduate of the American-run Amanzimtoti Institute (later named Adams College) and one of the first black faculty members there, Lutuli was a spokesman for the dignity of the individual, the right to equality, the importance of education, and the belief that freedom will unfold through history. Elected chief of Christian Zulus from 1935 until 1952, he led the Defiance Campaign against apartheid as a provincial president of the African National Congress until the government revoked his chieftainship. Lutuli responded to the annulment of his tribal authority with an essay, "The Road to Freedom Is via the Cross," advocating nonviolent resistance against the state, asserting that all parties to apartheid were degraded, and predicting the coming of a shared society. He became president-general of the ANC and he received the Nobel Peace Prize in 1961. (In a succinct expression of the animosity Lutuli faced, one South African newspaper called his receipt of the Nobel "an inexplicable pathological phenomenon.")[35]

As state-sponsored violence against blacks escalated, the black resistance movement became increasingly disenchanted with Christian liberalism and its white proponents. After becoming president of the Pan-African Congress in 1959, Robert Sobukwe (1924–1978) cut ties with multiracial churches and turned instead to independent, African churches for support. A spokesman for black consciousness, Sobukwe identified the racist oppressors of South Africa with those who crucified Christ, arguing that blacks had God on their side in the cause of justice and that whites would never relinquish power voluntarily. Steve Biko (1946–1977) carried Sobukwe's argument further by condemning otherworldly interpretations of Christianity and urging interpretation of biblical theology in light of the community-affirming, this-worldly ethics of traditional African religions. Biko died in jail from head injuries sustained during his detention. At his funeral, Tutu, then bishop of Lesotho, gave an oration. Despite his opposition to the violent tactics Biko sometimes espoused, Tutu proclaimed, "Steve has started something that is quite unstoppable."[36]

Tutu also used the funeral sermon to express sentiments Biko probably would not have agreed with. Anticipating a day when the black majority and the white minority would coexist in South Africa in a peaceful democracy, he called for forgiveness as well as justice. In the years following, Tutu led the way in carrying forward a nonviolent interpretation of Christian theology and in making explicit the equation between Christian healing and recovery from political violence and construction of a just peace. The Anglican Church made him archbishop of South Africa in 1986 and, in 1995, Nelson Mandela, the first democratically elected president of South Africa, appointed him to head a Truth and Reconciliation Committee. Using public testimony and written evidence to identify institutions and persons responsible for violating human rights between 1960 and 1994, this committee found the state to be primarily responsible for violent crimes against humanity. In an effort at fair moral discernment with antecedents that reach back to the judges of Hebrew scripture, the committee also found the black Inkatha Freedom Party, which operated in collusion with state security forces, responsible for the deaths of three thousand people and the ANC responsible for the deaths of one thousand others. The committee established procedures to grant amnesty to some perpetrators of violence who stepped forward to admit what they had done in what amounted, more or less, to public confession of sin.

Numerous complaints have been lodged about the insufficiency of this process, and South Africa today is far from a peaceful society. Nonetheless, the work of Desmond Tutu represents the ongoing importance that healing plays in Christianity's success as a robust and expansive religion. His political interpretation of healing also represents the culmination of a process of infusing Christianity with political meaning in a way that typifies modern Christian mission history and differentiates it from its antecedents. The global expansion of Western culture, and the disease, conflict, and tumultuous social change it entailed, prompted people faced by these ills to define the meaning of Christian suffering and healing in social, economic, and political terms. For Christians saturated in modern political conflict like Tutu, Christianity had to mean something politically to retain its authority in modern life, and Christians couldn't flinch from translating Christianity into political terms if history was going to progress. "We are looking to the healing of relationships," Tutu explained in an interview in 1999. "We are seeking to open wounds, yes, but to open them so we can cleanse them and they don't fester; we cleanse them and then pour oil on them, and then we can move into the glorious future that God is opening up for us."[37]

6

Christianity and the Global Development of Scientific Medicine

As a result of their long interest in human suffering and religious healing, Christians have constantly found themselves involved with medicine and concerned about the relationship between medical practice and religious faith. Over the centuries, many Christians practiced medicine as part of their religious outreach and employed it to recover natural health as God allowed. But the relationship between Christianity and medicine, and the boundaries between them, have always been complicated. Even when extreme Christians denied themselves natural remedies in order to prove their faith, they used medicine as a metaphor for Christ, the sacraments, the scriptures, and the blessings of the saints. Toward the other end of the spectrum, Christians enthusiastic about medicine as a primary expression of Christian service often insisted on its secondary status with respect to conversion. And even further along that spectrum, many Christians in the twentieth and twenty-first centuries put medicine first.

The global expansion of Western Christianity in the modern period coincided with the development of scientific medicine and its worldwide preeminence as a resource for human welfare. Christian missionaries figured importantly in these developments. They were the first to introduce scientific medicine in many parts of the world, and their leadership as practitioners and proponents of scientific medicine played historic roles in making health care an important component of global development. At the same time, the partnership between Christianity and scientific medicine was always complex, and often uneasy. In many places, it was complicated by competing ideas about spiritual healing. While many Christians who promoted scientific medicine discounted practices associated with indigenous forms of religious healing, reliance on prayer and other Christian approaches to spiritual healing contributed to ambiguities surrounding the relationship between Christianity and medicine, as did popular perceptions that certain scientific procedures, such as curing blindness through corneal incision, or anesthesia during surgery, were feats of spiritual power. To complicate matters further, many people found Christian healing to be more encompassing—and far more accessible—than scientific medicine. The shortcomings of medicine, including lack of availability, worked against its acceptance. Moreover, on issues related to reproduction and sexuality, proponents of world Christianity and proponents of world health did not always see eye to eye.

Medical Missions

Despite ambiguity about its relationship to Christian faith, the growing prominence of scientific medicine as a branch of missionary outreach contributed to important changes in how many Protestants in Europe and North America conceptualized healing, and in how they acted on their devotion to a God and desire to follow Christ. As scientific discoveries involving asepsis, anesthesia, and infectious disease dramatically increased the effectiveness of Western medicine, medical missions became increasingly useful as a means of showing the positive benefits of Christianity and increasingly relevant as a way to emulate Jesus and his compassion and care of the sick. Medical missionaries and their supporters even imagined that Jesus might have been a medical missionary if he had lived in their day.

Despite reluctance to divert funds from gospel preaching, Bible translation, and the establishment of new churches, Protestants took the lead in developing modern medicine as a form of missionary outreach. Largely because of greater enthusiasm for science and modern life generally among Protestants, they established medical service as part of their missionary programs much earlier and more readily than Catholics. But even some Protestants who believed that modern Western culture was superior to all others were hesitant about making medicine a missionary priority, especially when funds were tight and choices had to be made between medical service and explicitly religious forms of missionary outreach.

For example, in 1834, shortly after receiving Presbyterian ordination and a medical degree from Yale, Peter Parker left New York for Canton, where he established the first missionary hospital in China. Before leaving, he received explicit instructions from the American Board of Commissioners for Foreign Missions to subordinate his care for bodies to his care for souls. "The medical and surgical knowledge you have acquired, you will employ, as you have opportunity, in relieving the bodily afflictions of the people," Parker's superiors ordered. "But these, you will never forget, are to receive your attention only as they can be made handmaids to the gospel." Focusing on the "character" he should adopt, the Board gave him an explicit command: "The character of a physician, or a man of science, respectable as they are, or useful as they may be in evangelizing China—you will never suffer to supersede or interfere with your character of a teacher of religion."[1]

Once in China, Parker agonized over the conflict between his instructions from the mission Board and his commitment as a physician. "In the deep-growing interest I have felt for the sick and dying among the Chinese, I have in a degree deviated from those instructions," he confessed, "and have become involved in medical and surgical practice in a manner that I know not how to extricate myself." The American Board was not happy with Parker's neglect of his duties as a religious teacher, and when he took on diplomatic responsibilities in the 1840s, they cut off his support. Parker's friends responded by emphasizing the usefulness of medical work as a means of disarming Chinese suspicions about Christians, not only by demonstrating the good intentions of Christian missionaries and their willingness to be helpful, but also as a form of work that was intrinsically Christian. As one supporter wrote in defense of Parker's work, "His medical practice is itself preaching."[2]

In 1861, the English physician William Lockhart, founder of hospitals in Shanghai and Peking, made a corresponding point when he urged that the medical missionary be "sent out on an equal footing with the ordained missionary." Of course, the medical missionary would still "take every opportunity of Bible distribution, and avail himself of the occasions, peculiarly his own, of speaking to his patients privately," Lockhart assured. But the growing professionalization of both medicine and ministry meant that each job was too demanding, and too specialized, to be combined with the other: "Either a good surgeon or a good pastor was spoiled," he warned, if people expected one man to be both.[3]

Holy people throughout Christian history had dispensed medical advice, drafts, and unguents along with blessings, prayers, and spiritual advice. Catholic and Protestant missionaries continued this tradition (and still do) of representing spiritual concern for human sickness as emblematic of Christian faith. But the medical missions that emerged among Protestants from western

Europe and North America during the nineteenth century involved a highly systematic and rationalized form of medicine characterized by scientific concepts derived from anatomy, physiology, chemistry, and biology. The clinical spaces, structures, practices, and theories of scientific medicine did not always lend themselves to religious interpretation. Indeed, some proponents of scientific medicine, especially in France and other parts of continental Europe, criticized all forms of religious revelation and authority.[4]

Yet, missionary interest in establishing medical clinics and hospitals grew with the strength of the medical establishment. In the early nineteenth century, physicians wanting to advance medicine as a profession cultivated relationships with mission societies as a way to prove that doctors were morally reputable. As befitting their subordinate status with respect to ordained clergy, physicians first joined mission teams in the field as assistant missionaries. According to British historian Peter Williams, "For the first fifty or sixty years of the [nineteenth] century the talents of the medical doctor were seldom sought and, when they were, it was most often to provide protection for missionaries in areas of particular health hazard." But as the status of physicians improved, demand for medical missionaries increased along with their responsibilities and prestige in relation to other missionaries. Only thirteen European doctors worked out of mission stations in 1852. By 1900, there were 650 Protestant physicians working as medical missionaries, many of whom supervised clinics and hospitals independent of clerical supervision.[5] Andrew Walls described this dramatic change: "When the professional medical missionary first became noticeable in the middle of the nineteenth century he was a lay auxiliary worker alongside his clerical brother; by the end of the century missionary societies were taking responsibility for an entire University medical faculty and teaching hospitals to serve the entire Chinese Empire."[6]

Scientific Medicine in Missionary Outreach

The scientific medicine that came to be associated with Western missionary outreach had several interrelated characteristics that set it apart from traditional forms of medical practices around the world. The intellectual concepts of scientific medicine derived from materialistic disciplines—anatomy, physiology, chemistry, and biology—that, for the most part, denied spiritual interpretation. Neoplatonist approaches to medicine that ascribed spiritual causes to material elements, signs, and forces never disappeared, and in Western cultures today, they inform or complement alternative forms of medicine, such as homeopathy, massage, yoga, and macrobiotics. But by the end of the nineteenth century, the medical establishment had succeeded, for the most part, in excluding approaches based on spiritual causation from licensed medical practice on the grounds that they violated scientific principles. These principles included commitment to a method of empirical observation based on experiments that could be replicated by other researchers, ideally under laboratory conditions. Explanations based on such experiments could be disproved if later experiments proved them insufficient or false.

In the second half of the nineteenth century, new theories of biological evolution contributed both to the design of scientific experiments and to the effectiveness of medical treatments resulting from scientific experiments. Louis Pasteur (1822–1895) and other biological researchers showed that disease-causing bacteria and viruses were living organisms that reproduced and adapted to their environments. Pasteur and others proved the importance of antiseptic procedures in minimizing contact with these organisms during surgery. They also developed vaccines derived from disease-causing microbes that stimulated animals (including people) to develop immunities, enabling them to resist disease. New surgical procedures, such as chloroform for anesthesia and corneal incisions to remove cataracts, along with more effective treatments for diseases, such as injections of quinine for malaria, and new means of preventing disease, such as purifying water supplies to prevent cholera and eradicating tsetse flies to prevent sleeping sickness, also contributed to the utility of Western medicine and to the growing prestige of the medical establishment in the nineteenth and early twentieth centuries. As Western missionaries relied increasingly on medical personnel and facilities, scientific discoveries and new procedures contributed to Christianity's reputation and expansion in the non-Western world.

Important shifts in Protestant theology coincided with medicine's increasing authority and power. In the late nineteenth and early twentieth centuries, medicine's usefulness as the "heavy artillery" of Protestant missions developed along with optimism about improving the conditions of human life around the world, and along with enthusiasm about science and Christianity assisting one another in bringing the world together in peace and health. Since miracles had ceased, according to John Lowe, the influential proponent of medical missions appointed superintendent of the missionary training hospital in Edinburgh in 1871, "it is the welfare of my brother, the welfare of his body, the welfare of his soul—his welfare for time, his welfare for eternity" that counted. The old image of Christ as healer took on new meaning in the context of such discussions of human welfare. For many Christians in the West, the medical missionary came to embody the self-sacrificing compassion of Christ and his service to humanity. Saving souls still defined the missionary's work, but that work could be conducted by the physician who served as "an embodiment of the Divine idea," rather than by an exorcist or spiritual healer who combated demons and infused patients with the healing powers of spiritual forces. According to medical historian Peter Williams, just as Christ had conducted "a ministry of sympathy with suffering humanity, as He healed the sick, and went about continually doing good," so the medical missionaries who served as "His ambassadors must 'preach the Gospel,' not by word alone, but likewise, by a compassionate Christ-like ministry."[7]

Medical Missions in Africa

The most well-known exemplar of this modern notion of the medical missionary as the embodiment of Christ-like compassion for human suffering is Albert Schweitzer. He did as much as anyone to develop the concept of Christ's personality as part of a rationale for supporting the work of medical missions. Reverence for Jesus was the guiding principle of Schweitzer's life and the key to understanding his work as a medical missionary in French Equatorial Africa. For Schweitzer, Jesus was more than a teacher of ethics; he was the embodiment of ethical life, and his willingness to sacrifice everything, including his life, inspired an ultimate form of hero worship.

In deciding to become a medical doctor in Africa, Schweitzer expressed his commitment to ethical fellowship with Jesus and his desire to become a moral force in the twentieth century, as Jesus had been in his own day.[8] In Schweitzer's existential version of Protestant theology, religious life sprang from subjective experience and flowed out from there in acts of love and compassion for humanity. His emulation of Jesus harmonized with the secular practice of medicine and illustrates the attractiveness of medical outreach for Protestant missionaries in the late nineteenth and early twentieth centuries and their contributions to the development of modern medicine and science.

In *The Quest of the Historical Jesus*, published while studying for his medical degree, Schweitzer distinguished the "thought-forms" of first-century Palestine from the forceful personality of Jesus, arguing that the latter, not the former, commanded emulation. He celebrated Jesus as the man who fully realized the moral force at the heart of human nature. Jesus "grasped the entire truth and immediacy" of this force, Schweitzer believed, "and imbued it with his will and his great personality." Through the example of Jesus, modern men and women could apprehend the same moral force and embody it in their own time and way.[9]

The Quest of the Historical Jesus made Schweitzer a world figure in New

Testament studies, and books on Johann Sebastian Bach and the history of the organ established his influence in musicology. But his primary mission in life was medical service in Africa. He financed supplies for a hospital in Lambarene on the Ogowe River in Gabon with donations from friends and money earned from organ concerts, married Helene Bresslau, who studied nursing in order to assist him, and embarked for Lambarene in 1913. Despite nearly over-whelming obstacles, including devastating epidemics of sleeping sickness and dysentery and military internment, Schweitzer made thirteen journeys to Lam-barene, building and equipping a hospital and a leprosarium that, by 1963, provided care for five hundred inpatients and many relatives and outpatients. Having received numerous awards and honors for his work as a humanitarian, scholar, and artist, including the Nobel Peace Prize in 1952, he made his four-teenth and final trip to Lambarene in 1959 and died there in 1965, a few months short of his ninety-first birthday.

Schweitzer's practical, focused commitment to relieving human suffering deepened his appreciation of the common humanity that Europeans shared with the people of Africa and enabled him to refute one of the arguments used by friends to dissuade him from going to Africa: "The natives who live in the bosom of Nature are never so ill as we are, and do not feel pain so much." To the contrary, Schweitzer discovered, there existed a "Fellowship of those who bear the Mark of Pain." As if "by a secret bond," it joined people everywhere "who have learnt by experience what physical pain and bodily anguish mean." Membership in the fellowship of pain entailed a special burden of ethical re-sponsibility: "He who has been delivered from pain must not think he is now free again, and at liberty to take life up just as it was before," Schweitzer wrote in the memoir of his first journey to Lambarene. "He is now a 'man whose eyes are open' with regard to pain and anguish, and he must help to overcome those two enemies (so far as human power can control them) and to bring to others the deliverance which he has himself enjoyed."[10] This heightened aware-ness of human suffering inspired the principle of "reverence for life" that defined his later thought and led him to discern a fundamental moral sense in Christianity, Stoicism, and Chinese philosophy that he believed was missing in many forms of modern scientific enterprise.[11]

Schweitzer was quick to criticize the harm done to the people of Africa by colonial rule: "Who can describe the injustice and the cruelties that in the course of centuries they have suffered at the hands of Europeans? Who can measure the misery produced among them by the fiery drinks and hideous diseases that we have taken to them?" In light of this history, Schweitzer went on, "we are not free to confer benefits on these men, or not, as we please; it is our duty. Anything we give them is not benevolence but atonement." Schweitzer challenged the conservative European view "that Christianity is something too high for primitive man" and was quick to say "that the child of nature thinks a great deal more than is generally supposed."[12] But he never thought of Africans as equals. His sense of duty toward Africans was paternalistic. The burden of responsibility he expressed presupposed a fundamental connection between Christianity and Western culture, and consequently led him away from interest in African cultures, African approaches to leadership, and African forms of healing.

Schweitzer knew that religious experience was always mediated through cultural patterns and historical situations, and he readily admitted that no one could really anticipate what Jesus would be like if he appeared in the twentieth century. The famous final paragraph of his *Quest of the Historical Jesus* reflected his belief that personalities embodying the ethical force of Christ would continue to appear in human history and in the context of different cultures:

> He comes to us as one unknown, without a name, as of old, by the lakeside, he came to those men who did not know who he was. He says the same words, "Follow me!," and sets us to those tasks which he must fulfill in our time. He commands. And to those who hearken to him, whether wise or unwise, he will reveal himself in the peace, the labors, the conflicts and the suffering that they may experience in his fellowship, and as an ineffable mystery they will learn who he is.[13]

There is an element of irony in the fact that even though he undertook the practice of medicine as a means of emulating Jesus' ethic of love, Schweitzer paid little attention to Jesus' work as an exorcist and healer. Although profoundly aware that medicine put him in touch with the suffering that joined humanity together and with the compassion for suffering that Jesus embodied and inspired, he never described medicine as a religious practice. Conversely, he never described Jesus as a medical practitioner, or even took very seriously his reputed skill in expelling demons and performing other cures. Schweitzer had as little interest in the healing techniques of Jesus, or in the lore about healing that enveloped him, as he did in the healing practices and beliefs of African cultures. Even though he recognized that the doctoring performed by traditional religious healers in central Africa was more like the healing practices in Jesus' day than the medicine he practiced as a modern missionary, Schweitzer had little interest in the assumptions about reality underlying it or in how those assumptions shaped African perceptions of his own work and character.

Medical Science and Colonialism

In recent decades, scholars have explored the linkage between scientific medicine and colonialism, especially in Africa, and found a lot to criticize. Historian
John Farley coined the term "imperial tropical medicine" (ITM) to characterize
the imperialist agendas built into scientific approaches to infectious disease in
the non-Western world. Farley argued that ITM benefited Europeans first and
foremost. The virulence of tropical diseases made life in Africa debilitating and
often deadly for Europeans until new treatments for those diseases, and vac-
cinations against them, expedited Western entry and enabled colonial officials,
soldiers, entrepreneurs, and missionaries to work in Africa without sacrificing
their health. When Western medicine trickled down to benefit Africans, Farley
argued, Western providers boasted about the superiority and know-how of
Western civilization, elaborating on the contrast between their wonderful ability to control disease and the relative worthlessness of African remedies as
evidence of the inferiority of the dark race and as justification for the imposition
of Western ideas and practices.[14]

But as Michael Worboys pointed out in a challenge to this interpretation,
Farley's ITM paradigm is overly simplistic and does not differentiate between
the deployment of medical science by colonial governments and the medical
work of Christian missionaries. Although colonial governments may have util-
ized medicine as a vertical strategy of political and cultural dominance, missionaries were engaged in horizontal strategies of personal interaction as well
as in vertical strategies of religious conquest. The missionaries' emphasis on
personal interaction, and their use of medicine as a means of promoting Christianity and getting close to people, distinguished their approach to medicine
from that of colonial officials. Even the scientific discoveries that missionaries
made challenge the picture of top-down centralized domination of indigenous
people by agents of colonial rule. Medical missionaries often studied diseases,
with native help, in small laboratories at remote distances from the centers of
colonial government, making advances in medical science on the furthest bor-
ders of Western culture.

Missionaries were often sure of their cultural superiority and disdainful
of native healers. But their religion obligated them to attend to the suffering
and humanity of people they hoped to convert. Worboys wrote, "Missionaries
concentrated on individual patients and their care, while civil and military
doctors focused on disease agents, vectors, and populations." Although medical
missionaries were also interested in "disease agents" and the managers of

missionary programs sometimes counted souls as if they were beans, the interpersonal contact that missionaries acknowledged as necessary to reaching
people had the effect of opening their work to native agency, interpretation,
and at least partial control.[15] As a result of this human interaction, Western
missionaries never controlled the meaning of Christianity or the practice of
medicine, even if they liked to think they did.

Non-Western ideas about the nature of reality and about illness and its
remedies shaped the historical development of Christianity in Africa and in
other parts of the world. Non-Western ideas about reality also shaped perceptions of medicine, scientific or otherwise, and its relationship to religious healing. In Africa, people understood Western medicine in the context of a well-
established, general distinction between diseases of man and diseases of God
that underlay more specific spiritual practices and natural remedies that varied
from tribe to tribe. God allowed certain diseases as part of the natural order of
things, and Africans had considerable understanding of them. The historian
of international medicine Paul Basch noted, "Some African peoples were aware
of the transmission of sleeping sickness by tsetse flies, and of malaria by mos-
quitoes long before a Nobel Prize was awarded for the same observation."[16] In
African thinking, natural cures and medicines existed for these ailments and
were also part of God's plans. Diseases of man, on the other hand, violated the
natural order of things and God's intentions for human life. Because diseases
of man derived from witchcraft and other actions and feelings offensive to the
ancestral spirits, combat against these diseases required rituals of spiritual
healing.

Western medicine fell in alongside the herbal remedies and natural procedures Africans already used to cope with diseases that were part of God's
creation of the world. Many Africans admired and accepted the secular utility
of Western medicine and allowed it to replace traditional remedies when it
proved superior. As Terence Ranger observed, when Western medicine cured
a disease previously thought to be caused by witchcraft, people reclassified that
disease as part of God's plan and accepted it as a problem that no longer
triggered religious alarm.[17]

But if Western ideas about medicine corresponded fairly well with African
ideas about the natural diseases God allowed as part of creation, considerable
dissonance developed over diseases that, from African perspectives, were
caused by witchcraft and required spiritual intervention and combat against
witchcraft. Many Western missionaries did not believe that such diseases existed. On the other hand, many Africans embraced Christianity because it offered relief from the diseases of man.

In the late twentieth and early twenty-first centuries, practices of spiritual healing associated with Pentecostalism spread rapidly in Africa in response to horrendous widespread suffering. Pentecostals called on the Holy Spirit and its healing power to drive out demons, combat illness, and restore vitality in believers. The tremendous increase in African Pentecostalism in the late twentieth century reflected fear of the growing threat of diseases beyond the rational order of creation and the corresponding appeal of biblical stories about the healing power of Jesus, his victory over demons, evil, and death, and the ongoing enactment of that victory through the power of the Holy Spirit.

The sheer magnitude of human suffering in Africa heightened the relevance of these stories. The end of colonialism, the rise of independent nations, the withdrawal of Western infrastructures, the neglect and indifference of Western political powers, rampant corruption, and devastating internecine warfare led to famine and epidemics of biblical proportion. And the enormity of human suffering is only increasing. Historian Philip Jenkins observed in 2002, "Sub-Saharan Africa presently accounts for over two-thirds of known cases of HIV infection. In some regions of the continent, perhaps 40 percent of inhabitants carry the AIDS virus, and by 2015, Africa may be home to 16 million orphans." Jenkins estimated that 17 million people in Africa died from AIDS between the late 1970s and the beginning of the new century. "In Kenya alone, perhaps a million have already died from AIDS-related illnesses, and 2 million more carry the HIV virus." Without access to medical intervention, the demand for spiritual healing is enormous. "Today," according to Jenkins, "rising African churches stand or fall by their success in healing, and elaborate rituals have formed around healing practices." Even mainline denominations originating in the West rely on spiritual healing; thus, in Tanzania, a Lutheran bishop supervises an active program of spiritual healing.[18]

For many people in Africa, the sicknesses and deaths caused by AIDS fall into the category of diseases of man. If more drugs were available for treating the HIV virus, those diseases might be reclassified as natural aspects of God's creation, much as other diseases, such as certain forms of blindness, have been. But the scarcity of medicine works against this reclassification. In addition, medical efforts to prevent and treat the HIV virus have sometimes been resisted. In South Africa and elsewhere, some political and religious leaders rejected scientific theories about the AIDS virus as a Western hoax and objected to the idea that the epidemic could be controlled by natural means. And in many places, natural means of prevention, such as the use of condoms, are morally unacceptable and not widely practiced. Of course, Christians in other times and places have turned to prayer and other forms of spiritual practice to combat epidemics. But there have never been epidemics in which natural remedies and effective means of prevention known to some were unavailable to so many others, and in which the ambivalent relationship between Christianity and medicine had consequences of such enormity.

In Africa and also in Latin America and many parts of Asia, religious principle exacts a high price in terms of public health, especially for women and children. If overpopulation is a cause of poverty, famine, and environmental degradation, and high birthrates tend to have debilitating effects on women and children, then lack of support by conservative Protestants and the Roman Catholic Church for international programs that enable birth control carries significant health costs. Of course, Christians have long viewed suffering as a means of spiritual purification and celebrated poverty as proper for religious life. Sacrifices of health, wealth, and comfort are part of a long tradition of Christian asceticism and martyrdom. But asceticism and martyrdom have always been understood as voluntary acts of renunciation, and thus different from so much of the massive suffering in the world today.

Medical Missions in China

If medical science faltered in Africa as Christianity flourished, the opposite occurred in China. There the promotion of scientific medicine by Western Christians proved so effective that the Chinese incorporated it into their own society while by and large eschewing Christianity. In terms of missionary hopes for saving souls, China was a dismal defeat. Many Christian groups did not survive the Communist Revolution. Those that did survive were persecuted, driven into hiding, and, in some cases at least, forced to compromise their beliefs.[19] But with respect to relief from suffering and promotion of public health, the effect of Christianity was more positive.

When Jesuit missionaries arrived in China in the sixteenth century, they encountered a wide range of religious and philosophical traditions—Confucian, Buddhist, Daoist, and shamanic—along with a diverse array of healing practices. Learned physicians ministered to state officials and their families, and a wide range of local apothecaries, surgeons, acupuncturists, and midwives served a broader populace, as did Buddhist, Daoist, and shamanic healers. During the Taiping Rebellion in the early nineteenth century, the God Worshippers embraced exorcism and charismatic healing but expressed suspicion about medicine, a highly developed art in China involving considerable erudition and technical skill and strongly tied to the political elite. When they built the Heavenly City of Tianjing, the Taiping tried to recruit doctors to hospitals to care for the wounded and sick, but most fled the city as enemies of the rebellion.[20]

The politicization of medicine and religious healing under the Taiping affected the subsequent reception of medical missionaries from the United States and Europe, as did deep-seated Chinese resistance to "foreign devils" who sought to penetrate China's self-enclosed and highly rational culture. In the late nineteenth and early twentieth centuries, Western missionaries encountered suspicions about the political as well as religious dimensions of the medical services they offered. Given the fact that Western medicine arrived in the context of Western exploration, market expansion, military conflict, and missionary zeal, this should not have been surprising. But Western Christians sometimes missed these connections. Medical missionaries tended to think of both Western medicine and Christianity as being above politics, and thus able to pull politics up to a higher level. They viewed Western medicine and Christianity as universally valid means of elevating humanity that would enable the Chinese to develop a democratic form of government and, eventually, leave their feudal dynasties and oppressive economic policies behind.

Even as they contributed to revolutionary forces of social change, Western missionaries sometimes misjudged the political implications of their work by failing to grasp the necessity, as far as many Chinese were concerned, of incorporating new ideas on Chinese terms. Complicating the situation further, Western critics of medical missions often portrayed missionaries as more heavy-handed and more politically insensitive than, in fact, they were.

The career of Edward Bliss (1865–1960), an American missionary doctor in the walled city of Shaowu on the Min River between 1892 and 1932, illustrates these points. Bliss exemplified the religious and scientific idealism associated with medical missions and, more specifically, the idealism associated with the work of the physician whose compassion and service to humanity was, to recall the words of John Lowe, the late nineteenth-century superintendent of the famous missionary training hospital in Edinburgh, the "embodiment of the Divine idea." Bliss's career also reveals something of the political turmoil that enveloped this idealism and its effect on the development of scientific medicine, which continued to spread in China, and on the development of Christianity, which did not.

Bliss was inspired to become a medical missionary by the story of David Livingstone (1813–1873), the legendary Scottish explorer and first medical missionary in Africa, particularly by Livingstone's identification with the life and ministry of Christ. "The words of David Livingstone express my feelings better than any words of my own," Bliss wrote. " 'God had an only Son, and He was a missionary and a physician.' A poor, poor imitation of Him I am, or hope to be. In this service I hope to live; in it I wish to die."[21]

A native of Massachusetts and a heroically energetic and dedicated man,

Bliss built a dispensary, laboratory, and hospital in Shaowu and worked at isolating and combating the rinderpest virus that decimated cattle herds and led to famine, malnutrition, poverty, and disease in people. He rebuilt and resupplied the hospital after it was destroyed during the Boxer Rebellion in 1900 and again after a flood in 1922. Finally, in the Communist Revolution of the 1930s, the revolutionaries took over the hospital, animal barns, and whole missionary compound while the missionaries remaining in Shaowu escaped with their lives.

Bliss perceived Chinese "superstition" as a major obstacle to his work as a medical missionary and contrasted the soundness of Western scientific medicine with the follies of traditional Chinese medicine. He justified the need for Christian missions and the legitimacy of Western expansion through disdain for "Chinese 'doctors' who treated cancer by puncturing the skin with gold and silver needles" and performed other silly practices. "They prescribed bile from the gallbladders of bears for eye sores," he reported, focusing on what appeared to him to be the most outlandish remedies, "uncooked pears for malarial fever, snake meat for rheumatism, and the ginseng root for almost every ailment known." As a particularly outrageous example of worthless, wasteful treatment, he described a woman who came to his hospital with a massive ear infection after having spent a considerable portion of her family income "for prayers to idols and some powder made from beetle wings."[22]

Back in the United States as a medical missionary forced into retirement by political events, Bliss was devastated to learn that one of the younger American doctors associated with him in Shaowu had given the Mission Board a critical report of his work. Walter Judd, a congressman and spokesman for Republican policy in China, argued that "although Dr. Bliss was one of the finest, most benevolent, loving men who ever lived, from my point of view he was a failure as a missionary." Bliss never encouraged Chinese young people to attend medical school so that they might take charge of the hospital as doctors themselves, Judd charged. Taking Bliss as a symbol of what Americans had done wrong in China, Judd complained, somewhat unfairly, that he "did things *for* people, always *for* people."[23] Bliss was bitter about this characterization, arguing that he had instructed many young Chinese in how to treat wounds and diseases and that the communists had established a dairy in Shaowu based on his ideas. Whatever Bliss contributed to social welfare and self-determination in China, his work and reputation were caught up in politics, both Chinese and American. The enormity of surrounding political events and interpretations complicated and undermined his work as a medical missionary, both with respect to its impact and outcome and with respect to his own self-representation as a man of purpose and moral clarity.

From the holistic perspective of Chinese medicine, which presumed connections between emotional and physical states and concentrated on symptoms and disease prevention, Western medicine's relatively narrow focus on material but invisible causes of disease could be useful but often seemed incomplete. A Chinese diplomat remarked in the late nineteenth century, "Apart from timing the pulse," the Western physician knew little else about the pulse, which Chinese doctors analyzed closely. In addition, "his prescription deals only with one ailment, taking cognizance of nothing else. Even when treating a fever, he does not inquire whether the illness comes from external or internal causes, from 'substantive' or 'insubstantive' (*shih* or *hsu*) causes. His is indeed a piecemeal sort of medicine."[24]

Although Western medicine lacked the holistic perspective Chinese healers admired, its benefits in treating accidents, gunshot wounds, and numerous diseases became increasingly evident in the early decades of the twentieth century. Medical historians Yeut-Wah Cheung and Peter Kong-Ming New cite the 1910–1911 epidemic of pneumonic plague in Manchuria as "a turning point" in Chinese acceptance of Western medicine. Wu Lien-teh, a Chinese physician trained in England, managed the suppression of the outbreak, after traditional remedies proved useless against it.[25]

Although all foreign missionaries were evicted by 1950 and many churches outlawed, Western missions to China had a lasting effect. To quote historian Kaiyi Chen: "As many authors have pointed out, the work of missionaries contributed not only to the propagation of new techniques and knowledge in China, but, indirectly, to the awakening of the sense of democracy in the population."[26] The medical missionary played a leading role in this propagation of new techniques and knowledge, as well as in the dissemination of Christian ideas in China. As another historian observed, the partnership between medicine and Christianity in China served proponents of each, at least for a few decades: "It was only through the wonders of medical treatment that the message of the Church's teachings could reach the people, and on the other hand it was only through the respectability of religious affiliation that the medical missionaries could bring credit to the medical profession."[27] The conflict Peter Parker faced in the early nineteenth century with regard to his double character as a physician and a religious teacher in China had diminished considerably. A complementary relationship developed between medicine and Christianity that stimulated the growth of both, until political resistance to Western control in China halted the spread of the latter.

During the late nineteenth and early twentieth centuries, Western missionary agencies, especially those in the United States and England, invested a major proportion of their medical resources in China; in 1887, these agencies supported forty-one American and thirty-three British medical missionaries in China. By 1923, half of all missionary doctors and half of all missionary hospital beds were in China.[28] Protestant missionaries introduced Western medicine and opened the first hospitals and medical schools in many provinces. In the early twentieth century, support for medical missions in China poured in from nondenominational philanthropic agencies such as the Rockefeller Foundation, as well as from Protestant churches and mission societies. Judith Sealander and others have shown that American foundations placed considerable investments in scientific philanthropy before World War II, and these foundations were established by wealthy Americans—Rockefeller, Ford, Carnegie—who understood the dissemination of scientific practice throughout the world as an extension of Protestant missionary strategy.[29] The impact on international health of scientific philanthropy motivated by Christian idealism was significant. For example, one of the most famous ventures of the Rockefeller Foundation, the Peking Union Medical College, the so-called Johns Hopkins of the Orient, established in 1917, trained "a large proportion of the leaders of modern medicine in China," according to Oxford's 1999 *Textbook of International Health*. "Many of the 'patriotic health campaigns' in the early years of the People's Republic of China were based on knowledge derived from investigations carried out by the old PUMC, which has had a profound long-term effect upon the health of the Chinese people."[30]

Granting the importance of hospitals and medical schools founded by the Rockefeller Foundation and by Harvard and Yale Universities, Cheung and New argued that missionaries carried most of the responsibility for the development of modern health care and medical education in China prior to the Communist Revolution. Calling Western missionaries "the backbone of China's modern medical infrastructure before 1949," Cheung and New pointed to the importance of medical and nursing schools run by missionaries, the hospitals and clinics they established in both urban and rural areas, their public health campaigns, and their translations of medical texts as evidence that Christian missionaries were the most effective promoters of scientific medicine in early twentieth-century China.[31]

Nursing schools established by missionaries beginning in the 1880s encountered prejudice against female education and against forms of physical contact with strangers that violated traditional ideas about dignified behavior. Despite these obstacles, Protestant and Catholic missionaries had established two hundred nursing schools in China by the late 1930s, and nurses trained in these facilities contributed to a significant decline in infant mortality and to other improvements, especially in women's health. The Nursing Association of China, established in around 1910, listed six thousand members in the late

1930s. To quote Chen: "Although the number of medical missionaries, physicians and nurses was tiny compared to the size of the nation's population, and although their interest in 'healing the sick' aimed to serve their primary goal of 'saving the soul,' their contribution to nursing development in China, especially their efforts in training native nurses at numerous missionary hospitals and nursing schools, can hardly be overestimated."[32]

The impact of Western Christian enthusiasm for medicine on Chinese health care was significant, but only because the Chinese incorporated Western medicine on their own terms. In contrast to the belief of many missionaries that Christian teaching and scientific medicine were deeply, even uniquely compatible, and that extending Christian compassion through medical service would bring Chinese people to Christ, the Chinese found it relatively easy to take Western medicine without Christianity and to incorporate it into a pre-existing understanding of medicine as a heterogeneous art that could be sub-divided into different categories. Although many conversions did occur through missionary auspices in China, when Christianity was driven underground after the Communist Revolution, Western medicine stayed above ground as an integral part of Chinese institutions. Health care leaders in China incorporated scientific medicine as "an alternative pathway to health care," according to Cheung and New, in "an already pluralistic system" that included learned practitioners of traditional Chinese medicine as well as herbalists, astrologers, and family caregivers.[33]

Religious and Scientific Healing in the Context of Political Change

New demands for healing emerged in the context of Western expansion, and differences over the meaning of Christianity, the nature of spiritual healing, and the relationship between Christianity and scientific medicine proved central in Western Christianity's expansion and encounters with people from other traditions. In Africa, China, and elsewhere, healing served as a medium for negotiating social changes associated with modernization and Western influence, and indigenous leaders led the way in this process. Closer both to the power of religious healing as it was traditionally experienced and performed, and to the social problems associated with Western influence, indigenous leaders in various parts of the world interpreted Christianity, religious healing, and Western medicine in political and cultural terms that differed, in certain crucial respects, from the terms according to which Western missionaries thought.

Along with global expansion of Western religious and scientific influence, the twentieth century also witnessed the rise of fundamentalism and its resistance to modernist interpretations of Christianity. But at the turn of the twentieth century, often characterized as the high point of Protestant missions, humanitarian interpretations of missionary service coexisted for many supporters with commitment to "the evangelization of the world in this generation."[34] After World War I, Western optimism declined considerably, especially in Europe, and hostility to Western imperialism and colonialism increased in many parts of the world, leading to Indian independence from Britain in 1947, the expulsion of all Westerners from China in 1948, the withdrawal of western European powers from numerous regions in Africa, and the commencement of the cold war.

The face of Christian medical missions changed considerably during and after this time, with increasing reliance on indigenous leadership, the increasing presence of female specialists, the increasing importance and visibility of Catholic workers, and the increasingly complicated political worlds that medical missionaries and their supporters had to negotiate in obtaining on-the-ground support for their work. Today, thousands of private voluntary organizations and philanthropic foundations work to prevent disease and provide medical care around the world, and many people support and participate in these agencies for religious reasons. Although Christians are certainly not the only people involved in medical philanthropy, they play a major role, on a global scale, in that outreach.

Even as many aspects of medical philanthropy continue to grow more complex, the medical work sponsored by Christians has also become more centralized. Many Christian churches, groups, and individuals support such global agencies as Caritas International Medical Mission Board and Catholic Relief Services of the Roman Catholic Church, the Church World Service, which involves thirty Protestant and Orthodox churches, the Evangelical Foreign Missions Association, the American Friends Service Committee, Lutheran World Relief, the Mennonite Central Committee, and Seventh-day Adventist World Service.[35]

Despite these concerted efforts, the benefits of medical research and technology fail to reach vast portions of the world's population, and global health crises challenge existing resources and lines of support. In this situation, Christianity's appeal as a source of spiritual healing predominates over medical missionary work today as it did for centuries before the scientific discoveries of modern medicine. And medicine continues to play a secondary role as an expression of Christian compassion and missionary outreach to the world.

7

Christian Healing in the Shadow of Modern Technology and Science

Over the centuries, Christian healing has revolved around divine and holy persons. In the New Testament stories, Jesus' close relationship with God enabled him to heal the sick and command demons to leave the persons they possessed. Followers of Jesus drew on their faithful relationships with him and invoked his name in their healing work, and some of these followers became saints with healing cults of their own. Through visualization, prayer, pilgrimage, and acts of penance, believers established personal relationships with Jesus and his saints, especially Mary, and Christians to this day depend on these relationships for healing, strength, and solace.

Beginning in the early modern era among Christians in the West, a new interest in the Spirit of God developed alongside this investment in divine and holy persons. This interest coincided with modern ideas about spiritual power in the universe, as well as increasing interest in personal inspiration as an expression of individuality and source of authority for social reform. Modern invocations of the Spirit of God harked back to the reference in Matthew to Jesus casting out demons "by the Spirit of God" (12:28; cf. Luke 11:20) and to other New Testament references to spirits and spiritual gifts. At the same time, they resonated with scientific discoveries about unseen forces, such as gravity and electricity, operating in the natural world. Modern religious interest in the Spirit's power to inspire, transform, cleanse, and heal people coincided with modern theories about invisible forces that moved planets and created light. As the authority of science increased, and as inventors found new and ever more ingenious technologies to harness the forces of nature, Christians looked differently at references to the Spirit in the Bible and ancient creeds of the church.

Ancient and medieval theologians conceptualized the Holy Spirit as a person, although one less distinct and less human than Jesus or Mary. The men who crafted early church doctrine believed that the world was created through the agency of divine knowledge, which also revealed the mysteries of the world to believers. Their concepts of the Holy Spirit were Christian versions of the Platonic belief that material reality derived from ideal forms. Thus, the liturgy of St. John Chrysostom asked God to "Send down Thy Holy Spirit upon us and upon these gifts here offered, and make this Bread the precious Body of Thy Christ, and that which is in this Cup, the precious Blood of thy Christ, making the change by the Holy Spirit." The church fathers also incorporated Neoplatonic ideas about the discovery of truth as a spiritual journey. As the liturgy indicated, the Holy Spirit enabled people to repent, turn away from sin, and purify themselves in readiness for God. Thus, God made the sacramental elements "change by the Holy Spirit, so that they may be to those who partake for the purification of soul, for the communion of Thy Holy Spirit, for the fulfillment of the Kingdom of Heaven."[1]

In some ways, modern religious interest in the Holy Spirit was an extension of Neoplatonic thinking, which was revitalized in the Renaissance through the works of the sixteenth-century philosopher Paracelsus and others who believed that impersonal spiritual forces animated the material world. Later on, followers of the Swedish philosopher Emanuel Swedenborg (1688–1772) carried Neoplatonic thinking further in theories about currents of spiritual energy pervading material reality, and devised techniques for enabling people to become better attuned to those currents.[2] Christians attracted to these modern forms of Neoplatonism faced a variant of the same problem that the early church fathers faced, namely, how to integrate the person-oriented, suffering-attuned sensibility of Christianity, which anthropomorphized the entire cosmos and drew God's attention to the suffering of humanity, with the more impersonal, unemotional realm of ideas. But they also faced a problem the church fathers did not have, namely, the increasingly obvious difference between modern scientific conceptions of reality and idealistic conceptions derived from Platonic philosophy. Modern Christians faced the dilemma of how to live with scientific means of testing and verifying knowledge and with scientific challenges to the idea that the universe was governed by intelligent design.

The new authority of science and the appeal of science-based technologies altered the way many Christians thought about healing. Medicine had long served as a metaphor for Christ's efficacy as the antidote for the sickness of sin, and Christians had often used medicine as part of their outreach to the sick. But with the development of scientific medicine, Christianity's dominant status and close relationship to medicine were more difficult to maintain. Of course, competition between Christianity and medicine had existed for centuries, and many theologians found it necessary to remind people to rely more on Christ than on ordinary medicine. Faith healers argued along much the same lines in modern times, but their case was more difficult to make, given the new prestige, authority, and efficacy that scientific medicine enjoyed. At least in some cases, modern believers wanted Christianity to command the kind of validity people attribute to science.

As an example of this modern desire for scientific validation, some Pentecostal and charismatic believers blend Christianity and medicine in ways that present Christian faith as scientifically true, if not yet fully demonstrated to be so. As religion scholar Joseph Williams pointed out, Don Colbert's 2001 book, *Toxic Relief: Restore Health and Energy through Fasting and Detoxification*, described physical and spiritual detoxification as complementary therapies, each as transparent and empirically valid as the other. Similarly, Reginald Cherry's 1998 book, *The Bible Cure*, argued that physical maladies from allergies to cancer could be cured by "deciphering the ancient Hebrew dietary laws" and by "understanding how Jesus anointed natural substances to heal, and how we can pray specifically for healing and overcoming the mountain of our illness." Cherry claimed that strictures against fat in Leviticus 3:17 anticipated recent scientific studies about low-density lipoproteins and that, in many other ways, modern science validated biblical ideas. Divine guidance and supernatural intervention also played a role in Christian medicine, Cherry maintained, as important supplements to what science already confirmed.[3]

The Power of Prayer

Scientific ideas and technologies also influenced Christian prayer. Although prayer has long figured prominently in Christian healing, high-speed forms of communication developed since the late nineteenth century influenced the way people thought about prayer, healing, and communication with God. According to a recent study by the Pew Internet and American Life Project, despite the fact that Internet users tend to be less religious than the general population, "64% of wired Americans have used the Internet for spiritual or religious purposes."[4] And a growing number of these users turn to the Internet for prayer. Thousands of Christian groups, individual congregations as well as large denominations and affiliated groups, offer Web sites that enable people to use the Internet as a means of asking for prayer and praying for others. Religion scholar Thomas Lloyd argued that the Internet is not simply a convenience for believers; it allows people to reveal diseases and obsessions that they might not otherwise reveal or seek prayer for in face-to-face gatherings like church.[5] At the same time, the speed and virtual reality of Internet communication affect the way people think about divine communication.

Recent studies of remote prayer illustrate how scientific thinking and desire for scientific validation also influence the way some people think about healing. Between 1988 and 2000, researchers conducted more than one hundred clinical studies attempting to measure the effects of remote prayer on patients suffering a variety of different maladies. The salutary effects of prayer on people who prayed or knew that others prayed in their behalf is well-known.[6] Most of the researchers conducting studies of remote prayer wanted to prove something else, namely, that prayer conducted without patients knowing they were being prayed for improved the health of those patients in significant and measurable ways. The best-known of these studies, conducted by Randolph Byrd at San Francisco General Hospital, reported significant benefits from remote prayer for coronary disease. Subsequent studies attempted to replicate Byrd's findings for coronary patients, and researchers also attempted to show positive effects of remote prayer on AIDS, alcoholism, and in vitro fertilization.[7]

Other researchers conducted studies demonstrating no significant effect from remote prayer, and some pointed to "numerous possible mechanisms for error and bias" in all of the studies that claimed significant effects, including those conducted by Byrd and his followers.[8] The interest and controversy generated by these studies illustrate how scientific thinking can frame contemporary religious expression. Current fascination with remote prayer also suggests how recourse to scientific validation turns discussion of spiritual healing toward quantification of impersonal forces at work in disease and recovery and away from the emotional response to human suffering so typical of Christian healing in the past.

Today's interest in scientifically validating the therapeutic effects of religious faith grows out of several centuries of effort to establish a relationship between religion and science in which religious claims about spiritual reality can be made to harmonize with scientific claims about nature. Within Christianity, Protestants have been the most eager to square religion and science because of their confidence, prior to the late nineteenth century at least, that because God created nature, scientific investigation of nature should confirm God's existence and complement scriptural revelation. Protestant confidence in this complemetarity contributed to an enthusiasm for scientific work that enabled many new discoveries about nature. It also led Protestants to employ scientific terminology in their conceptualizations of religious experience. Even when scientists challenged Christian claims about creation, some of the staunchest supporters of Christian healing envisioned the spiritual force of God as something like the natural forces harnessed by science, only superior.

Electricity as a Way of Thinking about Spiritual Power

Christian understanding of healing began to change in Europe, Britain, and North America in the eighteenth century in response to new discoveries about electricity. The practice of healing changed, too, as healers of various sorts worked to open the way for divine power to enter believers as an electrifying force. Different methods of invoking and channeling this force developed, as did different understandings of its relationship to Christ. But beneath these important differences, a tendency to focus on healing as a revitalizing process stimulated by a spark, jolt, or flow of divine energy began to influence the rhetoric and performance of Christian healing.

One of the first and foremost proponents of the compatibility between electricity and divine power was John Wesley (1703–1791), the pathbreaking Anglican leader whose innovations in religious thought and practice led to the founding of the Methodist Church. Wesley viewed electricity as a subtle form of fire pervading and animating the universe, enlivening the air, and running through the blood and nervous system, making the human body "a kind of fire machine."[9] He formulated these ideas after experiments performed in the late 1740s by Benjamin Franklin (1706–1790) showed that lightning carried an electrical charge and after Franklin described electricity as an "Electrical fire" conducted through matter, especially water and metal.[10] An avid reader of texts on anatomy and medicine, Wesley was particularly interested in the functions of electricity inside the human body. He promoted electric therapy as a means of revivifying the human machine, and thus as a means of relieving pain and disability in cases of muscle spasm, toothache, deafness, and other ills. In the 1750s, he established several clinics for electrifying patients who suffered from a variety of complaints. He regarded this new treatment as an important advance in health care that physicians, much to their shame, were slow to endorse. Thus, in 1756, he reported that "while hundreds, perhaps thousands, have received unspeakable good" from operations at his clinics, "I have not known one man, woman, or child, who has received any hurt thereby:

so that when I hear any talk of the danger of being electrified (especially if they are medical men who talk so), I cannot but impute it to great want either of sense or honesty."[11]

Wesley's enthusiasm for electricity was part of a general excitement about breakthroughs in mastering natural phenomena long known to exist but hitherto not fully understood or exploited. Ancient Greek philosophers had observed electrical and magnetic effects in nature, and by the twelfth century, English navigators were using magnetic compasses. In 1600, the English scientist William Gilbert (1544–1603) used the term "electric" to describe the force between objects charged by friction and distinguished magnetic forces of alignment from electrical forces of attraction and repulsion. Benjamin Franklin assigned (+) and (−) to the attractive and repulsive forms of electrical charge, but it was not until 1791 that the Italian professor of anatomy Luigi Galvani (1738–1798) published the results of his experiments showing that electricity conducted through the leg of a dissected frog caused it to contract. In the decades preceding Galvani's demonstration of the effect of electricity on animal tissue, Wesley and others speculated about the role that electricity played in living mechanisms and developed instruments to explore and utilize its therapeutic effects.

Wesley never thought of God as being limited to electricity, but he did think of electricity as an elemental form of power, derived from God, working in and through nature. Thus, Wesley viewed discoveries about electricity and other natural phenomena as complements and aids to Christian life, not threats. His enthusiasm for science dovetailed with religious zeal for healthy living; he regarded the maintenance of good personal health as a Christian discipline. Like Benjamin Franklin, who recommended early rising as a form of virtue and means to prosperity, Wesley promoted exercise and temperance in food, drink, and sleep as means of keeping body and soul in good working order. He also encouraged use of simple herbal remedies as means of restoring the body's natural balance and vitality and published a popular book of such remedies for domestic use.[12]

Wesley's investment in religious experience complemented this interest in health and healing. His understanding of religious conversion affirmed the presence of bodily sensation in that spiritual transformation. Unlike his contemporary Jonathan Edwards (1703–1758), who argued that bodily feelings and expressions might not accompany a work of grace and should not be treated as evidence one way or the other, Wesley expected grace to stimulate feeling. Indeed, his effective methods of eliciting remorse for sin, hope of salvation, and joyful assurance of grace earned him the title "methodist" and prompted numerous critics to tar him with the disreputable brush of "religious enthusiasm." In spite of his detractors, Wesley's openness to bodily sensation as a natural part of Christian life proved enormously popular both in Britain and North America. His promotion of religious experience and encouragement of sensory and emotional feeling as part of that experience contributed to revivals on both sides of the Atlantic. By the early nineteenth century, these revivals made the Methodist Church the fastest-growing denomination in North America.

Sources and Development of Wesley's Thought

As an Anglican schooled in Puritan theology, Wesley was concerned about the problem of original sin, the need for salvation, and the pivotal role that faith in Christ played in personal transformation. Like many Anglicans, he espoused a moderate form of Puritanism that emphasized the importance of reason, self-discipline, and civic responsibility, along with the conviction that grace led to a virtuous and ultimately happy life. As an Anglican, Wesley was also heir to the rich language of the King James Bible, the effusion of English vocabulary and poetry it inspired, and to the emotional impact of its hymns to the beauty of creation and promise of new creation in Christ.

Along with a solid Anglican respect for virtue, reason, and beauty, Wesley shared with Quakers and other, more radical Puritan types a strong interest in the work of the Holy Spirit. Although he never approved of the antinomian ideas espoused by seventeenth-century Quakers who defied convention and gloried in their transcendence of ordinary law, his regard for the work of the Spirit in Christian life was similar to that of more moderate Quakers in his own day, who looked to, and relied on, inspiration from the Holy Spirit as the prime motivator of religious life. Wesley's reverence for Spirit's light and guidance resonated in the most interesting way with his fascination with electricity as the vital force in nature. Echoes of Wesley's respect for the light and power of electricity and of his reverence for the light and power of the Holy Spirit reverberated in the discourses of both his Pentecostal and spiritualist successors.

Wesley's reverence for the Holy Spirit was rooted in English Puritanism. Seventeenth-century Puritans found reference to the Holy Spirit and its operations useful in working through difficult issues about the nature of subjective experience and the extent of its authority. They pondered questions about how the Holy Spirit acted, and whether the Christian knew when it acted, and their answers to these questions reflected varying degrees of willingness to supplant political and clerical authority with individual conscience and inspiration. Radicals believed that the Spirit inspired Christians directly and that Christians knew when it happened. Conservatives, on the other hand, believed that the Spirit's work in individual hearts was always mediated through biblical texts. They also believed that Christians did not know for sure when or if this work had happened. On questions about the appropriateness of lay witness and spontaneous prayer, radicals emphasized the authority of subjective experience, and conservatives emphasized the Spirit's conformity to social hierarchy and reason.[13]

Closely related differences characterized expectations of religious healing. Radical Puritans expected the Holy Spirit to work the same kind of miracles through them as it had for the first Christians, and consequently reinstated the laying on of hands method of healing described in the New Testament. More conservative Puritans, including many who stayed in the Anglican Church, did not perform the laying on of hands for healing or expect to be able to perform miracles as the apostles had. Without denying God's power to intervene in nature to cause miraculous cures, they put more emphasis on the way divine power worked through nature, in conformity with natural order and law.

Although essentially a moderate in his expectation of divine power working through nature, Wesley also emphasized the importance of subjective experience of the Spirit. His exposure to German pietism and its influence at a critical juncture in his own religious life contributed to his commitment to intensely personal, subjective experience. German pietism helped him frame his understanding of the Spirit's work in individual hearts in terms of identification with the person and suffering of Christ. Whereas others would develop more impersonal, scientistic notions of the Spirit and its healing and redeeming power, Wesley always equated the Spirit with a personal Jesus and with surrender to him.

German pietists put Wesley in closer touch with the sensuality of late medieval German mysticism, especially with those elements developed by Martin Luther and carried forward by some of Luther's followers. Pastoral counseling from German pietists pushed Wesley to seek a clear feeling of the Spirit's presence in his own heart and to associate that feeling with the indwelling love of his redeemer. His conversations with German pietists lent definition to his own spiritual struggles and to his sensations of spiritual activity. He developed this definition further through his penchant for methodical organization and rational order. In systematically identifying and ranking different forms of inward feeling, Wesley and his followers joined the rationalism of Enlightenment culture to a complementary appreciation of emotional life and expression.

In 1735, Wesley sought counsel from Augustus G. Spangenberg (1704–1792), a charismatic leader of the Moravian Church, while he and his brother,

Charles Wesley (1707–1788), were in Georgia participating in a Moravian mission to Creek and Cherokee Indians. Through Spangenberg's questioning, Wesley discovered that he lacked the closeness to Jesus that marked true conversion. As Wesley recorded it, the future bishop dissected his spiritual state by asking, "Do you know Jesus Christ?" Taken aback, Wesley responded in intellectual and doctrinal terms. "I know He is the Savior of the world," Wesley replied. "True," responded Spangenberg, "but do you know He has saved you?" Wesley recalled, "I answered, 'I hope He has died to save me.' He only added, 'Do you know yourself?' I said, 'I do.' But I fear they were vain words."[14]

Spurred by this encounter, Wesley sought more spiritual guidance from Moravians after returning to London in 1737, and the result was significant. Advised "not to stop short of the grace of God," Wesley attained the grace he desired during a prayer meeting on Aldersgate Street, in a moment that came to epitomize the experience of sanctification prized by his followers. Reading from Luther's commentary on Romans "describing the change which God works in the heart through faith in Christ, Wesley felt the sensation of grace." As he famously explained in his journal, "I felt my heart strangely warmed. I felt I did trust in Christ, Christ alone, for salvation; and an assurance was given me that He had taken away my sins."[15]

This interest in identifying the sensation of religious experience held important implications for the future of Christian healing. Wesley's fusion of pietistical sensation with Puritan investment in the practical outcomes of grace stimulated new expectations for religious healing and new experiments in methods of producing it. Wesley stood at the crux of important new developments in religious healing, some of which he probably would have resisted.

Scholars disagree about Wesley's attitude toward miracles. Historian Henry Rack argued that "Wesley's love of the supernatural made it difficult for him to show where limits had to be defined."[16] On the other hand, historians Donald Dayton and Harold Vanderpool suggest that Wesley was never as preoccupied with miracles as some of his successors, and that although he affirmed the Spirit's work in effecting sudden cures and acknowledged his own participation in some of that work, he devoted more effort to promoting electric therapy, herbal remedies, and the disciplines of healthy living. Both his belief in healing miracles and his restraint in participating in them are evident in a journal entry for December 1742, where he wrote of praying for a man whose physician had pronounced his condition beyond hope. The man recovered. "But what does all this prove?" Wesley demanded. "Not that I claim any gift above other men, but only that I believe that God now hears and answers prayer even beyond the ordinary course of nature."[17]

Sources of Pentecostal Healing

Pentecostalism derived from numerous sources, including the Holiness branch of the Methodist Church, where believers looked beyond conversion to the more advanced stage of sanctification that purified and perfected them as followers of Christ. Pentecostalism also derived from the larger tradition of evangelical revivalism, to which African Americans made significant contributions, as well as from a variety of Anglo and European pietistic groups, including the Plymouth Brethren, who rediscovered Christian exorcism, and participants in the "Higher Life" movement and other forms of Christian perfectionism. American revivalist Maria Woodworth Etter (1844–1924) and other charismatic preachers incorporated healing into their religious meetings in the Midwest, and in Topeka, Kansas, Charles Fox Parham (1873–1929) began speaking in tongues as a sign of Holy Ghost baptism. Parham carried his Apostolic Faith to Houston, where he met the African American preacher William J. Seymour. In Los Angeles in 1906, Seymour led blacks and whites together in an outpouring of Pentecostal spirit known as the Azuza Street revival.[18]

Folklorist Elaine Lawless pointed to African Caribbean culture as an important source of Pentecostalism, arguing that new forms of Christian practice that incorporated African healing and spirit possession moved through New Orleans up the Mississippi in the late nineteenth century. Maria Woodworth Etter and other white preachers incorporated these new practices into Protestant revival meetings. Already a mix of Scottish, English, German, and African traditions, these meetings became more exciting with a second infusion of African healing practices growing out of African Caribbean traditions.[19]

Beginning in the eighteenth century, African expression became part of the larger phenomena of revivalism through frontier camp meetings and outdoor city services that drew black and white participants together. Torn from indigenous cultures where ancestral spirits carried the authority of tribal lineages and territories, and where religious adepts demonstrated the power of these spirits acting through their bodies, Africans in America found some of the healing power previously associated with ancestral spirits in the Holy Spirit of Christianity.[20] At the same time, the infusion of African forms of spirit possession into Christianity gave new meaning and new life to biblical stories about the healing gifts bestowed on the followers of Jesus.

On the Kentucky frontier at the turn of the nineteenth century, a series of extraordinary religious revivals made Wesley's sensitivity to the connection between electrification and religious experience more explicit. Isolated from traditional forms of community, the people who came to these camp meetings by foot, horseback, and wagon brought various forms of personal intensity with them, even as they found new experience through Methodist-inspired preaching. Young Peter Cartwright (1785–1872) found his life transformed at the big meeting in 1801 at Cane Ridge, where "the power of God was wonderfully displayed." The future revivalist was already concerned about God and desperate for a sign of God's acceptance, when, a few months before, he "heard a voice from heaven, saying, 'Peter, look at me.'" On hearing that call, Cartwright wrote, "A feeling of relief flashed over me as quick as an electric shock." But he could not sustain this initial burst of "hopeful feelings" and sank back into darkness. Then, at Cane Ridge, on a Saturday night, amid "weeping multitudes" of other frontier people, he "earnestly prayed for mercy." In the course of these prayers, "an impression was made on my mind, as though a voice said to me, 'Thy sins are all forgiven thee.'" The power of this moment changed his life forever: "Divine light flashed all round me, unspeakable joy sprung up on my soul. I rose to my feet, opened my eyes, and it really seemed as if I was in heaven; the trees, the leaves on them, and everything seemed, and I really thought were, praising God."[21]

Another participant at Cane Ridge, Colonel Robert Patterson, described how "the flame spread more and more" when the Lord's Supper was celebrated at nearby Stony Creek.[22] Patterson's estimate of eight thousand participants reflected more excitement than accurate count, but it suggests the thrill people felt coming together from so many different backgrounds as they did in the first Pentecost, "when cloven tongues of fire sat upon the apostles and amid a rushing, mighty wind they spoke to an untoward generation of Parthians, Medes and Elamites, each in his own tongue."[23] Patterson used electric and medical terminology to describe the Pentecost in Kentucky:

Of all ages, from 8 years and upwards; male and female; rich and poor; the blacks; and of every denomination; those in favor of it, as well as those, at the instant in opposition to it, and railing against it, have instantaneously laid motionless on the ground. Some feel the approaching symptoms by being under deep convictions; their heart swells, their nerves relax, and in an instant they become motionless and speechless, but generally retain their senses. It comes upon others like an electric shock, as if felt in the great arteries of the arms or thighs; closes quick into the heart, which swells, like to burst. The body relaxes and falls motionless; the hands and feet become cold, and yet the pulse is as formerly, though sometimes rather slow. Some grow weak, so as not to be able to stand, but do not lose their

speech altogether. They are all opposed to any medical application.
. . . Many have not recovered, so that it is not certain that they will.—
Others will recover in an hour, and speak of salvation sure, and are
in possession of great gifts in praying and exhortation, which they
often perform in an incredible manner.[24]

In the most concrete ways, both Patterson and Cartwright invoked electric
images and sensations to describe revival experience. In Patterson's description
of "experimental" knowledge of religion, God literally struck down sinners with
electric force. In Cartwright's account of his sanctification, God lit up the world
with electrifying brightness. In these reports, Wesley's suggestion about a possible relationship between electricity and divine power had acquired a life of
its own.

At one level, the association of religious experience with electrification can
be understood as a metaphor for conveying the transformational impact of
conversion and sanctification. As such, it was not the same thing as a scientific
proposition subject to empirical verification: Patterson was not interested in
proving that sanctification was a form of electricity in the same way that Benjamin Franklin wanted to prove that lightning carried an electric charge. But
at another level, Patterson's use of clinical, scientific language imputed a kind
of objective reality to the metaphysical power and subjective experience he
described. In this respect, electrification was more than a metaphor for describing conversion and sanctification; it was also a way of making those experiences real.

Sister Aimee

In subsequent expressions of healing influenced by Wesley's interest in physical sensations of religious experience, believers took care to emphasize, just
as Wesley had, that they were only conduits for the Spirit's healing power, not
healers in their own right. Even the flamboyant Pentecostal healer Aimee (Kennedy) Semple McPherson (1890–1944) minimized the significance of healing
in relation to other aspects of Christian life and downplayed her role in the
faith healing process. Despite the fact that she was often flooded with requests
for healing prayer and held special "Stretcher Day" services to accommodate
the many invalids who sought her help, she claimed that "her meetings were
99 percent salvation and 1 percent healing" and that she had no power of her
own. "My healings?" she exclaimed in Denver in 1921, when she heard that
reports of her healings preceded her visit there. "I do nothing. If the eyes of

the people are set on ME, nothing will happen. I pray and believe with others who pray and believe, and power of Christ works the cure."[25]

By the turn of the twentieth century, people attached to the revival tradition had become keenly aware of the dangers involved in allowing scientific thinking free rein in discussions of religious experience. Still invested in promoting these as sensory phenomena with real physical effects, many proponents of conversion and sanctification made it clear that they had come to a parting of the ways with modern science. Thus, high school biology precipitated a religious crisis for young Aimee Kennedy, who felt she had to choose between being a Christian and accepting the principles of evolutionary science. She made the choice for Jesus, and never looked back. Yet, as a charismatic preacher and Pentecostal healer, she continued to rely on the association between sanctification and electrification. Twenty years after his death, she attributed her commitment to Pentecostal experience to the "liquid fiery eloquence" of her first husband, Robert Semple (1882?–1910), who "swept me clear from a quiet Canadian farm and whirled me into neighboring fields and then afar, then 'round the world and back again, so swift speeding in the Master's work that I am going yet." In response to his preaching, she "went down" under the power of the Holy Spirit. Later, as an American citizen through her marriage to Harold McPherson (1890–1978), and a famous preacher and healer in her own right, she regularly led her congregants, at the culminating moment of her own healing services, in singing Edward Perronet's hymn, "All hail the power of Jesus' name;/Let angels prostrate fall." During these services, she often said that she "felt the power of God working through me," and at her Temple in Los Angeles, she built a separate room she called the "power house," where she and her followers gathered for the sole purpose of praying for the Holy Spirit's baptizing fire.[26]

McPherson's embrace of electrical technology to promote her revivals went along with her enthusiasm for literal and sensational descriptions of the Holy Spirit's power. In Roanoke in 1918, amid a controversy with a local Pentecostal church that declined to let her use their building, the local power company responded positively to McPherson's request to wire an open lot with electric lights, thus promoting their business as well as God's. In the Bronx in 1919, McPherson hired another local power company to put up electric signs in an empty lot, one of which read, "Do you want to be Baptised with the Holy Ghost and Fire? Come!" In another expression of her enthusiasm for the literal signs from heaven, she was the first to preach from an airplane and, in a related tactic, sold burial plots next to her own with the slogan "Go Up with Aimee." She was the first woman to own a radio license and one of the first to preach over the air. When Herbert Hoover, then secretary of commerce, called her to task for using an undesignated frequency, she made adjustments, but only after glorying in the literal implications of broadcasting for God: "You cannot expect the almighty to abide by your wave length nonsense. When I offer my prayers to Him I must fit into His wave reception."[27]

For all her corny gimmickry, McPherson was perfectly serious about the literal reality of the Holy Spirit and its transformational effects. She believed that the Holy Spirit acted on people in much the same visceral way that electricity did, that God communicated messages in much the same way radio towers did, and that Christians would be transported to heaven, not by airplane, but through a divine technology no less concrete or practical than modern forms of aviation. Of course, the Holy Spirit could not be reduced or confined to electricity, radio waves, or manipulations of gravitational force, but these phenomena provided timely ways of thinking about how the Holy Spirit worked, and thus of accepting and affirming the Spirit's reality. Belief in the healing of the Spirit of God did go back to Jesus and the apostles, as modern Pentecostals claimed. But the rhetoric and sensations that Pentecostals associated with the Spirit derived from modern science and technology as well as from the gospels and acts of the apostles.

McPherson's career epitomized the increasing prominence of faith healing and its association with modern technology among Wesley's Pentecostal successors. In hindsight, this development seems almost inevitable given the Wesleyan emphasis on religious sensation and the coincidence of new developments in electrification and communication technologies that inspired new ways of thinking and talking about divine power. In a world increasingly filled with these technologies, healing performances stood as empirical proofs of divine power that carried forward Wesley's respect for bodily sensation as an appropriate medium of religious expression.

Pentecostal Healing as a Global Phenomenon

More than any other modern expression of Christianity, Pentecostalism carried the stimulating charge of cross-cultural and interracial fellowship. In a world becoming smaller through new technologies of communication, speaking in tongues (glossolalia) reflected the excitement of crossing boundaries between social groups and creating community with people who had different languages and ways of talking. The fear and excitement born of social dislocation and desire for new community coincided with powerful needs for physical healing born of the stresses of modern life. In new situations of cultural upheaval and dislocation, Wesley's "methods" of eliciting religious feeling coincided, and partly merged, with forms of Christian expression developed by African Americans, and Protestant revivalism provided a new home for ecstatic forms of worship rooted in African spirit possession. As revivalism turned into Pentecostalism, and Pentecostalism spread, these African-rooted elements contributed to its appeal in many places where traditional forms of healing persisted in combination with new elements from Christianity, especially in Africa.

In Korea, in the United Kingdom, in Russia and Italy, in Brazil, Mexico, Chile, and other parts of Latin America as well as in Africa and North America, indigenous forms of religious healing combine with belief in the literal truth of the Bible and the restoration of spiritual gifts, and expectations of Jesus' return. In Seoul and other cities in South Korea, Pentecostalism fuses evangelical Protestantism with indigenous forms of shamanic healing. In the United Kingdom, Pentecostalism attracts immigrants from the Caribbean and other regions where spirit possession and shamanic healing are well known. In Russia, Pentecostalism stimulates growth in the Orthodox Church, as well as competition to it. In Italy, especially in Sicily, it contributes to renewal movements within the Catholic Church, as well as conversions to Protestant churches. In many regions of the world, Assemblies of God and other international forms of Pentecostal Christianity draw millions of adherents and coexist with smaller churches that incorporate elements of Christianity within the framework of indigenous beliefs and healing practices.[28]

Pentecostalism today not only has a global reach, but also reflects the nature of globalization as a mass cultural, economic, and technological process. Along with its fusion of Christianity with indigenous forms of healing, Pentecostalism is a universalizing social movement, drawing people together from different ethnic, cultural, and religious backgrounds. Like globalization itself, Pentecostalism is a predominantly urban phenomenon that attracts people with diminished ties to traditional forms of community. When it emerged in early twentieth-century North America, Pentecostalism caught on in Los Angeles, Chicago, Kansas City, Denver, and Indianapolis among immigrants from rural areas nostalgic for old-time religion and the intimate experiences of community characteristic of their previous lifestyles. In Seoul, São Paulo, Santiago, and East London today, Pentecostalism resonates with experiences of shamanic healing associated with indigenous cultures while at the same time promoting a strict behavioral code that enables migrants from rural areas to reorganize their lives and cope with the poverty, disease, loneliness, and other stresses of urban life. Pentecostalism helps newcomers find themselves among the fast-paced and often brutal realities of the multinational cultures and economies of city life. It also gives people a second, third, and fourth chance at establishing themselves and a means of forging new ties of interpersonal and institutional support.

In this context, healing is very much at the center of what people need and want from religion. Poor health is one of the principal dangers of the poverty that urban immigrants face, away from tighter communities where doctoring, nursing, and other forms of health care were more informal, comforting, intimate, inexpensive, and ready to hand than in many cities. Much as Christianity succeeded during its first centuries as a relatively effective form of health care, Pentecostalism succeeds today for some of the same reasons. And much as Christianity's effectiveness as a healing cult facilitated its spread throughout the far-flung Roman Empire in late antiquity, healing performances enable Pentecostalism to grow in many parts of the early twenty-first-century world.

At the same time, the modern character of Pentecostalism is evident in its depictions of the Holy Spirit as a force of energy analogous to electricity and high-speed communications. As one witness described the work of the Argentine evangelist Carlos Annacondia, "With a high-volume, high-energy, prolonged challenge he actually taunts the spirits until they manifest in one way or another." Much as medieval artists conveyed the blessings of saints in heaven through the sights and sounds of spectacular cathedrals and pageants, many Pentecostal preachers use compelling audiovisual aids to represent the transforming power of the Holy Spirit, the malevolence of Satan, and the final redemption in heaven. Emotion-packed performances, like those conducted in Argentinia, fuse local knowledge of spiritual pain and misfortune with gospel stories about the healing and demon-slaying power of Jesus: "To the skilled, experienced members of Annacondia's crusade ministry teams, it is just another evening of power encounters in which the power of Jesus Christ over demonic forces is being displayed for all to see."[29]

Spiritualist Influences in Christian Healing

Although the histories of spiritualism and Pentecostalism are usually treated separately, their idealizations of spiritual power are similar. To be sure, many Christians in the charismatic or Pentecostal tradition regard spiritualism as anathema. Their focus on the person of Jesus and strict adherence to biblical precepts does distinguish them from spiritualists, who interpret the Bible symbolically and embrace teachings from a variety of different religious traditions. But belief in the power of a spiritual force akin to electricity plays a significant role in the historical development of both traditions. As several scholars have shown, spiritualism figured importantly in European, British, and American religious thinking in the nineteenth century and helped shape the religious thinking of many Protestants who condemned it.[30]

Spiritualism derived from theories about magnetic forces developed in the eighteenth and nineteenth centuries. Working on the premise that invisible magnetic forces influenced the human mind, experimenters devised mechanical and rhetorical procedures for manipulating these forces to produce states of mesmerism, or hypnotic trance, in willing subjects. In addition to blocking pain and offering relief from a variety of symptoms, mesmerists claimed to provide scientific demonstration of the existence of unseen metaphysical forces akin to electricity.

Efforts to manage magnetic forces and to produce religious experience through them grew out of the work of the Austrian physician Franz Anton Mesmer (1734–1815). Inspired by the astrological theories of disease promoted by Paracelsus, who believed that invisible toxins originating in the stars, and essentially spiritual in nature, could invade human bodies and cause disease,[31] Mesmer theorized about the existence of planetary forces transmitted throughout the universe through invisible ether, and about the possibility of harnessing these forces for use in curing human ailments. He devised magnetic treatments in which patients held hands, or iron bars, around containers of dilute sulfuric acid believed to expedite the flow of magnetic current. He rose to fame by challenging Johan Gassner, a Tirolean priest who conducted thousands of exorcisms in southern Germany, Austria, and Switzerland in the 1760s and early 1770s. Mesmer's attempts to refute Gassner's teachings about demon possession drew criticism from physicians in Vienna who forced his exile in 1778 for practicing magic. He reestablished his practice in Paris, where he treated an affluent clientele until the French Revolution forced to him to escape to London.

Mesmer's theories about "animal magnetism" influenced thinking in several different religious and scientific arenas. Perhaps most famously, his theories contributed to new ideas and experiences associated with occult phenomena, such as spirit rapping, messages from the dead, and extrasensory perception. The esoteric religion of Theosophy, which involved communications with Tibetan lamas from an elevated plane of existence, derived in part from Mesmer's beliefs about animal magnetism, as did later forms of esoteric spirituality and alternative forms of healing associated with New Age religions and various forms of neopaganism.

In the arena of academic medicine, Mesmer's theories about animal magnetism led to the discovery of hypnotism and laid some of the ground for later theories of somaticization and hysteria developed by Jean-Martin Charcot

(1825–1893), Josef Breuer (1842–1925), and Sigmund Freud (1856–1939). Those pioneers in neuropsychology studied "conversion" in suggestible, "hysterical" patients, a phenomenon they identified, not with the infusion of saving grace as American revivalists used the term, but with the transformation of emotional distress into physical symptoms. Charcot, Breuer, and Freud laid the groundwork for current theories about hypnosis and for current applications of hypnosis in the treatment of tobacco addiction and other bad habits. In a less direct way, they also laid some of the groundwork for current understanding of the placebo effect. Their interest in somatic conversion contributed to later ideas about psychological stress as a major contributor to disease and to later interest in persuasion, belief, and expectation as means of amplifying the effects obtained from taking medicine.

Mesmerism also stimulated new thinking within Christianity. In this arena, mesmerism was both a challenge and an inspiration. As a challenge, it offered explanations of religious experience quite different from those of traditional theology. Trance states, messages from beyond the grave, sudden physical and instantaneous recovery—mesmerists offered explanations for all of these through a quasi-scientific terminology, often without reference to theological language about new birth in Christ. But if it worked as an alternative to the rhetorical conventions of traditional Christian theology, mesmerism could also insinuate itself into Christian thought. Thus, mesmerism stimulated new ideas about how divine power worked in Christian healing and new developments in the practice of Christian healing, even as it seemed to threaten the integrity of Christian thought. Even when they denounced spiritualism and animal magnetism as anti-Christian, more than a few Christians borrowed ideas from them.

For example, spiritualism influenced Ellen G. White (1827–1915), the founder of Seventh-day Adventism, at least as the bogeyman she tried to fight off. A semi-invalid in Portland, Maine, following a blow on the face in childhood, this visionary prophet suffered a variety of ailments, especially nervous problems, and sought relief in many corners. Swept up in the religious excitement caused by William Miller's predictions that Christ would return to earth sometime around 1843, she felt sure that she was a saint and would shortly attain relief from her sufferings. When a revised date of October 22, 1844, passed without apparent event, she sought divine guidance to surmount her bewilderment and disappointment. Praying with friends, she fell into a trance that suffused her with the light of the Holy Spirit and lifted her "far above the dark world."[32] In a subsequent experience she identified with sanctification, she described how "wave after wave of glory rolled over me, until my body grew stiff." Her visions multiplied, and in a number of instances, she underwent episodes of paralysis or involuntary movement, much like manifestations of religious enthusiasm seen in camp meetings, and also much like the effects of mesmerist trance. She arranged to be observed during some of these episodes, and several physicians noted slowed rates of heartbeat and respiration. One physician commented that her behavior corresponded exactly to that induced by magnetic trance and explained to her that she "was a very easy subject." He offered to prove this by inducing a vision through mesmerist technique, but she refused, warning him that "mesmerism was from the devil, from the bottomless pit, and that it would soon go there, with those who continued to use it."[33]

Even as she set herself against mesmerism as the work of the Devil, White feared she might have become one of the "channels for Satan's electric currents."[34] This fear struck with special intensity one morning during family prayer, when she felt God's power upon her but then wondered if it might be mesmerism instead. With this thought, she immediately became mute and did not recover her power of speech until the next day, when it returned in loud praises to God. After the crisis was over and her indecision passed, White said she had been "struck dumb" for questioning the godly origin of her religious experiences. She also preached that opponents of true religion were so vicious they would even have accused Jesus of mesmerism. Signaling her staunch commitment to evangelical theology, but also her worrisome preoccupation with mesmerism as an explanation for religious experience, White remarked that if her opponents had seen the disciples' shouting as Jesus entered Jerusalem, "they would doubtless raise the cry, 'Fanaticism! Mesmerism! Mesmerism!'"[35]

White reaffirmed her belief in the Christ-centered, Bible-oriented thrust of evangelical Christianity, combining it with investment in natural means of maintaining good health, including vegetarianism, exercise, fresh air, water cures, and abstinence from alcohol, tobacco, drugs, and excessive indulgence in sex. In its synthesis of disease prevention, holistic treatment, and an apocalyptic form of Protestant theology, White's Adventism represented a distinctively modern approach to Christian healing and health care. Inspired by her teachings, Adventists established health care centers in many parts of the world and built an international network of churches whose members' good health and longevity today well exceeds that of the general population.

Ellen White consigned mesmerism to the Devil partly because she felt its insidious attraction. In positing the existence of subtle currents of magnetic force that many of its adherents presumed to be spiritual in nature, mesmerism offered a metaphysical alternative to evangelical theology in the guise of science, claiming to confirm the essentially spiritual nature of reality through experiments, depersonalized observation, and empirical evidence. For Ellen White and others attached to Christian supernaturalism but also keen on health reform and enamored of the growing ethos of experiment, observation, and scientific evidence in Victorian culture, mesmerism was a variant of the fusion of religion and health they sought, but a dangerous one that substituted currents of magnetic force for the biblical God and redemption through Christ.

Another heir to Wesley's understanding of Christian healing, Mary Baker Eddy (1821–1910) also emphasized the power of Christ's Spirit in effecting cures. For Eddy, the "El Dorado of Christianity" was Christian Science, which "recognizes only the divine control of Spirit, in which Soul is our master, and material sense and human will have no place." Although Eddy and her followers hinted broadly that she might be a female counterpart to Jesus, identical to the "woman clothed with the sun" depicted in the Book of Revelation, they ultimately backed away from deifying her and from equating the Science of Christianity with her person. Instead, they claimed that Eddy "discovered the Christ Science or divine laws of Life, Truth, and Love," much as Jesus had centuries before. Eddy explained in *Science and Health*, the main repository of her teaching, "The physical healing of Christian Science results now, as in Jesus' time, from the operation of divine Principle." Recognizing the power of divine Mind was the first step to overcoming sickness, sin, and death. The power of divine "Thought passes from God to man," she explained, although "neither sensation nor report goes from the material body to Mind," as they did in materialist forms of communication like electricity and magnetism.[36]

Eddy's engagement with mesmerism led her to relinquish many aspects of evangelical theology in a search for scientific understanding of Christian healing. By the time she formulated her concept of Christian Science, Eddy had also come to reject mesmerism, equating it with the "malicious animal magnetism" that she thought her rivals were using against her. Promoting Christian Science as the rediscovery of methods Jesus used to expel demons, Eddy invoked the power of Christ against erroneous thoughts that led to sickness and death. She believed that any attempt to explain spiritual power in materialist terms was dangerously erroneous, and she identified mesmerists as chief among the evildoers advocating such debilitating and life-threatening thoughts.

In her break with the materialist elements of mesmerism, Eddy followed her mentor, Phineas P. Quimby (1802–1866), but also went beyond him. A clockmaker from Ellen White's hometown of Portland, Maine, Quimby experimented with mesmerist techniques for alleviating pain and breaking bad habits until he discovered that he could produce remarkable changes in his patients' feelings and behavior through the power of suggestion alone.

Dispensing with all the stuff about magnetic forces and invisible fluids, he rejected mesmerism as "the greatest humbug of the age." Enthused by Ralph Waldo Emerson's ideas about the Oversoul manifest in nature, and by his own discovery of the power of man's own creative intelligence to free itself from negative thinking and the needless suffering it imposed on the body, he identified this creative intelligence in Christ, the savior of mankind. He described Christ as the great Scientific Man, existing within each mind, able to break through the darkness and bondage of suffering. Interpreting resurrection to mean the reemergence of a sick person's "own Christ or health," he explained to one of his patients, "Your belief is the sepulcher in which your wisdom is confined." To readers he proclaimed, "Disease is a belief; health is in Wisdom." Jesus understood this completely, Quimby argued, and healed people by stimulating the creative intelligence of their minds. In the case of a paralyzed arm, for example, "Jesus knew that the arm was not the cause but the effect, and he addressed Himself to the intelligence, and applied His wisdom to the cause."[37]

In emphasizing the mind's power over illness, Eddy went further than Quimby to claim that disease and death did not really exist at all, but were erroneous beliefs that caused pain when people accepted them. She also went further than Quimby in interpreting the whole Bible as an allegory about the divine power of Mind and its ultimate triumph over the evils of materialism. For example, "When a new spiritual idea is borne to earth," she wrote in *Science and Health*, "the prophetic Scripture of Isaiah is renewedly fulfilled: 'Unto us a child is born . . . and his name shall be called Wonderful.'" Similarly, she defined the proclamation in Genesis, "Let there be light," as "the perpetual demand of Truth and Love, changing chaos into order and discord into the music of the spheres." With regard to the disclosure of divine truth, Eddy interpreted the rediscovery of Christian Science in "the present age" as "the opening of the sixth seal" described in the Book of Revelation, suggesting that her own life and teaching had been foretold: "And there appeared a great wonder in heaven; a woman clothed with the sun, and the moon under her feet, and upon her head a crown of twelve stars."[38]

The New Thought movement associated with Quimby, including Christian Science, represented an important development in religious conceptions of healing. Before the medical analysis of somatic conversion conducted by Charcot, Breuer, and Freud showed that emotional distress could produce physical symptoms, Quimby found that physical symptoms could be relieved by mental suggestion. Although later research on hypnosis and the placebo effect emerged independently, Quimby developed a similar understanding of the power of suggestion. If Quimby was a scientific investigator insofar as he revised his theories on the basis of experiments he attempted to replicate, Eddy's concept of science as the application of universal ideas had little to do with scientific method. Nevertheless, in an era bringing new authority, prestige, and resources to medical science, the appeal of science was so strong that she chose "Christ Science" as the name for her understanding of the Word of God's healing power.

Along with Ellen White and Aimee McPherson, Eddy represents the difficulties of integrating Christian claims to healing with science. All three women embraced idealistic versions of Christian theology that conflicted with natural science. Yet, all were stimulated by the truth claims, empirical ethos, and technologies of science and brought strong echoes of them into their religious practice and thought.

In their belief in an invisible spiritual force that stimulates healing, Eddy, White, and McPherson also represent a patch of common ground between Protestant faith healing and metaphysical practices available today as alternatives or supplements to Christian healing. To be sure, many followers of Eddy, White, and McPherson would shun healing practices associated with crystals, stones, and dream catchers and alternative forms of healing like yoga, macrobiotics, and acupuncture. Yet, followers of these alternative practices share with followers of faith healing and Christian Science the belief that spiritual power is a force permeating material reality that could conceivably be measured, or at least detected, by scientific instruments.

Catholic Devotion to Miracles in the Age of Science

While Protestants sought to recover the healing force of the Holy Spirit, join holistic health reform to expectations of heaven, and invoke Christ as a dispeller of negative thoughts, nineteenth- and twentieth-century Catholics also pursued religious healing in cultural contexts infiltrated with the rhetoric of modern science and the inventions of modern technology. Like Protestants, Catholics found science and technology challenging stimuli to beliefs and practices associated with healing. But unlike Protestants, many Catholics retained beliefs about the healing powers of saints, and thus participated in a relatively unbroken tradition of healing that reached back to antiquity. While Pentecostals, Adventists, and Christian Scientists believed that they had recovered the healing power of faith that had been lost for centuries, Catholics venerated healing saints, especially the Blessed Virgin Mary, as Christians had for centuries. But modern Catholics were not immune to the stimulus of modern science. In fact, Catholic religious orders and lay people developed effective ways of enabling miracles and modern science to coexist, and even support each other, with relatively little interference.

The popularity of the shrine of Notre Dame at Lourdes is a good example of how Catholic faith in the healing power of saints could be maintained and even revitalized in the context of modern science and technology. Countless instances of Marian devotion exist today, and local shrines where Mary has appeared and healed people can be found throughout Latin America, in many parts of Africa, and in virtually every part of the world where Catholic, Ortho-dox, and other non-Protestant churches can be found. The shrine at Lourdes is particularly noteworthy because of its worldwide fame as a pilgrimage center, because of the role that Catholic physicians played in the shrine's development, and because of the fine scholarly treatment it has received.

The origins of the shrine at Lourdes date to 1858, when a peasant girl, Bernadette Soubrious, experienced visions of a small white lady, later identified as the Virgin Mary. Following the lady's instructions, Bernadette unearthed a spring of holy water in the grotto near the garbage dump where the lady ap-peared. After eighteen visions, numerous healings at the spring, and a ground-swell of popular devotion, Church authorities relaxed their disapproval of Ber-nadette's visions and stepped in with cautious support for some of the miraculous claims attributed to the waters of the spring. Through a combi-nation of popular enthusiasm and clerical management, the remote village of Lourdes became a thriving town with many profitable businesses and excellent rail connections.

As historian Ruth Harris explained, Lourdes became associated with con-servative politics through its affiliations with the French church and with pop-ular culture in rural France. In the 1870s, penitents flocked to Lourdes in the hope of enlisting the Virgin's help in restoring the French monarchy. The reestablishment of secular government in the Third Republic hardly dimin-ished the shrine's popularity as a healing center or its association with con-servative religion as it developed into one of the world's major pilgrimage centers of the twentieth century. In 1908, the fiftieth anniversary of the original visions, more than 1.5 million believers made the pilgrimage to Lourdes. In the 1990s, close to 5 million pilgrims a year came to Lourdes from many corners of the world, many on chartered planes as part of package excursions.[39]

At one level, the shrine at Lourdes signaled the resistance of pious Cath-olics to secular and scientific rationalism. From the beginning, believers em-braced the healing miracles of Lourdes in defiance of secular authority. When police summoned her for questioning and threatened her with jail if she re-turned to the grotto, popular support escalated for the shepherd girl, her visions, and her sanctuary in the rubble heap on the edge of the village. As the magnitude of popular support became apparent, so did the commercial advantages of becoming part of a pilgrimage center, and local businessmen and politicians stepped in to promote the shrine and to develop shops, hotels, restaurants, and hospitals. The shrine's success as a religious center derived as much from the cooperation of secular authorities and their help in developing Lourdes as an economic market as it did from the apparent defiance of secular and scientific rationalism manifest in the celebration of miracles.

In another form of cooperation, the French church extended a degree of official support for miracles occurring at Lourdes, despite the fact that more than a few members of the hierarchy viewed the activities there as too much like paganism to be condoned. The church might have studiously ignored or even attempted to squelch belief in Bernadette's apparitions, had it not been for the remarkable way the Virgin identified herself: when pressed by the village priest to identify the white lady, Bernadette relayed the message, "I am the Immaculate Conception." Bernadette had probably heard the name in homilies from the village priest celebrating the official declaration by Pius IX in 1854 that Mary was spotless of sin from the moment of conception. Although the feast celebrating Mary's conception dated to the seventh century and belief in her absolute purity had been popular since the sixteenth century, Bernadette's delivery of a message from the Virgin in which the Virgin affirmed the new dogma herself established a bridge between the piety of common folk and the theology of a pope who perceived the Church as besieged by the forces of modernity.[40]

Medical science played a subordinate but important role at Lourdes, an arrangement that exemplified the way Catholic piety and modern science often coexisted. Although belief in miracles flew against the most thoroughgoing forms of scientific empiricism and rationality, many physicians allowed for the possibility of miracles. Even among those who were skeptical, many acknowledged that *belief* in miracles could produce cures. Moreover, the medical establishment's involvement at Lourdes gave physicians opportunity to observe the healing effects of prayer, ritual bathing, and drafts of holy water, as well as the consolations that belief in the Virgin offered.

The development of procedures for verifying healings at Lourdes reveals a history of cooperation between physicians and priests that served both groups well, at the same time regulating the expectations of patients and their helpers streaming into the shrine. In the first decades after the shrine opened, an Episcopal Commission of Inquiry, established by the Catholic Church, passed judgment on the authenticity of healing claims presented to it for approval. The Commission adhered to relatively strict requirements laid down in canon law for certifying the authenticity of miracles and called in physicians to verify the existence, nature, and disappearance of particular maladies. In 1883, apparently at the request of Garaison Fathers stationed in Lourdes, much of the responsibility for adjudicating healing claims passed to a Medical Bureau, staffed primarily by physicians but including priests as advisors.[41] Under this arrangement, a pilgrim might obtain medical certification of a cure, although requirements were stiff and certification fairly rare. As the focus of attention shifted to medical criteria for validating a cure, ecclesiastical certification for miracles quietly disappeared.

This disappearance served the church hierarchy in France by helping them avoid embarrassing public disputes with unbelievers without discouraging believers from expressing their religious devotion. For their part, physicians not only had opportunity to examine interesting cases of religious healing, but also to set a different tone from that struck at the medical clinics in Paris, where neuropsychologists were conducting experiments and making misogynist pronouncements about histrionic women. While Charcot was sticking needles through the arms of hypnotized women to demonstrate the hysteric's pathological vulnerability to suggestion, the physicians at Lourdes took a kindlier and more respectful view, not only of the relationship between religion and healing, but also of religious believers themselves, most of whom were women who made pilgrimages to Lourdes in search of help in suffering or who came to Lourdes to care for others who suffered. Over the course of the twentieth century, the softer and more pragmatic approach to the relationship between religion and medicine at Lourdes seemed almost open-minded in contrast to the narrow-minded and even cruel positivism of the Paris clinics.

While conservative politics inflected hateful, corrosive elements, especially in the virulent association between anti-Semitism and conservative politics in France, the overwhelming presence of human suffering at Lourdes made visits there emotionally compelling. Indeed, after Ruth Harris visited the shrine and found herself assisting a mother with an "adult son who was incontinent, paralysed, blind and deaf," she wrote that the manifestations of suffering at Lourdes, and the compassion for suffering revealed there, enabled her to see "where the appeal of Lourdes lies." She determined to integrate this sense of the shrine's emotional appeal with analysis of its cultural history prior to World War I, when it emerged as a modern pilgrimage center:

Despite the great differences between my experience and that of the nineteenth-century pilgrim, at the core there was the same intense physicality, backbreaking labour, and centrality of pain and suffering. The body in pain was the focus of our collective and personal minis-

trations in a world that was rendered spiritual by ritual. This spirituality was invested in rites such as the Eucharistic processions and
bathing in the pools, activities that seemed to have a timeless, un-
changing character. In fact, they originated out of specific nineteenth-
century conditions, and encapsulated a particular vision of body and
spirit.[42]

In her analysis of healing at Lourdes, Harris identified elements of modern
culture that coexisted with Christianity's sensitivity to and participation in human suffering as an almost timeless reality. In its modern aspect, the "particular vision of body and spirit" that emerged at Lourdes in the nineteenth century centered on a vision of "self" in accounts by believers that "did not
privilege spirit over body; on the contrary, both bathing and taking the Eucharist were rituals that broke down the boundaries between the two." A modern
expression of spirituality was emerging that focused with increasing precision
on the subjective experience of bodily pain. This religious development not
only coincided with the emergence of psychiatry as a medical science focusing
on much the same thing, but also reflected an infusion of scientific and technological ideas into religious experience. Thus, in a familiar image, one ar-
thritic patient felt "as if electrified, an internal strength drove me to rise."[43]

Christian Healing as Response to Suffering

Heightened attention to the self characterizes Christian healing in the modern
era. New investigations into religious experience associated with science co-
incide with increasingly dramatic and compelling ways of expressing emotional
feeling, especially emotional pain. Thus, even as they depersonalize the world
in some ways, science and modern technology also stimulate new ways of
analyzing and experiencing human suffering.

The emotional self and its expressions in bodily pain may be a modern
preoccupation, yet Christian healing has been associated from the beginning
with care for human bodies and with willingness to touch and cleanse them.
Christians have not always believed that Christ suffered; Basil argued in the
fourth century that Christ excelled as the soul's physician because he was not
infected with feelings of suffering as he conveyed the impression of vitality
onto his patients. Yet they have always linked the body of Christ with care for
human suffering. If devotion to the sufferings of Jesus only emerged in the
medieval period as part of increasingly refined explorations of human feeling,
Christian healing has always been directed to human suffering and to bodies—

the body of Christ, the bodies of believers, the body of the church, and frag-
ments and images of the bodies of saints—as sites of transformation and
transcendence.

The symbolism of Christ's body originated in Judaism and brought with
it attitudes toward creation and assumptions about the connection between
suffering and sin in creation, laid out in Hebrew scriptures. As a healing cult
that branched out of Judaism, early Christianity caught on as a way of remedying suffering and explaining it as a consequence of sin, and as a way of
imputing meaning to suffering as the context for personal salvation and communal strength and vitality. One writer put it this way: Christian "is not a
'religious' epithet, it is a cosmic vision."[44]

The beliefs and practices associated with Christian healing changed profoundly through Christianity's expansions and incorporations into many different cultures and through influences derived from numerous sources, including modern science. Yet, persisting through these changes, Christian
healing carried the idea, derived from Judaism, that sin and evil were the cause
of suffering. In some cases, suffering was caused by sinful behavior in the
person who suffered. This was God's way of teaching people to repent and
obey him. In other cases, innocent people suffered because of the sins of others
and the forces of evil surrounding them. Either way, suffering was important
and could be explained, redeemed, and healed.

Contributing both to the development of modern science and to the emergence of a modern sense of self, Christian healing has exerted enormous influence in human history and affected the behavior and thinking of billions of
people. The linkage between suffering and sin prompts Christians to action,
both to combat evil and seek forgiveness of sin within themselves, and to press
for change in other people and in the world around them. In the modern era,
the advent of science and scientific technologies increases the power of Christians to fight against people and forces they perceive to be evil. It also opens
new opportunities to Christians for relieving suffering in the world and for
understanding its material causes, giving people a sense of being at home in
the universe, with the assurance that human suffering matters.

Notes

INTRODUCTION

1. Essays by Edward Schieffelin, Thomas J. Csordas, Robert R. Desjarlais, and Charles L. Briggs, in *The Performance of Healing*, ed. Carol Laderman and Marina Roseman (New York: Routledge, 1996) have been particularly important in the development of my understanding of religious healing.

2. An important source on the history of Christian forgiveness and its relation to healing is John T. McNeill, *A History of the Cure of Souls* (1951; New York: Harper & Row, 1977).

3. John Winthrop, "A Model of Christian Charity" (1629), in *The American Puritans: Their Prose and Poetry*, ed. Perry Miller (New York: Anchor Books, 1956), 83.

4. Catherine Bell, *Ritual Theory, Ritual Practice* (New York: Oxford University Press, 1992), 81–93.

5. Janet Hoskins, "From Diagnosis to Performance: Medical Practice and the Politics of Exchange in Kodi, West Sumba," in Laderman and Roseman, *The Performance of Healing*, 288.

6. Anne Harrington, introduction to *The Placebo Effect: An Interdisciplinary Exploration*, ed. Anne Harrington (Cambridge, MA: Harvard University Press, 1997), 4–6.

7. R. J. Herrnstein, "Placebo Effect in the Rat," *Science* 138 (1962): 677–678.

8. William James, *Varieties of Religious Experience* (1902; New York: New American Library, 1958), 30.

9. For representation of these trends, see Harold G. Koenig, Michael E. McCullough, and David B. Larson, *Handbook of Religion and Health* (New York: Oxford University Press, 2001).

10. Albert S. Lyons and R. Joseph Petrucelli II, *Medicine: An Illustrated History* (New York: Harry N. Abrams, 1987), 164–217, 251–261.

11. Quoted in ibid., 313.

12. Alan K. Shapiro, "The Placebo Effect in the History of Medical Treatment: Implications for Psychiatry," *American Journal of Psychiatry* 116 (1959): 303.

13. Lawrence Power, *San Francisco Chronicle*, March 15, 1978, 24; quoted in Michael Ross and James M. Olson, "Placebo Effects in Medical Research and Practice," *Social Psychology and Behavioral Medicine*, ed. J. Richard Eiser (New York: Wiley, 1982), 442.

14. Harrington, 1–12.

15. Ross and Olson, "Placebo Effects," 445.

16. E. G. Dimond, C. F. Kittle, and J. E. Crockett, "Comparisons of Internal Mammary Artery Ligation and Sham Operation for Angina Pectoris," *American Journal of Cardiology* 5 (1960): 483–486; L. A. Cobb, G. I. Thomas, D. H. Dillard, K. A. Merendino, and E. A. Bruce, "An Evaluation of Internal-Mammary-Artery Ligation by a Double-Blind Technic," *New England Journal of Medicine*, 260 (1959): 1115–1118; Ross and Olson, "Placebo Effects."

17. Jerome Frank, *Persuasion and Healing: A Comparative Study of Psychotherapy*, rev.ed. (1961; Baltimore: Johns Hopkins University Press, 1974), 147.

18. Ibid., 47.

19. Peter Brown, "The Rise and Function of the Holy Man in Late Antiquity" (1971), in Peter Brown, *Society and the Holy in Late Antiquity* (Berkeley: University of California Press, 1982), 142, 147.

20. Peter Brown, *The Cult of the Saints: Its Rise and Function in Latin Christianity* (Chicago: University of Chicago Press, 1981), 83–84.

21. Quoted in John de Cuevas, "Mind/Brain/Behavior: The Pleasing Placebo," available at http://www.med.harvard.edu/publications/Focus/Jan20_1995/Mind.html.

22. E. Ernst and K. L. Resch, "Concept of True and Perceived Placebo Effects," *British Medical Journal* 311, no. 7004 (August 26, 1995): 551–553; Peter C. Gotzsche, "Is There Logic in the Placebo?," *The Lancet* 344, no. 8927 (October 1, 1994): 925–926; Peter C. Gotzsche, "Placebo Effects: Concept of Placebo Should Be Discarded," *The Lancet* 311, no. 7020 (December 16, 1995): 1640–1641.

23. Randolph C. Byrd, "Positive Therapeutic Effects of Intercessory Prayer in a Coronary Care Unit Population," *Southern Medical Journal* 81, no. 7 (July 1988): 826–829; Kwang Y. Cha, Daniel P. Wirth, and Rogerio A. Lobo, "Does Prayer Influence the Success of in Vitro Fertilization-Embryo Transfer?," *Journal of Reproductive Medicine* 46, no. 9 (September 2001): 781–787. For criticism of the methodologies employed by Byrd and others claiming similar findings, see Gary P. Posner, "Study Yields No Evidence for Medical Efficacy of Distant Intercessory Prayer," *Scientific Review of Alternative Medicine* 6, no. 1 (winter 2002): 44–46; Bruce L. Flamm, "Faith Healing by Prayer," *Scientific Review of Alternative Medicine* 6, no. 1 (winter 2002): 47–50; Irwin Tessman and Jack Tessman, "Efficacy of Prayer: A Critical Examination of Claims," *Skeptical Inquirer* 24 (May/June 2000): 31–33. Thanks to Ron Numbers for sending me these articles.

24. Thomas J. Csordas, "Imaginal Performance and Memory in Ritual Healing," in Laderman and Roseman, *The Performance of Healing*, 94.

25. Personal communication from Gene Mills, September 10, 2004.

26. Csordas, "Imaginal Performance," 107–108.

27. Charles L. Briggs, "The Meaning of Nonsense, the Poetics of Embodiment, and the Production of Power in Warao Healing," in Laderman and Roseman, *The Performance of Healing*, 212–217.

CHAPTER I

1. Morton Kelsey, *Healing and Christianity: A Classic Study* (1973; Minneapolis: Fortress Press, 1995), 42–46; also see John J. Pilch, *Healing in the New Testament: Insights from Medical and Mediterranean Anthropology* (Minneapolis: Fortress Press, 2000).

2. Augustine, *Concerning the City of God, Against the Pagans* (413–426), trans. Henry Bettenson, ed. David Knowles (Baltimore: Penguin, 1972), book 22, chap. 8, 1034; book 18, chap. 46, 827.

3. John Meyendorff, *Byzantine Theology: Historical Trends and Doctrinal Themes*, 2nd ed. (New York: Fordham University Press, 1983), 1–15; Dumitru Staniloae, *Orthodox Spirituality: A Practical Guide for the Faithful and a Definitive Manual for the Scholar*, trans. Jerome Newville and Otilia Kloos (South Canaan, PA: St. Tikhon's Seminary Press, 2002), 21–29.

4. Robert Bruce Mullin, *Miracles and the Modern Religious Imagination* (New Haven: Yale University Press, 1996).

5. Martin Luther, "What Fasting Was Like in the Monastery" (1539) and "Questions about Purgatory, Prayer, Free Will" (1538), in *Luther's Works*, vol. 54, *Table Talk*, nos. 4422 and 3695, ed. and trans. Theodore G. Tappert (Philadelphia: Fortress Press, 1967), 340, 266. In "What It Means to Be Delivered to Satan" (1540), no. 5074, Luther declared: "At the time of the apostles miracles still occurred often" (*Table Talk*, 386).

6. John Calvin, *Institutes of the Christian Religion* (1559), 2 vols., trans. John Allen (Philadelphia: Presbyterian Board of Publication, 1909), 1: 182, 2: 479, 2: 467; 1: 185.

7. Albert Schweitzer, *The Quest of the Historical Jesus* (1906 in German), trans. W. Montgomery, J. R. Coates, Susan Cupitt, and John Bowden (Minneapolis: Fortress Press, 2001), 486–487.

8. Albert Schweitzer, *Out of My Life and Thought* (1933), trans. Antje Bultmann Lemke (Baltimore: Johns Hopkins University Press, 1998), 219.

9. Søren Kierkegaard, *The Sickness Unto Death* (1849 in Danish), in *Fear and Trembling and The Sickness Unto Death*, ed. and trans. Walter Lowrie (1941; Garden City, NJ: Doubleday Anchor,1954), 146–147.

10. Rudolph Bultmann, *Jesus Christ and Mythology* (New York: Scribner's, 1958), 63, 61, 53; also see Rudolf Bultmann, *Primitive Christianity in Its Contemporary Setting*, trans. Reginald H. Fuller (Cleveland: Meridian Books, 1956); and Rudolf Bultmann and Five Critics, *Kerygma and Myth: A Theological Debate* (1948 in German),

ed. Hans Werner Bartsch, trans. and rev. Reginald H. Fuller (New York: Harper Torchbook, 1961). For Bultmann's discussion of Kierkegaard, see *Jesus Christ and Mythology*, 55–59.

11. Morton Smith, *Jesus the Magician: Charlatan or Son of God?* (San Francisco: Harper & Collins, 1978), 181; also see Morton Smith, *Clement of Alexandria and the Secret Gospel of Mark* (Cambridge, MA: Harvard University Press, 1973).

12. Smith, *Jesus the Magician*, 10–11.

13. Ibid., 141, 142.

14. Harold Remus, *Jesus as Healer* (Cambridge, UK: Cambridge University Press, 1997), 104–118.

15. Leo Sternberg, "Divine Election in Primitive Religion," in *Compte-Rendu de la XXI session, Pt. 2 (1924)* (Goteborg, Sweden: Congres International des Americanistes, 1925), 472–1925; Mircea Eliade, *Shamanism: Archaic Techniques of Ecstasy* (1951 in French), trans. Willard R. Trask (Princeton: Princeton University Press, 1972), 33–66; C. G. Jung, "Transformation Symbolism in the Mass," in *Collected Works of C. G. Jung*, vol. 11, *Psychology and Religion West and East*, 2nd ed., trans. R. F. C. Hull (Princeton: Princeton University Press, 1969), 227.

16. Remus, *Jesus as Healer*; also see Paula Fredriksen, *From Jesus to Christ: The Origins of the New Testament Images of Jesus* (New Haven: Yale University Press, 1988).

17. Remus, *Jesus as Healer*, 70–91.

18. David Rhoads, Joanna Dewey, and Donald Michie, *Mark as Story: An Introduction to the Narrative of a Gospel*, 2nd ed. (Minneapolis: Fortress Press, 1999), 2, 3–4.

19. Ibid., 4.

20. Christopher D. Marshall, *Faith as a Theme in Mark's Narrative* (Cambridge, UK: Cambridge University Press, 1989), 57–74; also see Adela Yarbro Collins, *The Beginning of the Gospel: Probings of Mark in Context* (Minneapolis: Fortress Press, 1992), 58–61; and James G. Williams, *Gospel against Parable: Mark's Language of Mystery* (Sheffield, UK: Almond Press, 1985).

21. Marshall, *Faith as a Theme*, 59, 58.

22. Ibid., 63, 64.

23. Geza Vermes, *Jesus the Jew: A Historian's Reading of the Gospels* (New York: Macmillan, 1973), 58–69. Also see Norman Cohn, *Cosmos, Chaos and the World to Come: The Ancient Roots of Apocalyptic Faith* (New Haven: Yale University Press, 1993).

24. Elaine Pagels, *The Origin of Satan* (New York: Vintage Books, 1996).

25. Richard A. Horsley, "The Historical Context of Q" and "Israelite Traditions in Q," in Richard A. Horsley with Jonathan A. Draper, *Whoever Hears You Hears Me: Prophets, Performance, and Tradition in Q* (Harrisburg, PA: Trinity Press International, 1999), 46–60, 94–122.

26. John Dominic Crossan, *The Birth of Christianity: Discovering What Happened in the Years Immediately after the Execution of Jesus* (San Francisco: HarperSanFranciso, 1998), 343; also see John Dominic Crossan, *The Historical Jesus: The Life of a Mediterranean Jewish Peasant* (San Francisco: HarperSanFrancisco, 1992).

27. Ben Witherington III, "Jesus the Talking Head: The Jesus of the Jesus Semi-

nar," in *The Jesus Quest: The Third Search for the Jew of Nazareth* (Downers Grove, IL: InterVarsity Press, 1995), 42–57.

28. John P. Meier, *A Marginal Jew: Rethinking the Historical Jesus*, vol. 2, *Mentor, Message, and Miracles* (New York: Doubleday, 1994), 607.

29. Edwin K. Broadhead, "Echoes of an Exorcism in the Fourth Gospel?," *Zeitschrift fur die Neutestamentliche Wissenschaft* 86, nos. 1–2 (1995): 111–119.

30. Meier, *Marginal Jew*, 650–653.

31. Graham H. Twelftree, *Jesus the Exorcist: A Contribution to the Study of the Historical Jesus* (Peabody, MA: Henrickson, 1993), 170.

32. Meier, *Marginal Jew*, 656–657, 648.

33. Twelftree, *Jesus the Exorcist*, 190–207.

34. Christian Strecker, "Jesus and the Demoniacs," in *The Social Setting of Jesus and the Gospels*, ed. Wolfgang Stegemann, Bruce J. Malina, and Gerd Theissen (Minneapolis: Augsburg Fortress, 2002), 120; also see Santiago Guijarro, "The Politics of Exorcism," in *Social Setting*, 159–174.

CHAPTER 2

1. Samuel Hugh Moffett, *A History of Christianity in Asia*, vol. 1, *Beginnings to 1500* (San Francisco: HarperSanFrancisco, 1992), 79.

2. Bengt Sundkler and Christopher Steed, *A History of the Church in Africa* (Cambridge, UK: Cambridge University Press, 2000); Richard C. Foltz, *Religions of the Silk Road: Overland Trade and Cultural Exchange from Antiquity to the Fifteenth Century* (New York: St. Martin's Press, 1999).

3. Adolph von Harnack, "Medicinisches aus der altesten Kirchengeschichte," *Texte und Untersuchungen zur Geschichte der altchristlichen Literatur (TUGAL)* 8, no. 4 (1892): 37–152; Hector Avalos, *Health Care and the Rise of Christianity* (Peabody, MA: Hendrickson, 1999); Rodney Stark, *The Rise of Christianity: How the Obscure, Marginal Jesus Movement Became the Dominant Religious Force in the Western World in a Few Centuries* (San Francisco: HarperCollins, 1996).

4. Darrel W. Amundsen, "Medicine and Faith in Early Christianity," in *Medicine, Society, and Faith in the Ancient and Medieval Worlds* (Baltimore: Johns Hopkins University Press, 1996), 127–157; Michael Dornemann, *Krankheit und Heilung in der Theologie der frühen Kirchenvater* (Tubingen: J.C.B. Mohr, 2003); R. J. S. Barrett-Lennard, *Christian Healing after the New Testament: Some Approaches to Illness in the Second, Third and Fourth Centuries* (Lanham, MD: University Press of America, 1994).

5. Ignatius, bishop of Antioch, "To the Ephesians," in *The Apostolic Fathers: Greek Texts and English Translations*, rev. ed., ed. Michael W. Holmes (Grand Rapids, MI: Baker Books, 1992), 141.

6. "An Ancient Christian Sermon Commonly Known as Second Clement," in Holmes, *Apostolic Fathers*, 121.

7. Shannon Burkes, *God, Self, and Death: The Shape of Religious Transformation in the Second Temple Period* (Leiden: Brill, 2003).

8. Elaine Pagels, *The Origin of Satan* (New York: Vintage, 1996).

9. Wendy Cotter, *Miracles in Greco-Roman Antiquity: A Sourcebook* (New York: Routledge, 1999); Jan N. Bremmer and Jan R. Veenstra, eds., *The Metamorphosis of Magic from Late Antiquity to the Early Modern Period* (Leuven, Belgium: Peeters, 2002), 13–103; Jill Kamil, *Christianity in the Land of the Pharaohs: The Coptic Orthodox Church* (New York: Routledge, 2002).

10. "An Ancient Christian Sermon" (commonly but erroneously attributed to Clement), in Holmes, *Apostolic Fathers*, 115.

11. Barrett-Lennard, *Christian Healing*, 9–41, 85–86, 31 n. 129.

12. Stanley Samuel Harakas, "The Eastern Orthodox Tradition," in *Caring and Curing: Health and Medicine in the Western Religious Tradition*, ed. Ronald L. Numbers and Darrel W. Amundsen (Baltimore: Johns Hopkins University Press, 1986), 151.

13. Avalos, *Health Care*, esp. 21.

14. Dionysius, "Festival Letters" in Eusebius, *The Church History*, trans. and ed. Paul L. Maier (Grand Rapids, MI: Kregel, 1999), 269.

15. Ibid.

16. Eusebius, *Church History*, 328–329.

17. Stark, *Rise of Christianity*, 73–94.

18. Ibid., 93, 94.

19. Ignatius, "To the Ephesians" and "To the Romans," in Holmes, *Apostolic Fathers*, 141, 139, 173.

20. Timothy S. Miller, *The Birth of the Hospital in the Byzantine Empire*, rev. ed. (1985; Baltimore: Johns Hopkins University Press, 1997).

21. Moffett, *Christianity in Asia*, 186, 187.

22. Arthur Voobus, *History of the School of Nisibis* (Louvain, Belgium: Secretariat du Corpus SCO, 1965), 1–5, 144–145, 283.

23. Moffett, *Christianity in Asia*, 299–300, 297. Also see P. Yoshiro Saeki, *The Nestorian Documents and Relics in China* (Toyko: Maruzen Company, 1951); A. C. Moule, *Christians in China before the Year 1550* (London: Society for Promoting Christian Knowledge, 1930).

24. Miller, *Birth of the Hospital*, 52–61, 86; Dornemann, *Krankheit und Heilung* 195–218.

25. Amundsen, "Medicine and Faith,"142.

26. Basil, "Homily on the Words, 'Give Heed to Thyself,'" trans. M. Monica Wagner, in *Writings of Saint Basil*, vol. 1 (New York: Fathers of the Church, 1950), 436.

27. Dornemann, *Krankheit und Heilung*, 204–207, esp. n. 129. Thanks to David Levenron for help translating Basil and Hippocrates.

28. Irenaeus, *Against Heresies*, book 5, chaps. 8, 12–13; quotation from book 2, chap. 32, 4; Barrett-Lennard, *Christian Healing*, 96, 99, 116–117.

29. For example, Hans Jonas, *The Gnostic Religion: The Message of the Alien God and the Beginnings of Christinaity*, 2nd ed. (Boston: Beacon Press, 1958).

30. Elaine Pagels, *The Gnostic Gospels* (New York: Random House, 1979).

31. W. H. C. Frend, *The Rise of Christianity* (Philadelphia: Fortress Press, 1984), 194–218, esp. 212–217.

32. C. Kingsley Barrett, "John and Judaism," in *Anti-Judaism in the Fourth Gospel*,

ed. Reimund Bieringer, Didier Pollefeyt, and Frederique Vandecasteele-Vanneuville (Louisville, KY: Westminster John Knox Press, 2001), 231–246, esp. 232–237.

33. Barrett-Lennard, *Christian Healing*, 96.

34. Elaine Pagels, *Adam, Eve, and the Serpent* (New York: Random House, 1988), 16–18.

35. Jean Danielou, *Gospel Message and Hellenistic Culture*, trans. J. A. Baker (Philadelphia: Westminster, 1973), 396; Amundsen, "Medicine and Faith," 127–157.

36. Troels Engberg-Pedersen, *Paul and the Stoics* (Louisville, KY: Westminster John Knox Press, 2000).

37. John G. Gager, *Reinventing Paul* (New York: Oxford University Press, 2000), 61. Like many recent historians, Gaeger rejected the theory, advanced in the nineteenth century by D. F. Strauss, F. C. Baur, and other members of the Tubingen school of New Testament interpretation, that a conflict existed between a Gentile faction of the early church associated with Paul and a Jewish faction associated with Peter.

38. "The Epistle of Barnabas, in Holmes, *Apostolic Fathers*, 289.

39. Peter Cramer, *Baptism and Change in the Early Middle Ages, c. 200–c. 1150* (Cambridge, UK: Cambridge University Press, 1993), 9–45. For the earliest source of directives on baptism outside the New Testament, see the late first-century *Didache* or *The Teaching of the Twelve Apostles* in Holmes, *Apostolic Fathers*, 259. For baptism in Syria, see Moffett, *Christianity in Asia*, 55.

40. "The Epistle of Barnabas," in Holmes, *Apostolic Fathers*, 259; and the early third-century Hippolytus, *Apostolic Tradition*, ed. B. Botte (Munster-in-Westfalen: Liturgiewissenschaftliche Quellen and Forschungen, 1963), 275.

41. Wayne A. Meeks, *The First Urban Christians: The Social World of the Apostle Paul* (New Haven: Yale University Press, 1983), 150–157, esp. 153; G. R. Beasley-Murray, *Baptism in the New Testament* (1962; Grand Rapids, MI: William B. Eerdmans, 1994).

42. S. V. MacCasland, *By the Finger of God: Demon-Possession and Exorcism in Early Christianity in Light of Modern Views on Mental Illness* (New York: Macmillan, 1951), 104.

43. Ramsay MacMullen, *Christianizing the Roman Empire A.D. 100–400* (New Haven: Yale University Press, 1984), 28, 62.

44. Athanasius, *The Life of Antony and the Letter to Marcellinus*, trans. Robert C. Gregg (Mahwah, NJ: Paulist Press, 1980), 38, 41, 42.

45. Georgia Frank, " 'Taste and See': The Eucharist and the Eyes of Faith in the Fourth Century," *Church History: Studies in Christianity and Culture* 70, no. 4 (December 2001): 619.

CHAPTER 3

1. Gregory of Tours, *The History of the Franks*, trans. Lewis Thorpe (London: Penguin Books, 1974), 333, 335.

2. Darrel W. Amundsen, *Medicine, Society, and Faith in the Ancient and Medieval*

Worlds (Baltimore: Johns Hopkins University Press, 1996), 191; also see Patrick J. Geary, *Before France and Germany: The Creation and Transformation of the Merovingian World* (New York: Oxford University Press, 1988); James C. Russell, *The Germanization of Early Medieval Christianity: A Sociohistorical Approach to Religious Transformation* (New York: Oxford University Press, 1994).

3. Bede, *Ecclesiastical History of the English People*, trans. Leo Sherley-Price, rev. R. E. Latham (orig. trans. 1955; London: Penguin Books, 1990), book 3, chap. 9, 157–158.

4. Valerie I. J. Flint, *The Rise of Magic in Early Medieval Europe* (Princeton: Princeton University Press, 1991), n. 30, 184.

5. Barbara Abou-El-Haj, *The Medieval Cult of the Saints: Formations and Transformations* (Cambridge, UK: Cambridge University Press, 1997), 50; also see 3.

6. Ronald C. Finucane, *Miracles and Pilgrims: Popular Beliefs in Medieval England* (1977; New York: St. Martin's Press, 1995), 69.

7. Gregory of Tours, *History of the Franks*, 263–264.

8. Darrel W. Amundsen, "The Medieval Catholic Tradition," in *Caring and Curing: Health and Medicine in the Western Religious Traditions*, ed. Ronald L. Numbers and Darrel W. Amundsen (1986; Baltimore: Johns Hopkins University Press, 1998), 82.

9. Flint, *Rise of Magic*, 163; Finucane, *Miracles and Pilgrims*, 68.

10. Flint, *Rise of Magic*, 150; Finucane, *Miracles and Pilgrims*, 67.

11. Flint, *Rise of Magic*, 89.

12. Ibid., 187–192.

13. See discussion of the unfortunate "leakage of reality" that Edward Gibbon, in *The Decline and Fall of the Roman Empire* (1914) perceived to characterize the early medieval era in Peter Brown, "Gibbon's Views on Culture and Society in the Fifth and Sixth Centuries" (1976), in *Society and the Holy in Late Antiquity* (Berkeley: University of California Press, 1982), 22–48.

14. Miri Rubin, *Corpus Christi: The Eucharist in Late Medieval Culture* (Cambridge, UK: Cambridge University Press, 1991), 112.

15. In his classic discussion of the relationship between magic and science, Bronislaw Malinowski emphasized that magic was guided by desire, whereas science was less subjective and emotional. But he also pointed out that "magic is akin to science in that it always has a definite aim intimately associated with human instincts, needs, and pursuits." Although Malinowski minimized some of the important differences between scientific and magical reasoning, his insight into magic as a forerunner to science is suggestive. Bronislaw Malinowski, "Magic, Science, and Religion" (1925), in *Magic, Science, and Religion and Other Essays* (Garden City, NJ: Doubleday Anchor Books, 1954), 86.

16. Florence Eliza Glaze, "Medical Writer," in *Voice of the Living Light: Hildegard of Bingen and Her World*, ed. Barbara Newman (Berkeley: University of California Press, 1998), 136. Also see Sabina Flanagan, *Hildegard of Bingen, 1098–1179: A Visonary Life*, 2nd ed. (New York: Routledge, 1998).

17. Hildegard von Bingen, *Physica*, trans. Priscilla Throop (Rochester, VT: Healing Arts Press, 1998), 229, 60.

18. Quoted in Glaze, "Medical Writer," 125.

19. Timothy S. Miller, *The Birth of the Hospital in the Byzantine Empire* (1985; Baltimore: Johns Hopkins University Press, 1997), 97.

20. John Meyendorff, *Byzantine Theology: Historical Trends and Doctrinal Themes* (New York: Fordham University Press, 1974), 1–15; Elaine Pagels, *Adam, Eve, and the Serpent* (New York: Random House, 1988), 116, 124–125.

21. Meyendorff, *Byzantine Theology*, 6; Jaroslav Pelikan, *The Spirit of Eastern Christendom (600–1700)*, vol. 2, *The Christian Tradition: A History of the Development of Doctrine* (Chicago: University of Chicago Press, 1974).

22. Miller, *Birth of the Hospital*, 57, 111.

23. Ibid., 100–110, 182–185.

24. Demetrios J. Constantelos, *Byzantine Philanthropy and Social Welfare* (New Brunswick, NJ: Rutgers University Press, 1968), 152, 153.

25. J. F. Haldon, *Byzantium: The Transformation of a Culture*, rev. ed. (Cambridge, UK: Cambridge University Press, 1990), 403–435.

26. Leslie Brubaker, *Vision and Meaning in Ninth-Century Byzantium: Image as Exegesis in the Homilies of Gregory of Nazianzus* (Cambridge, UK: Cambridge University Press, 1999), 20, 28–29.

27. John Julius Norwich, *A Short History of Byzantium* (New York: Knopf, 1997), 109–141; Ken Parry et al., eds., *The Blackwell Dictionary of Eastern Christianity* (Oxford: Blackwell, 1999), 325–326.

28. John McManners, ed. *The Oxford History of Christianity* (New York: Oxford University Press, 1993), 150.

29. Dumitru Staniloae, *Orthodox Spirituality: A Practical Guide for the Faithful and a Definitive Manual for the Scholar*, trans. Jerome Newville and Otilia Kloos (South Canaan, PA: St. Tikhon's Seminary Press, 2002), 21–39.

30. Amundsen, "Medieval Catholic Tradition," 83; also see C. H. Lawrence, *Medieval Monasticism*, 3rd ed. (1984; Harlow, UK: Longman, 2001), 117–119.

31. Described in Glaze, "Medical Writer," 127.

32. Stanley Samuel Harakas, "The Eastern Orthodox Tradition," in Numbers and Amundsen, *Caring and Curing*, 155.

33. Darrel W. Amundsen, "Medieval Canon Law on Medical and Surgical Practice by the Clergy," *Bulletin of the History of Medicine* 52 (1978): 22–44; Nancy G. Siraisi, *Medieval and Early Renaissance Medicine: An Introduction to Knowledge and Practice* (Chicago: University of Chicago Press, 1990), 13–14.

34. Peter Brown, "The Holy Man in Late Antiquity" (1971), in *Society and the Holy in Late Antiquity* (Berkeley: University of California Press, 1982), 103–152.

35. Marilyn Dunn, *The Emergence of Monasticism: From the Desert Fathers to the Early Middle Ages* (Oxford: Blackwell, 2000); Lawrence, *Medieval Monasticism*; Herbert Grundmann, *Religious Movements in the Middle Ages: The Historical Links between Heresy, the Mendicant Orders, and the Women's Religious Movement in the Twelfth and Thirteenth Century, with the Historical Foundations of German Mysticism* (1935 in German), trans. Steven Rowan (Notre Dame, IN: University of Notre Dame Press, 1995).

36. Basil, "Homily on the Words, 'Give Heed to Thyself,'" in *Writings of Saint*

Basil, vol. 1, *Ascetical Works*, trans. M. Monica Wagner (New York: Fathers of the Church, 1950), 436.

37. Lisa M. Bitel, *Isle of the Saints: Monastic Settlement and Christian Community in Early Ireland* (Ithaca, NY: Cornell University Press, 1990).

38. Quoted and translated in Dunn, *Emergence of Monasticism*, 169–170.

39. For discussion of the historical development of the system of penance and its growing arbitrariness, see Thomas N. Tentler, *Sin and Confession on the Eve of the Reformation* (Princeton: Princeton University Press, 1977).

40. Gregory of Tours, *History of the Franks*, 497–498.

41. Translated and quoted in Russell, *Germanization*, 195.

42. Peter Cramer, *Baptism and Change in the Early Middle Ages, c. 200–c.1150* (Cambridge, UK: Cambridge University Press, 1993), 179.

43. Ibid., 143–145.

44. See Flint, *Rise of Magic*, 168–172.

45. Finucane, *Miracles and Pilgrims*, 72.

46. Donald Weinstein and Rudoph M. Bell, *Saints and Society: The Two Worlds of Western Christendom, 1000–1700* (Chicago: University of Chicago Press, 1982), 124.

47. Flanagan, *Hildegard*, 160–165.

48. Larry W. Hurtado, *At the Origins of Christian Worship: The Context and Character of Earliest Christian Devotion* (Grand Rapids, MI: William B. Eerdmans, 2000), 59; Paul Bradshaw, *Early Christian Worship: A Basic Introduction to Ideas and Practice* (Collegeville, MN: Liturgical Press, 1996), 64.

49. Meyendorff, *Byzantine Theology*, 204, 205; Pelikan, *Spirit of Eastern Christendom*.

50. Rubin, *Corpus Christi*, 143, 339.

51. Dmitri Obolensky, *The Byzantine Commonwealth: Eastern Europe, 500–1453* (New York: Praeger, 1971), illus. 46, ff., 210.

52. Caroline Walker Bynum, *Holy Feast and Holy Fast: The Religious Significance of Food to Medieval Women* (Berkeley: University of California Press, 1987), 172–173; also see Rubin, *Corpus Christi*, 302–316.

53. Robert E. Lerner, "Introduction to the Translation," in Grundmann, *Religious Movements*, xxi–xxiv.

54. Christopher J. Kauffman, *Tamers of Death: The History of the Alexian Brothers from 1300 to 1789* (New York: Seabury Press, 1976), 142–143.

CHAPTER 4

1. Carlos Eire, *War against the Idols: The Reformation of Worship from Erasmus to Calvin* (New York: Cambridge University Press, 1986), 13.

2. Kenneth Scott Latourette, *A History of Christianity*, vol. 2, rev. ed, A.D. 1500–A.D. 1975 (San Francisco: HarperSanFrancisco, 1975), 923–966.

3. Eire, *War against the Idols*, 37–38, 95.

4. Peter Matheson, *The Imaginative World of the Reformation* (Minneapolis: Fortress Press, 2001), 7.

5. Keith Thomas, *Religion and the Decline of Magic* (New York: Scribner's, 1971), 125–128.

6. John Calvin, *Calvin: Institutes of the Christian Religion* (1559), in *Library of Christian Classics*, vol. 20, trans. Ford Lewis Battles, ed. John T. McNeill (Louisville, KY: Westminster John Knox Press, 1960), book 4, chap. 3, 1061.

7. Ibid.

8. Ibid., book 4, chap. 10, 1203.

9. Martin Luther, *Luther's Works*, ed. J. Pelikan et al. (St. Louis: Fortress Press, 1955), 40: 146; Eire, *War against the Idols*, 65–86.

10. Eire, *War against the Idols*, 224.

11. Calvin, *Institutes*, book 1, chap. 17, 223.

12. William J. Bouwsma, *John Calvin: A Sixteenth Century Portrait* (New York: Oxford University Press, 1988), 32; also see Ronald S. Wallace, *Calvin, Geneva and the Reformation: A Study of Calvin as Social Reformer, Churchman, Pastor and Theologian* (Edinburgh: Scottish Academic Press, 1988).

13. Euan Cameron, *The European Reformation* (New York: Oxford University Press, 1991), 64–69; Bouwsma, *John Calvin*, 12–15; Hugh R. Trevor-Roper, *Religion, the Reformation, and Social Change* (New York: Harper & Row, 1967).

14. Eire, *War against the Idols*, 43, 2–3; Ronald S. Wallace, *Calvin's Doctrine of the Word and Sacrament* (Eugene, OR: Wipf and Stock Publishers, 1997), 1–2.

15. Calvin, *Institutes*, book 2, chap. 1; book 1, chap. 17, 250, 224.

16. Ibid., book 2, chap. 1; book 3, chap. 1, 242, 537. The worldwide restoration of God's creation was already beginning, as promised in the Second and Seventy-second Psalms: "The nations have been made his inheritance, and the ends of the earth his property that he may have unbroken dominion from sea to sea, and from the rivers even to the ends of the earth" (book 2, chap. 11, 461).

17. Ibid., book 3, chap. 8, 706.

18. John Calvin, "Commentary on 1 John 1:1," quoted in Wallace, *Calvin's Doctine*, 18.

19. Wallace, *Calvin's Doctrine*, 197–210, 237–242.

20. Calvin, *Institutes*, book 3, chap. 8, 706. See Thomas N. Tentler, *Sin and Confession on the Eve of the Reformation* (Princeton: Princeton University Press, 1977), esp. 3–27, 345–370.

21. Tentler, *Sin and Confession*, 263–264. In denying priests the power of the keys, Calvin followed Luther. Although he never entirely rejected the practice of private confession, Calvin went further than Luther in lack of enthusiasm for it. Luther emphasized the importance of the pastor's ritual pronouncement of the promise of absolution in Christ as an essential consolation; Calvin did not (349–363).

22. Herbert Grundmann, *Religious Movements in the Middle Ages: The Historical Links between Heresy, the Mendicant Orders, and the Women's Religious Movement in the Twelfth and Thirteenth Century, with the Historical Foundations of German Mysticism* (1935 in German), trans. Steven Rowan (Notre Dame, IN: University of Notre Dame Press, 1995); Caroline Walker Bynum, *Holy Feast and Holy Fast: The Religious Significance of Food to Medieval Women* (Berkeley: University of California Press, 1987).

23. Peter Iver Kaufman, *Prayer, Despair, and Drama: Elizabethan Introspection* (Urbana: University of Illinois Press, 1996), 103–143. Also see Barbara Kiefer Lewalski, *Protestant Poetics and the Seventeenth-Century Religious Lyric* (Princeton: Princeton University Press, 1979); and William H. Halewood, *The Poetry of Grace: Reformation Themes and Structures in English Seventeenth-Century Poetry* (New Haven: Yale University Press, 1970).

24. Albert S. Lyons and R. Joseph Petrucelli II, *Medicine: An Illustrated History* (New York: Harry N. Abrams, 1978), 456.

25. Michael MacDonald, "Psychological Healing in England, 1600–1800," in *The Church and Healing*, ed. W. J. Sheils (Oxford: Basil Blackwell, 1982), 116.

26. Democritus Junior [Robert Burton], *The Anatomy of Melancholy: What it is, with all the kinds, causes, symptoms, prognostics & several cures of it* (1621; London, 1652), 661.

27. Ibid., 738–739.

28. Mary Lindemann, *Medicine and Society in Early Modern Europe* (Cambridge, UK: Cambridge University Press, 1999), 71–74.

29. Michel Foucault, *Madness and Civilization: A History of Insanity in the Age of Reason* (New York: Random House, 1965).

30. Burton, "The Author's Abstract of Melancholy," in *Anatomy of Melancholy*, n.p.

31. Thomas Glanvill, *Saducismus triumphatus: or, full and plain evidence concerning witches and apparitions*, 3rd ed. (1689), ed. C. O. Parsons (Gainesville: University of Florida Press, 1966), 62; Stuart Clark, *Thinking with Demons: The Idea of Witchcraft in Early Modern Europe* (New York: Oxford University Press, 1997), 303.

32. Walter Stephens, *Demon Lovers: Witchcraft, Sex, and the Crisis of Belief* (Chicago: University of Chicago Press, 2002), 30–31; also see Clark, *Thinking with Demons*, 294–311; Armando Maggi, *Satan's Rhetoric: A Study of Renaissance Demonology* (Chicago: University of Chicago Press, 2001).

33. John W. O'Malley, *The First Jesuits* (Cambridge, MA: Harvard University Press, 1993), 38, 37; George E. Ganss, ed., *Ignatius of Loyola: The Spiritual Exercises and Selected Works*, (New York: Paulist Press, 1991), paragraph 1.

34. Cameron, *European Reformation*, 46–47.

35. Jill Raitt, "Calvin's Use of Bernard of Clairvaux," *Archive for Reformation History* 72 (1981): 98–121; Dennis E. Tamburello, *Union with Christ: John Calvin and the Mysticism of St. Bernard* (Louisville, KY: Westminster John Knox Press, 1994).

36. Christopher J. Kauffman, *Tamers of Death: The History of the Alexian Brothers from 1300 to 1789* (New York: Seabury Press, 1976), 121–128, 162.

37. Martin Luther, *Luther's Works*, 40, I, 282, 21–23, quoted in Marc Lienhard, "Luther and the Beginnings of the Reformation," in *Christian Spirituality: High Middle Ages and Reformation*, ed. Jill Raitt (New York: Crossroad, 1987), 277. Also see Martin Luther, "Lectures on Romans," in *Luther's Works*, vol. 25.

38. Nicholas Orme and Margaret Webster, *The English Hospital 1070–1570* (New Haven: Yale University Press, 1995), 150–166.

39. Martin Luther, *Luther's Works*, 43: 131, cited in Carter Lindberg, "The Lutheran Tradition," in *Caring and Curing: Health and Medicine in the Western Religious*

Traditions, ed. Ronald L. Numbers and Darrel W. Amundsen (1986; Baltimore: Johns Hopkins University Press, 1998), 181–182, 190–195.

40. Quoted in Lindberg, "Lutheran Tradition," 178; see 173–203.

41. Joanna Moody, ed.. *The Private Life of an Elizabethan Lady: The Diary of Lady Margaret Hoby, 1599–1605* (Phoenix Mill, Gloucesteshire, UK: Sutton Publishing, 1998), esp. 45–46, 75, 224.

42. Thomas, *Religion and the Decline of Magic*, 10.

43. Ibid., 190, 192.

44. Lindberg, "Lutheran Tradition," 180; Lindemann, *Medicine and Society*, 75–77.

45. Francis Bacon, "Preface," in *History of the Winds* (1623), quoted in Joseph Needham, "Mysticism and Empiricism in Philosophy of Science," in *Science, Medicine and History: Essays on the Evolution of Scientific Thought and Medical Practice Written in Honour of Charles Singer*, 2 vols., ed. E. Ashworth Underwood (London: Oxford University Press, 1953), 2: 382. Luther, *Luther's Works*, 5: 163, quoted in Lindberg, "Lutheran Tradition," 180. Also see Lindemann, *Medicine and Society*, 76.

46. Lindemann, *Medicine and Society*, 231.

47. Max Weber, *The Protestant Ethic and the Spirit of Capitalism* (1904–1905), trans. Talcott Parsons (New York: Scribner's, 1958).

48. C. John Sommerville, *The Secularization of Early Modern England: From Religious Culture to Religious Faith* (New York: Oxford University Press, 1992), 4. Also see Patrick Collinson, *The Birthpangs of Protestant England: Religious and Cultural Change in the Sixteenth and Seventeenth Centuries* (New York: St. Martin's Press, 1988); and Thomas, *Religion and the Decline of Magic*, to which Sommerville and many other scholars of religion in early modern society are indebted.

CHAPTER 5

1. Kenneth Scott Latourette, *A History of Christianity*, vol. 2, A.D. 1500–A.D. 1975 (San Francisco: HarperSanFrancisco, 1975); Andrew F. Walls, *The Missionary Movement in Christian History* (Maryknoll, NY: Orbis Books, 1996); David Chidester, *Christianity: A Global History* (San Francisco: HarperSanFrancisco, 2000); Stephen Neill, *A History of Christian Missions* (1964; London: Penguin Books, 1990); Dana L. Robert, *American Women in Mission: A Social History of Their Thought and Practice* (Macon, GA: Mercer University Press, 1997); Amanda Porterfield, *Mary Lyon and the Mount Holyoke Missionaries* (New York: Oxford University Press, 1997); Clifton Jackson Phillips, *Protestant America and the Pagan World: The First Half Century of the American Board of Commissioners for Foreign Missions, 1810–1860* (Cambridge, MA: Harvard University Press, 1969).

2. Mark A. Noll, *America's God: From Jonathan Edwards to Abraham Lincoln* (New York: Oxford University Press, 2002).

3. R. V. Modak, "History of the Native Churches Connected with the Marathi Mission," in *Memorial Papers of the American Marathi Mission, 1813–1881* (Bombay: Education Society's Press, 1882), 11.

4. Robert Hume, untitled report, *Dynanodya* 4, no. 12 (June 16, 1845).

5. Samuel Hugh Moffett, *A History of Christianity in Asia*, vol. 1, *Beginnings to 1500* (San Francisco: HarperSanFrancisco, 1992), 25–36.

6. Matteo Ricci quoted in Jonathan D. Spence, *The Memory Palace of Matteo Ricci* (New York: Penguin Books, 1984), 60.

7. Albert Schweitzer, "On the Edge of the Primeval Forest," *The Primeval Forest*, trans. W. Montgomery, J. R. Coates, Susan Cupitt, and John Bowden (Minneapolis: Fortress Press, 2001), 116.

8. Quoted in James D. Knowles, *Memoir of Ann H. Judson, Missionary to Burmah* (Boston: Gould, Kendall, and Lincoln, 1850), 162–163.

9. Johannes Du Plessis, *A History of Christian Missions in South Africa* (1911; Cape Town: C. Struik, 1965), 306; Lewis Grout, *Zulu-Land; or Life Among the Zulu-Kafirs of Natal and Zulu-Land, South Africa* (Philadelphia: Presbyterian Publication Committee, 1864), 217–218.

10. Rubem A. Alves, *A Theology of Human Hope* (Washington, DC: Corpus Books, 1969), 149–151.

11. Ibid., 149.

12. Andrew F. Walls, *The Cross-Cultural Process in Christian History* (Maryknoll, NY: Orbis Books, 2002), 121–133.

13. Amanda Porterfield, "Witchcraft and the Colonization of Algonquian and Iroquois Cultures," *Religion and American Culture: A Journal of Interpretation* 2, no. 1 (February 1992): 103–125.

14. Bruce G. Trigger, *The Children of Aataentsic: A History of the Huron People to 1660* (1976; Kingston, Canada: McGill-Queen's University Press, 1987), 590–593.

15. Ibid., 593, 723.

16. Christopher Vecsey, *The Paths of Kateri's Kin* (Notre Dame, IN: University of Notre Dame Press, 1997), 96–108; K. I. Koppedrayer, "The Making of the First Iroquois Virgin: Early Jesuit Biographies of the Blessed Kateri Tekakwitha," *Ethnohistory* 40 (1993): 277–306; Allan Greer, *Mohawk Saint: Catherine Tekakwitha and the Jesuits* (New York: Oxford University Pres, 2005).

17. Claudia McDonnell, "Kateri Tekakwitha, Native Americans' Gift to the Church," *St. Anthony Messenger* (July 1987) cited in Vecsey, *Kateri's Kin*, 103–104.

18. Anthony F. C. Wallace, "The Dekanawidah Myth Analyzed as the Record of a Revitalization Movement," *Ethnohistory* 5 1958: 118–130; Dean R. Snow, *The Iroquois* (Malden, MA: Blackwell, 1994), 52–76.

19. Anthony F. C. Wallace, *The Death and Rebirth of the Seneca* (New York: Vintage Books, 1972), 239–302.

20. Michael Hittman, Wovoka and the Ghost Dance, ed. Don Lynch, expanded ed. (Lincoln: University of Nebraska Press, 1997); Alice Kehoe, *The Ghost Dance: Ethnohistory and Revitalization* (Ft. Worth, TX: Holt, Rinehart, and Winston, 1989), 3–26.

21. Clyde Holler, ed., *The Black Elk Reader* (Syracuse, NY: Syracuse University Press, 2000); also see Joseph G. Jorgensen, *The Sun Dance Religion: Power for the Powerless* (Chicago: University of Chicago Press, 1974).

22. Joseph Epes Brown, ed., *The Sacred Pipe: Black Elk's Account of the Seven Rites of the Oglala Sioux* (1953; Norman: University of Oklahoma Press, 1974), 31.

23. Ibid., xx.

24. Robert P. Weller, *Resistance, Chaos and Control in China: Taiping Rebels, Taiwanese Ghosts and Tiananmen* (Seattle: University of Washington Press, 1994), 64–68.

25. Jonathan D. Spence, *God's Chinese Son: The Taiping Heavenly Kingdom of Hong Xiuquan* (New York: Norton, 1996); Weller, *Resistance*; Robert H. T. Lin, *The Taiping Revolution: A Failure of Two Missions* (Washington, DC: University Press of America, 1979).

26. Shelia S. Walker, "The Message as the Medium: The Harrist Churches of the Ivory Coast and Ghana," in *African Christianity: Patterns of Religious Continuity*, ed. George Bond, Walton Johnson, and Sheila S. Walker (New York: Academic Press, 1979), 9–32.

27. Ibid., 25–64, esp. 25–26.

28. Ibid., 26.

29. See, for example, Terence O. Ranger and John Weller, eds., *Themes in the Christian History of Central Africa* (Berkeley: University of California Press, 1975); Lyn S. Graybill, *Religion and Resistance Politics in South Africa* (Westport, CT: Praeger, 1995); and Bond et al., *African Christianity*.

30. Bengt G. M. Sundkler, *Bantu Prophets in South Africa* (1948; London: Oxford University Press, 1961), 297, 301; Norman Etherington, *Preachers, Peasants, and Politics in Southeast Africa, 1835–1880: African Christian Communities in Natal, Pondoland, and Zululand* (London: Royal Historical Society, 1978); Walls, *Cross-Cultural Process*, 123.

31. Terence Ranger, "Medical Science and Pentecost," in *The Church and Healing*, ed. W. J. Shiels (Oxford: Basil Blackwell, 1982), 333–365; Walls, *The Cross-Cultural Process*; Philip Jenkins, *The Next Christendom: The Coming of Global Christianity* (New York: Oxford University Press, 2002); Harvey Cox, *Fire from Heaven: The Rise of Pentecostal Spirituality and the Reshaping of Religion in the Twenty-First Century* (Cambridge, MA: Da Capo Press, 1995).

32. Patrick Kwesha, unpublished notebook, trans. Emilia Chiteka, in Ranger, "Medical Science and Pentecost," 351.

33. Ibid.

34. Sundkler, *Bantu Prophets*.

35. Thomas Karis and Gwendolen M. Carter, eds., *From Protest to Challenge: A Documentary History of African Politics in South Africa 1882–1964*, vol. 4, *Political Profiles* (Stanford: Hoover Institution Press, 1977), 60–63.

36. Graybill, *Religion and Resistance Politics*, 45–96.

37. Desmond Tutu, interview with Ray Suarez, June 2, 1999, *Online Newshour*, available at www.PBS.org.

CHAPTER 6

1. George B. Stevens, *The Life, Letters, and Journals of the Reverend and Honorable Peter Parker, M.D., Missionary, Physician, Diplomatist, the Father of Medical Missions, and Founder of the Ophthalmic Hospital in Canton* (Boston: Congregational Sunday

School and Publishing Society, 1896), 82; Theron Kue-Hing Young, "A Conflict of Professions: The Medical Missionary in China, 1835–1890," *Bulletin of the History of Medicine* 47, no. 3 (1973): 253–254.

2. Stevens, *Parker*, III; letter of January 22, 1846, from I. W. Newton Young to Rufus Anderson, in W. W. Cadbury and Mary H. Jones, *At the Point of a Lancet: One Hundred Years of the Canton Hospital* (Shanghai: Kelly, 1935), 96–98; Young, "Conflict of Professions," 253, 255.

3. William Lockhart, *The Medical Missionary in China, a Narrative of Twenty Years Experience* (London: Hurst & Blackett, 1861), vi, 115; Young, "A Conflict of Professions," 259–260.

4. John V. Pickstone, "Establishment and Dissent in Nineteenth-Century Medicine: An Exploration of Some Correspondence and Connections between Religious and Medical Belief-Systems in early Industrial England," in *The Church and Healing*, ed. W. J. Shiels (Oxford: Basil Blackwell, 1982), 165–189; Michel Foucault, *The Birth of the Clinic: An Archeology of Medical Perception* (New York: Vintage Books, 1975).

5. C. Peter Williams, "Healing and Evangelism: The Place of Medicine in Later Victorian Protestant Missionary Thinking," in Shiels, *The Church and Healing*, 271.

6. Andrew F. Walls, "The Nineteenth-Century Medical Missionary,"in Shiels, *The Church and Healing*, 288.

7. John Lowe, *Medical Missions: Their Place and Power* (London, 1886), 10–11; James Johnston, ed., *Report of the Centenary Conference on the Protestant Missions of the World, London 1888*, 2 vols., (London, 1889), 1: 389; Williams, "Healing and Evangelism," 281, 282.

8. In 1904, an article describing the need for missionaries in the northern Congo province of Gabon caught Schweitzer's attention. As he recalled, "The writer expressed the hope that his appeal would bring some of those 'on whom the Master's eyes already rested' to a decision to offer themselves for this urgent work." Inspired by this call, but aware that his liberal interpretations of scripture would cause most missionary societies to balk at sending him out as a preacher, Schweitzer resigned his seminary post to pursue medical study. Faced with resistance from family, friends, and colleagues who urged him not to throw away career and health, he tried to explain his commitment to missionary work by appealing to the sayings of Jesus. To his consternation, others questioned his motivations. As he lamented, reference "to the obedience that Jesus' command of love requires under certain circumstances earned me an accusation of conceit. How I suffered to see so many people assuming the right to tear open the doors and shutters to my inner self!" Schweitzer went ahead with his plans undeterred, but not oblivious to the question of whether giving up one's life to God and loving service of others could coexist with mental health. In the dissertation that culminated his medical study, he reviewed psychiatric studies of Jesus and concluded that "Jesus' high estimation of Himself and possible hallucinations at the time of his baptism—were far from sufficient to prove the presence of any medical disease." Albert Schweitzer, *Out of My Life and Thought* (1933 in German), trans. Antje Bultmann Lemke (Baltimore: Johns Hopkins University Press, 1998), 87, 108, 85.

9. Albert Schweitzer, *The Quest of the Historical Jesus* (1906 in German), trans.

W. Montgomery, J. R. Coates, Susan Cupitt, and John Bowden (Minneapolis: Fortress Press, 2001), 486–487.

10. Albert Schweitzer, "On the Edge of the Primeval Forest" (1931 in German), trans. C. T. Campion, in *The Primeval Forest* (Baltimore: Johns Hopkins University Press, 1998), 126, 128.

11. Schweitzer, *Out of My Life*, 228–232.

12. Schweitzer, "On the Edge," 127, 114.

13. Schweitzer, *Quest*, 487.

14. John Farley, *Bilharzia: A History of Imperial Tropical Medicine* (Cambridge, UK: Cambridge University Press, 1991); Michael Worboys, "The Colonial World as Mission and Mandate: Leprosy and Empire, 1900–1940," *Osiris* 15 (2001): 207–218.

15. Worboys, "Colonial World," 210.

16. Paul F. Basch, *Textbook of International Health*, 2nd ed. (New York: Oxford University Press, 1999), 329.

17. Terrence Ranger, "Medical Science and Pentecost," in Shiels, *The Church and Healing*, 333–365.

18. Philip Jenkins, *The Next Christendom: The Coming of Global Christianity* (New York: Oxford University Press, 2002), 125–127.

19. Joseph Tse-Hei Lee, "Watchman Nee and the Little Flock Movement in Maoist China," *Church History: Christianity and Culture* 17, no. 1 (March 2005): 68–96.

20. Robert P. Weller, *Resistance, Chaos and Control in China: Taiping Rebels, Taiwanese Ghosts and Tiananmen* (Seattle: University of Washington Press, 1994), 65; Jonathan D. Spence, *God's Chinese Son: The Taiping Heavenly Kingdom of Hong Xiuquan* (New York: Norton, 1996), 186, 188.

21. Edward Bliss Jr., *Beyond the Stone Arches: An American Missionary Doctor in China, 1892–1932* (New York: Wiley, 2001), 31.

22. Ibid., 43.

23. Quoted in ibid., 219.

24. Quoted in Jerome Ch'en, *China and the West: Society and Culture, 1815–1937* (Bloomington: Indiana University Press, 1979), 131.

25. Yuet-Wah Cheung and Peter Kong-Ming New, "Missionary Doctors vs. Chinese Patients: Credibility of Missionary Health Care in Early Twentieth Century China," *Social Science & Medicine* 21, no. 3 (1985): 313.

26. Kaiyi Chen, "Missionaries and the Early Development of Nursing in China," *Nursing History Review* 4 (1996): 143.

27. Theron Kue-Hing Young, "A Conflict of Professions: The Medical Missionary in China, 1835–1890," *Bulletin of the History of Medicine* XLVII, no. 3 (1973), 272.

28. Chen, "Missionaries," 129, 143.

29. Judith Sealander, "Curing Evils at Their Source: The Arrival of Scientific Giving," in *Charity, Philanthropy, and Civility in American History*, ed. Lawrence J. Friedman and Mark D. McGarvie (Cambridge, UK: Cambridge University Press, 2003), 217–239; Amanda Porterfield, "Protestant Missionaries: Pioneers of American Philanthropy," in *Charity*, 49–69.

30. Chen, "Missionaries," 137; Basch, *Textbook of International Health*, 47.

31. Cheung and New, "Missionary Doctors," 309.

32. Sonya J. Grypma, "Neither Angels of Mercy nor Foreign Devils: Revisioning Canadian Missionary Nurses in China, 1935–1947," *Nursing History Review* 12 (2004): 97–119; Chen, "Missionaries," 143.

33. Cheung and New, "Missionary Doctors," 312.

34. The title of a popular book, published in 1900, by John R. Mott (1865–1955), a Methodist layman, director of the Student Volunteer Movement, and prominent American spokesman for Protestant missionary work.

35. Basch, *Textbook of International Health*, 67.

CHAPTER 7

1. Liturgy of St. John Chysostom quoted in John Meyendorff, "The Role of Christ," in *Christian Spirituality: Origins to the Twelfth Century*, ed. Bernard McGinn, John Meyendorff, and Jean Leclercq (1985; New York: Crossroad, 2000), 246.

2. Catherine L. Albanese, *Nature Religion in America: From the Algonkian Indians to the New Age* (Chicago: University of Chicago Press, 1990).

3. Don Colbert, *Toxic Relief: Restore Health and Energy through Fasting and Detoxification* (Lake Mary, FL: Siloam, 2001); Reginald Cherry, *The Bible Cure* (Orlando, FL: Creation House, 1998), ix–x; Joseph Williams, "Psychology and Medicine in Pentecostal-Charismatic Healing Practices," unpublished seminar paper in author's possession, 20.

4. Stewart M. Hoover, Lynn Schofield Clark, and Lee Rainie, "Faith Online," Pew Internet & American Life Project, available at http://www.pewInternet.org/.

5. Thomas Lloyd, "Internet Prayer," unpublished seminar paper in the author's possession; also see John Corrigan, *Business of the Heart: Religion and Emotion in the Nineteenth Century* (Berkeley: University of California Press, 2002), 207–230; Rick Ostrander, *The Life of Prayer in a World of Science: Protestants, Prayer, and American Culture 1870–1930* (New York: Oxford University Press, 2000); and James Gilbert, *Redeeming Culture: American Religion in an Age of Science* (Chicago: University of Chicago Press, 1997).

6. Harold G. Koenig, Michael E. McCullough, and David B. Larson, *Handbook of Religion and Health* (New York: Oxford University Press, 2001), 81–83, 90–92, 151–152, 247–249, 318–319, 350–352.

7. John A. Astin, Elaine Harkness, and Edzard Ernst, "The Efficacy of 'Distant Healing': A Systematic Review of Randomized Trials," *Annals of Internal Medicine* 132, no. 11 (June 2000): 903–910; Randolph C. Byrd, "Positive Therapeutic Effects of Intercessory Prayer in a Coronary Care Unit Population," *Southern Medical Journal* 81, no. 7 (July 1988): 826–829; Kwang Y. Cha, Daniel P. Wirth, and Rogerio A. Lobo, "Does Prayer Influence the Success of *in vitro* Fertilization-Embyro Transfer?," *Journal of Reproductive Medicine* 46, no. 9 (September 2001): 781–787; Fred Sicher, Elisabeth Targ, Dan Moore II, and Helene S. Smith, "A Randomized Double-Blind Study of the Effect of Distant Healing in a Population with Advanced AIDS," *Western Journal of Medicine* 169, no. 6 (December 1998): 356–363; Scott R. Walker, J. Scott Tonigan, William R. Miller, Stephen Comer, and Linda Kahlich, "Intercessory Prayer in the Treat-

ment of Alcohol Abuse and Dependence: A Pilot Investigation," *Alternative Therapies in Health and Medicine* 3, no. 6 (November 1997): 79–86. Thanks to Ron Numbers for these articles.

8. Bruce L. Flam, "Faith Healing by Prayer," *Scientific Review of Alternative Medicine* 6, no. 1 (winter 2002): 47; Gary P. Posner, "Study Yields No Evidence for Medical Efficacy of Distant Intercessory Prayer," *Scientific Review of Alternative Medicine* 6, no. 1 (winter 2002): 44–46; Nicholas Humphrey, "The Power of Prayer," *Skeptical Inquirer* 24, no. 3 (May/June 2000): 61; Irwin Tessman and Jack Tessman, "Efficacy of Prayer: A Critical Examination of Claims," *Skeptical Inquirer* 24, no. 2 (March/April 2000): 31–33.

9. John Wesley, *The Desideratum; or, Electricity Made Plain and Useful*, in *The Works of the Rev. John Wesley* (Bristol, 1773), 24: 284–369; and Harold Y. Vanderpool, "The Wesleyan-Methodist Tradition," in *Caring and Curing: Health and Medicine in the Western Religious Traditions*, ed. Ronald L. Numbers and Darrel W. Amundsen (1986; Baltimore: Johns Hopkins University Press, 1998), 324.

10. Benjamin Franklin, *Experiments and Observations on Electricity* (1751), in *The Papers of Benjamin Franklin*, 22 vols., ed. Leonard W. Larabee et al. (New Haven: Yale University Press, 1959–1990), 4: 125–145.

11. John Wesley, *The Journal of John Wesley*, ed. Percy Livingstone Parker (Chicago: Moody Press, n.d.), 218.

12. John Wesley, *Primitive Physick; or, An Easy and Natural Method of Curing Most Diseases* (1747), 12th ed. (Philadelphia, 1764); John Wesley, *The Duty and Advantage of Early Rising* (London, 1789).

13. Geoffrey Nuttall, *The Holy Spirit in Puritan Faith and Experience* (Oxford: Basil Blackwell, 1946); also see Amanda Porterfield, *Female Piety in Puritan New England: The Emergence of Religious Humanism* (New York: Oxford University Press, 1992), 98–99.

14. Wesley, *Journal*, 36–37.

15. Ibid., 62, 64.

16. Henry D. Rack, "Early Methodist Healing," in *The Church and Healing*, ed. W. J. Sheils (Oxford: Basil Blackwell, 1982), 150.

17. Donald W. Dayton, *Theological Roots of Pentecostalism* (1987; Metuchen, NJ: Hendrickson, 2000), 118–119.

18. Ibid., 63–84, 115–141; Grant Wacker, *Heaven Below: Early Pentecostals and American Culture* (Cambridge, MA: Harvard University Press, 2001), 1–8; Wayne E. Warner, *The Woman Evangelist: The Life and Times of Charismatic Evangelist Maria B. Woodworth-Etter* (Metuchen, NJ: Scarecrow Press, 1986).

19. Elaine Lawless, "Performing Pentecostalism: Cultural Investment in an American Origins Narrative," paper presented at Crossing Boundaries: Religion in the Louisiana Purchase Conference, Columbia, MI, February 21, 2004; Leigh Eric Schmidt, *Holy Fairs: Scottish Communions and American Revivals in the Early Modern Period* (Princeton: Princeton University Press, 1989).

20. Albert Raboteau, *Slave Religion: The "Invisible Institution" in the Antebellum South* (New York: Oxford University Press, 1978); Mechel Sobel, *Trabel' On: The Slave*

Journey to an Afro-Baptist Faith (Westport, CT: Greenwood Press, 1979); John H. Wigger, *Taking Heaven by Storm: Methodism and the Popularization of American Christianity* (New York: Oxford University Press, 1998).

21. Quotations from Peter Cartright, *Autobiography* (1856), in *The American Evangelicals, 1800–1900: An Anthology*, ed. William G. McLoughlin (New York: Harper & Row, 1968), 43–44.

22. Robert Patterson, "Letter to the Rev. Dr. John King," September 25, 1801, in *American Christianity: An Historical Interpretation with Representative Documents*, 2 vols., ed. H. Shelton Smith, Robert T. Handy, and Lefferts A. Loetscher (New York: Scribner's, 1960), 1: 568.

23. Bernard A. Weisberger, *They Gathered at the River: The Story of the Great Revivalists and Their Impact upon Religion in America* (Boston: Little, Brown, 1958), 32.

24. Patterson, "Letter," 568.

25. Quotations from Edith L. Blumhofer and Aimee Semple McPherson in Edith L. Blumhofer, *Aimee Semple McPherson: Everybody's Sister* (Grand Rapids, MI: William B. Eerdman, 1993), 174, 169.

26. McPherson quoted in ibid., 93–94, 66, 161, 170, 277.

27. Blumhofer, *Aimee Semple McPherson*, 126, 194; Wacker, *Heaven Below*,33.

28. Harvey Cox, *Fire from Heaven: The Rise of Pentecostal Spirituality and the Reshaping of Religion in the Twenty-first Century* (Cambridge, MA: Da Capo Press, 1995); also see Vinson Synan, ed., *The Century of the Holy Spirit: 100 Years of Pentecostal and Charismatic Renewal, 1901–2001* (Nashville, TN: Thomas Nelson, 2001).

29. Synan, *Century of the Holy Spirit*, 317.

30. Ann Taves, *Fits, Trances, and Visions: Experiencing Religion and Explaining Experience from Wesley to James* (Princeton: Princeton University Press, 1999); Ronald L. Numbers and Rennie B. Schoepflin, "Ministries of Healing: Mary Baker Eddy, Ellen G. White, and the Religion of Health," in *Women and Health in America: A History*, ed. Judith Walzer Leavitt (Madison: University of Wisconsin Press, 1984), 376–389; Leigh Eric Schmidt, *Hearing Things: Religion, Illusion, and the American Enlightenment* (Cambridge, MA: Harvard University Pres, 2000).

31. Paracelsus, *Selected Writings* (1951), ed. Jolande Jacobi, trans. Norbert Guterman (Princeton: Princeton University Press, 1988); Mary Lindemann, *Medicine and Society in Early Modern Europe* (Cambridge, UK: Cambridge University Press, 1999), 75–77.

32. Numbers and Schoepflin, "Ministries of Healing," 382.

33. Ellen G. White, *Spiritual Gifts, My Christian Experience, Views and Labors* (Battle Creek, MI: James White, 1860), 20; and Ellen G. White, "Experience and Views" (August 1851), in *Early Writings of Ellen G. White* (Washington, DC: Review and Herald, 1882), 21; all quoted in Taves, *Fits, Trances, and Visions*, 156, 161–162.

34. White, *Early Writings*, quoted in Numbers and Schoepflin, "Ministries of Healing," 383.

35. White, *Spiritual Gifts*, 59; White, *Early Writings*, 109; all quoted in Taves, *Fits, Trances, and Visions*, 162, 164; also see Numbers and Schoepflin, "Ministries of Healing," 383.

36. Mary Baker Eddy, *Science and Health with Key to the Scriptures* (1875), 6th ed.

(Boston: First Church of Christ Scientist, 1971), 9, 560, 107, xi, 284, 286. Also see Edwin Franden Dakin, *Mrs. Eddy: The Biography of a Virginal Mind* (1929; New York: Scribner's, 1970), 157–287; David L. Keyston, *The Healer: The Healing Works of Mary Baker Eddy* (Boston: Healing Unlimited, 1996).

37. Phineas Parkhurst Quimby, *The Quimby Manuscripts* (1921), ed. Horatio W. Dresser (Seacaucus, NJ: Citadel Press, 1969), ix, 353, 354, 355.

38. Eddy, *Science and Health*, 109, 255, 560.

39. Ruth Harris, *Lourdes: Body and Spirit in the Secular Age* (New York: Viking Penguin, 1999), 3–18, esp. 10.

40. Ibid., 9, 14.

41. Ibid., 320–326.

42. Ibid., xiv-xv.

43. Ibid., 317–319; also see Elaine Scarry, *The Body in Pain: The Making and Unmaking of the World* (New York: Oxford University Press, 1985).

44. Nelly Richie, "Women and Christology," trans. Jeltje Aukema, in *Through Her Eyes: Women's Theology from Latin America*, ed. Elsa Tamez (1986 in Spanish; Maryknoll, NY: Orbis Books, 1989), 83.

Index